P9-DFA-895

# INTRODUCTION TO CORRECTIONS

## AN EVIDENCE-BASED APPROACH

RYAN ALEXANDER, PHD

WASHBURN UNIVERSITY

WEST
ACADEMIC
PUBLISHING

The publisher is not engaged in rendering legal or other professional advice, and this publication is not a substitute for the advice of an attorney. If you require legal or other expert advice, you should seek the services of a competent attorney or other professional.

© 2020 LEG, Inc. d/b/a West Academic
    444 Cedar Street, Suite 700
    St. Paul, MN 55101
    1-877-888-1330

West, West Academic Publishing, and West Academic are trademarks of West Publishing Corporation, used under license.

Printed in the United States of America

**ISBN:** 978-1-64242-592-5

# Table of Contents

# Table of Cases

# INTRODUCTION TO CORRECTIONS

## AN EVIDENCE-BASED APPROACH

# Corrections Today

**Chapter Objectives**

- Understand the current state of correction in the U.S.
- Explain the role of Corrections in the U.S. Criminal Justice System.
- Compare the historical policy and practices to current ones.
- Understand the role of early correctional historical figures.

## A. PICTURE OF CORRECTIONS IN AMERICA TODAY

Corrections is one of the three parts of our criminal justice system. Police determine who the suspect(s) are and the court determine **legal culpability**. Corrections serves to dispense punishment and potentially rehabilitation. Corrections in the U.S. today is an important part of society whether people are directly impacted by it such as having a family member somewhere involved in the system either as an inmate, probationer, parolee. There are approximately 6.5 million people under some form of corrections in the U.S., this is the highest incarceration rate of any country in the world.[1] Also there is a strong possibility a

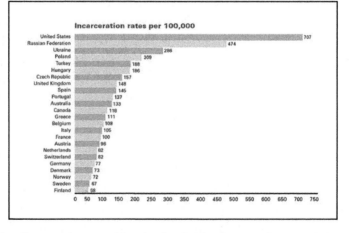

student knows or has a family member working in the field of corrections as there are a number of different occupational fields in institutional and community corrections. Not to mention hundreds of job possibilities that range from the medical field, psychology, food service, technology such as global positioning monitoring just to name a few. Corrections in the U.S. ranges far outside of traditional career opportunities.

Americans spend a large portion tax dollars on corrections. We pay approximately $80 billion dollars per year on corrections. In other words each U.S. resident pays $260 per year to incarcerate or to supervise people on probation or parole. This represents a 300% increase in correctional spending since 1980. Interestingly, the overall crime rate has fallen about 45% in the last twenty years[2]. The steep decline in the crime rate should signal a decrease in spending. Instead quite the opposite result has occurred. We can attribute these costs to being more punitive and using incarceration at unprecedented levels. For instance the incarceration rate has risen approximately 400% since the early 1980s. Also, consider that it costs about $30,000 a year to incarcerate an adult and as much as $90,000 a year to incarcerate a juvenile we can see the cost of incarceration alone is quite a burden on local, state, and federal budgets. Currently there are approximately 6,740,000 people under some type of correctional supervision or 1 in 37 Americans we can see that costs add up very quickly.[3]

The cost of incarceration, coupled with shifting public attitudes about punishment and the effectiveness of incarceration, along with research which has questioned punitive policies. These factors have resulted in a slow but steady shift toward alternatives to incarceration. Indeed, we have started to see a small decline (-0.6% from 2000 to 2015)[4] in the prison population and corrections overall.

We have begun to realize there is a toll associated with incarcerating large number of people beyond tax dollars. There are a number of issues that challenge correction in the U.S. today. The overrepresentation of minorities in the correctional system is an issue beyond sentencing disparity. Instead sentencing is one of a number of symptoms that facilitate this overrepresentation. Also, understanding the role that mental health plays in not only preventing crime but preventing those under correctional control from committing future crimes has been given more recognition. In subsequent chapters we will thoroughly investigate these issues and many more.

The shift toward using research and empirical data to guide correctional policy has begun to occur. Utilizing evidence-based practices allows agencies to be more effective with the resources or money allotted to their budgets. When agencies can show the public and ultimately the legislators that approve budgets that measures they employ are effective then they can stave off budget cuts or have more resources allotted to them. More state and local correctional agencies are utilizing programs and policies that are evidence-based. As a consequence agencies are in need of professionals that can conduct research, understand research reports, and are informed of best practices.

## 1. American Corrections

Corrections is split into two categories: Institutional corrections (i.e. jails and prisons) or community corrections (i.e. probation and parole). Although we will discuss these categories much more in depth later its important to gain context of the overall system here. Below we will briefly review the populations of community corrections and institutional corrections.

### a. *Probation*

The use of probation as a correctional measure is far more often used than prison or prole. There are well over 4 million people in the U.S. on probation, that is the approximate population of the state of Kentucky.[5,6] About 7 in 10 of people under correctional supervision were supervised on probation. Probation is widely used for many reasons. It's favored because people are held accountable for crimes but they are allowed to remain in the community. It's also very cost effective as the average yearly cost to supervise a person is $3,347.40[7]. However, the use of probation has been in decline since 2007. From 2007 to 2015, the total number of people on probation declined by -1.6%. That may seem like a small percentage but it marks a trend nonetheless.

### b. *Jail*

Jails are typically controlled at the local level of government and house a variety of inmates for a variety of reasons. The role of a jail as just a temporary holding facility is beginning to change as jails now provide more services to inmates such as education, various sorts of therapy (i.e. substance abuse or mental health treatment), and serving as day reporting centers or halfway houses. Even though jails act as sort of a "catch all" their populations have decreased slightly in recent years (-0.9% from 2007 to 2015).[8]

### c. *Prison*

When people think of corrections they often think of prisons with their high walls, barb wired lined perimeters, and all around imposing environs. The U.S. incarceration rate is the highest in the world. Our incarceration rate is 716 per 100,000 people. The average world incarceration rate per country is 150 per 100,000 people. As you can see the U.S. is far above average.[9] Even though we have the highest incarceration rate in the world we are starting to see prison populations decrease for the first time in decades. From 2007 to 2015, the overall prison population declined by -0.6%.[10]

### d. Parole

A person can be granted parole once they have served a period of time in prison. The term parole is a bit of a misnomer as we will discuss in Chapter 10 there are different types of early release from prison. We will use the term "parole" to encompass early release from prison. The number of people on parole is the only corrective method to increase since 2007. There are more people on parole supervision than any other time in our history (870,500 paroles in 2015). This number will most likely grow as those people who were convicted and received lengthy prison sentences in the 1990s and early 2000s are now becoming eligible for parole. There have also been various state and federal legislative and executive measures employed to allow people early opportunities at parole.[11]

### e. Alternatives to Traditional Corrections

Today there are many more opportunities for people charged with crimes or somehow involved with the criminal justice system to avoid the traditional criminal justice remedies of probation or incarceration. These alternatives arose as a result of a need for local, state, and federal governments to pursue less expensive measures of justice. The public also began to question the efficacy of traditional measures of incarceration or probation. Thus alternatives such as specialized courts like as drug courts and other diversionary courts became popular. These alternatives provide a measure of **restorative justice** which seeks accountability for the offender's actions, reparation for the victim, and rehabilitation of the offender.

## B.  WHAT IS CORRECTIONS?

The field of corrections is just one part of the American Criminal Justice system. Our system acts as a process or series of steps that ultimately end up with some type of corrective measure being administered by a governmental entity. The first step in the criminal justice process is policing. Police are given the responsibility of investigating behaviors deemed to crimes. Once they believe that probable cause exists and that a crime was committed and identify a suspect the person is arrested or otherwise brought to court where the second step in the process occurs. The court process is detailed and lengthy but essentially involves the prosecutor deciding to officially charge the defendant. The court determines

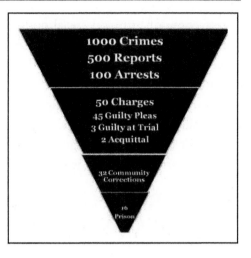

legal culpability through a trial or plea bargain, and then hands down a sentence. The sentence handed down by the court is crucial when considering the field of corrections. Without a sanction or punishment being given to a defendant then the field of corrections largely ceases to exist. As we can see illustrated by the Crime Funnel many crimes go unreported and even if they are reported there are many cases that for one reason or another do not result in a criminal conviction.

## 1. Social Control

There are two types of social control largely recognized by sociologists[12]. The first, informal social control, are loosely considered the "unwritten" rules of society. These controls may determine what sort of clothes you wear or how you behave at the dinner table. The other type of control is formal social control. This form of control are the written rules or laws of society. When a person violates the law the authorities or police are notified and the criminal justice system becomes engaged. Ultimately if a person is convicted of an offense they are typically given some type of punishment. Of course this punishment doesn't always result in a correctional measure such as probation or incarceration being utilized, but rather a fine or suspension of the privilege to drive are examples. A fine isn't as intrusive as probation but is none the less a corrective measure used to deter the speeder from speeding.

Corrections is a type of formal social control. Indeed, it's the essence of formal social control as it represents what the community views as behavior that is bad enough (i.e. a crime) that it rises to the level of using community resources to address or punish the behavior. The behavior is in need of publically holding the person accountable and applying some type of punishment. Corrections provides an identifiable punishment that is supposed to specifically deter a person from repeating criminal behavior and create a general deterrent whereby the public fears punishment.

It's important to consider the limits of formal social control. Of course we don't do things such as speed down a highway because we don't want to pay a large fine. That is no doubt a deterrent. However we cannot discount the effectiveness of informal social control on our behavior. We certainly want to avoid the formal punishment of a fine but the more effective deterrent toward speeding might be the reaction of the parents of a person caught speeding. This informal social control can exhibit a great deal of deterrent value. The importance of informal social control should not be overlooked by those studying, creating and implementing correctional policy. The only reason why we obey speeding limits isn't because of a singular fear of a fine just as the only reason why one person doesn't kill another is because they fear prison or execution.

## C. THE ROLE OF CORRECTIONS IN THE AMERICAN CRIMINAL JUSTICE SYSTEM

Corrections is a key part of our criminal justice system. Without corrections policing would provide little meaning. Courts could act and find someone guilty or accept a plea but if there was no entity or agency to provide carrying out a court ordered sanction or punishment then the court system's efficacy becomes questionable.

The role of corrections is ever changing. It's certainly a valuable part of our criminal justice system. In future chapters we will discuss the various purposes corrections has served in the U.S. The evolutionary nature of our corrections system is tied to what we find socially acceptable as punishment. For instance in colonial America there were several types of crimes that could result in the death penalty being utilized. Today the death penalty is still an option in about half of the states but even then is used very infrequently in most states. The use of **corporal punishment** was also utilized in early America. Today the idea of applying direct physical punishment for law violations isn't considered constitutional.

### 1. The Three Parts of the American Criminal Justice System

The American Criminal Justice System has three parts: police, courts, and corrections. We largely see these three entities working together as a system whereby each supports the other, much like the various systems of your body (i.e. vascular, skeletal, digestive, etc.) support your body. If all the various systems are healthy and functioning properly and harmoniously the entire person is healthy. It's certainly true that without any one entity the entire criminal justice system as we know it fails. However, it's questionable how harmoniously each piece supports the other. They might not be completely supportive, which isn't necessarily a negative aspect. For instance the courts have and continue to impact corrections in many ways. Legal precedents such as in *U.S. v. Knights*, 534 U.S. 112 (2001) is a case which set a legal precedent that allows parole officers to search parolees without a search warrant. The use of solitary confinement for inmates has come into question as a potential cruel and unusual punishment. These developments and others within law enforcement and the courts have served to impact corrections in many ways just as developments within corrections have impacted policing and the courts.

Overall, it appears that courts are atop the hierarchy of the criminal justice system as they can dictate the legality of correctional or police matters. However, for many years the court system was not involved in corrections. Indeed, it largely observed a "hands off" approach. Many referred to this as the **hands off doctrine,** whereby the courts saw corrections and more specifically the prison system as a function of the executive branch of government which they had no legal standing. Accordingly, many courts saw that involving themselves in corrections was outside their scope of authority. It wasn't until the U.S. Supreme Court era largely recognized at the **Warren Court** whose time-pan ranged from 1953–1969, became much more involved with corrections.

> **Warren Court**—United States Supreme Court Chief Justice Earl Warren presided in his post from 1953–1969. He led a court that was largely seen as progressive and expanded judicial power and civil liberties.

## D. WHY DOES HISTORY MATTER?

The subject of history can be a dry and mundane subject for students and instructors alike. Often the focus of history is lost on memorizing dates, names, and court cases. Instead knowing the history of the area under study helps provide a rich context or understanding of a field like corrections. We can see the evolution of the field materialize. We can see what sorts of correctional policies and measures that were employed in the past. We can see why these failed or were successful. We should certainly realize that what "worked" as effective correctional measure in the past may not be an efficient or even legal today. Conversely polices or measures that were not adopted of left out may in fact be an efficient measure today.

Correctional policy is representative of current cultural values and mores of society. This representation may lag for a bit but ultimately it seems that when changes occur in society they ultimately are mirrored within corrections. What is considered appropriate punishment for someone who has stolen a horse or cattle the 1800s certainly doesn't meet the same fate of someone committing the same offense today. We can see the type of punishments employed today being recycled in some form such as chain gangs or "boot camps". Boot camps became a popular form of punishment for juveniles or young first time offenders in the mid-1990s. The initial use and later large movement away from the use of boot camps appeared to be in large parts social reaction to a criminal justice problem.

## Correctional Focus Today

### Boot Camps

The first adult boot camp started in Georgia in 1983, the development of this new type of corrections[13,14] was in response to a rising crime rate and a search to find an alternative to incarceration. Boot camps were largely used in the juvenile justice system and to a much smaller degree in the adult criminal justice system as an alternative to sending someone to prison. Non-violent and/or first time offenders typically were sent to this type of placement. These types of offenders were seen as most likely to benefit from this program as opposed to those with a long criminal history.

Why did boot camps develop? One needs to consider the social or historical context of the time. The early 1980s into the 1990s was largely seen as the "get tough on crime" or "Just Desserts" era of criminal punishment. The social mood or environment was ripe for this type of punishment. The idea of having kids that were once out vandalizing, burglarizing, or otherwise causing havoc doing push-ups at 5:30 AM in the rain was appealing to many. Thus the purpose was two-fold. First the offender would receive some type training that resembled military basic training and discipline which was above the already strict institutional control of prison or jail. The hope was that the offender would internalize and appreciate goal setting and obtaining those goals. Although most of the goals were physical in nature. It was hoped that by internalizing self-discipline the offender would not recidivate. The second purpose was to relieve a strained and crowded prison system thereby decreasing costs.

Ultimately boot camps failed to deliver on both goals of reducing recidivism and saving money. This realization coupled with a few high profile abuse and death cases of boot camp offenders has led to many states no longer utilizing this type of punishment[15]. Today there are approximately 50 boot camps still in use today.

Examining correctional history allows us to see what we have done formerly to prevent people from continuing to or keep from committing crime. It gives us context to see why and how we punished people in the past and to be cognizant of the social factors impacting corrections in America today. Being familiar with the past helps us to explain why we continue to use the same policies and methods of corrections today yet allows us to be flexible and realize the inevitable changes in the future.

# E.  THE EARLY HISTORY OF CORRECTIONS

The evolutionary nature of society is critical to understand when discussing the history of corrections. People began to form cities and move away from a nomadic lifestyle in many parts of the world. Cities began to emerge thereby creating more of a need for written laws and punishments as populations concentrated. Here we will discuss origins of American corrections which is largely based in Western European common law practices and philosophies about punishment. This is not to say that corrections didn't exist in other parts of the world. Indeed, societies in Asia, India, Africa, and in early America certainly had their own laws and corresponding punishments. These are equally valuable and worthy of study. However, we have most closely aligned our punishment with Western European concepts of punishment.

## 1.   The Enlightenment

For well over a thousand years punishment for offenses committed against royalty or the church was harsh and usually involved some form or corporal punishment or death. These punishments were often carried out in public. The effect of public punishment was two-fold. First punishment carried out in public served as a general deterrent. Often punishments, especially executions, were largely regarded as public events whereby almost a carnival type atmosphere existed. Public executions served as an example or warning to others in a time when newspapers were largely non-existent. The second purpose of public punishment served to display the monarch's or churches' role as sovereign. These displays let the public know who was in power, that there was and is an authority. The rule of law established by the king or sovereign which eventually became the state began to become more socially acceptable. Today we take it for granted that the state has sovereignty over the population.

The age of Enlightenment is largely recognized to have occurred in the late 1600 and lasted well through the 1700s in Western Europe. This transitional period spurred many advances outside of the law and affected art, philosophy, business, politics, and religion. Of course we are most interested in the Enlightenments effects on punishment[16]. Also, we should remember that corrections evolves as society evolves. Thus the manner in which we punished people and why we punished people began to be questioned. People like Cesare Beccaria, John Howard and William Penn played important roles that affected corrections and how we view the concept of justice.

## 2.   Cesare Beccaria and the Classical School

Cesare Beccaria (1738–1794) played a very important role in shaping criminal law. He helped form "the academy of fists" in Milan, Italy. This organization was

emblematic of the Enlightenment period and thus dedicated to economic, political, and administrative reforms. His most important criminological work, *An Essay on Crimes and Punishment* (1764) questioned not only the use of the death penalty for any crime but the purpose for punishment altogether. It questioned the proportion of punishment, the deterrent value of punishment, and that people generally act in their own self-interest.

The major tenets of Beccaria's work formed the basis of the Classical School of criminology. The Classical School is largely regarded the original criminological theory. We can see much of the Classical School's thoughts in use in our criminal justice system today. Below is a chart that summarizes the connections between that school and today.

| Classical School | Practical use today |
|---|---|
| The notion of free will. This states that people behave of their own free will. | How blameworthy is a person for their own actions? If a person suffers from a mental health issue (legally insane) they may not be blameworthy and avoid criminal punishment. |
| Hedonistic Calculus concerns a rational person deciding the costs (i.e. punishment) of criminal behavior versus the benefit (i.e. the potential gain from the crime). Tis is often referred to as the pain vs. pleasure principle | A person may be specifically deterred or not from committing a crime based on their past experience with the legal system. |

| Manipulability is the notion that since we seek pleasure more than pain that we are predictable. | Since a rational person prefers pleasure to pain if we make the pain of punishment (i.e. incarceration) more than the potential pleasure of the crime people will chose to behave legally. He can see this best illustrated in sentencing grids |
|---|---|

The contributions of Beccaria are often credited within our own Bill of Rights. For instance the 5th amendment protection against double jeopardy and unreasonable bail, the 6th Amendment right to a speedy trial, and the 8th Amendment protection from cruel and unusual punishment all have roots in Beccaria's writings.

# F. ENGLISH COMMON LAW

A prime example of our roots of criminal law in the U.S. are expressed by our connection to English Common Law. Of course when under colonial rule from England the original 13 colonies adopted law and practices from "home" in this case England. English Common Law is largely based upon social customs and recognized by judicial pronouncements or **precedents**[17]. These customs and legal standards are maintained and adhered to by other courts and future cases. The common-law system continues today. There are various people responsible for establishing correctional customs that impact current U.S. correctional policy.

## 1. John Howard

Another product of the Enlightenment, John Howard (1726–1790), played a major role in reforming prisons and jails. Howard, an Englishman, upon his appointment as sheriff of Bedfordshire began to inspect not only prisons and jails in his jurisdiction but embarked upon a tour of prisons across Europe. What he found shocked him, as many prisons in England and across Europe housed prisoners in brutal conditions. He also saw that inmates were often treated unfairly based on economic disparity. Poor inmates lived in deplorable conditions while the wealthier were better fed and housed.

Howard's efforts led to Parliamentary Acts in 1774. These acts brought significant legislative changes which impacted overall prisoner health. His work also brought about a social focus on the plight of prisoners.[18]

## 2.   William Penn

William Penn (1644–1718) embodies the connection between social changes largely due to the environment and atmosphere of the Enlightenment and religion.

This social atmosphere coupled with the new opportunities and need for settlement in America fostered opportunities for change. The major impact these two forces had on early American corrections are important.

Penn was granted of a large tract of land by King Charles II of England. This tract of land later became the colony and then state of Pennsylvania. Penn's religion as a Quaker also impacted his humanitarian views on corrections. The social environment of the period coupled with Penn's religious views had a great effect on his correctional philosophy.

William Penn and thus Pennsylvania observed what was known as the "Great Law". This approach to law and punishment was much more humane than typical English law and punishment. For instance the death penalty was only allowed in murder cases, which was a big departure from the many crimes that could result in a person being executed in England. There was an emphasis on imprisonment instead of corporal punishments, helping inmates learn a trade, bail for minor offences, and humane prison conditions.[19] However, after William Penn's death in 1718, many of his reforms were nullified and punishment for the sake of retribution resumed until after the Revolutionary War.

# G. EARLY HISTORY OF CORRECTIONS IN THE U.S.

## 1.  Advent of Incarceration

Imprisonment is not a creation born in the U.S. However, we were among the first countries to utilize the prison as a major form of punishment. Punishment and reform have often been viewed at either ends of the justice spectrum. Whereby one philosophy is the overall dominant philosophy of the time. We often seek to find a balance between reform and punishment. Indeed this back and forth battle is representative of U.S. correctional eras.

We often see cadres or groups of like-minded people forcing change on corrections, such as the Quakers. These groups often seem to represent the social milieu or environment of the time. The historical context of changes in corrections cannot be discounted.

## 2.  Walnut Street Jail

The Walnut street jail is an example of an early American attempt to incarcerate people and use that time to reform the inmate as opposed to simply housing them. Initially the Walnut Street Jail was administered by the local sheriff it became the partial responsibility of the Commonwealth of Pennsylvania in 1790. A wing of the Walnut Street Jail essentially became a state prison. One of the first reforms was to house inmates in individual cells. Education for inmates and learning trades were also a staple at the prison. Religious services and safeguards for health were also given. This model soon caught the attention of reformers such as Dr. Benjamin Rush, an influential politician, and the Philadelphia Society for Alleviating the Miseries of Public Prisons as well as the local Board of Inspectors. The Pennsylvania legislature soon acted and in 1818 they called for the Western State Prison to be built and in 1821, the Eastern State Prison to be built. These prisons were modeled after the Walnut Street Jail.[20]

### 3.  Pennsylvania System

The Eastern State Prison was built outside of Philadelphia in 1829. There were seven rows of cell blocks that radiated out from a central hub, like spokes 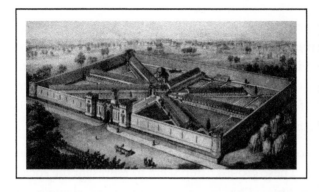 on a tire. The architectural plan served a purpose, whereby the guards could walk down each block and monitor inmates in their cells. Each cell housed one person. The prison was a technological marvel for the time. It had flushing toilets, and a shower in each cell as well as a central heating system. These luxuries were not even available in the White at that time. Inmates were kept in solitary confinement and their only contact was with prison guards through a small feeding hole. Inmates were given a Bible as their sole possession and also chores such as shoemaking or weaving. This method supposedly allowed the inmate to dwell in solitude on his or her crimes and provide time for a type of penitence, thus the term penitentiary was coined.

This treatment may not seem rehabilitative to us today but at the time represented a major way in which inmates were treated and prepared for eventual release. People from around the world came to Eastern State prison to study this new method of incarceration. More than 300 prisons throughout Europe, Russia, China, and South America adopted this model[21].

### 4.  Auburn System

Although the Pennsylvania system was studied and copied by many countries there was another competing model within the U.S. The Auburn System was largely an imitation of the Pennsylvania System[22]. In March 1796, Governor John Jay of New York signed sweeping legislation that put an end to the death penalty for all crimes except murder and treason. Corporal punishment was also replaced with periods of imprisonment. An initial prison, Newgate Prison, was opened in 1797, but is soon became clear that Newgate was too small and discipline was difficult to achieve. Thus in 1816, a new prison in Auburn New York was built.

Although the Auburn System and Pennsylvania System shared some similarities they differed in others. Respectively, the Auburn system directed by

Warden Elam Lynds allowed inmates to work together during the day. Inmates were still not allowed to communicate with each other but they at least were allowed outside of their cells and some type of human contact. They worked as groups on various types of jobs. Often time inmates were contracted for

jobs in private manufacturing. This **contract labor** became profitable in many respects and would offset costs of running the prison. Although many have called into question the use of very inexpensive inmate labor to do jobs that others outside of prison could do, inmate labor still occurs in many forms in U.S. prisons today. Discipline was still very much a part of the Auburn System inmates were forced to march in lockstep much like a military formation does. The Auburn System soon began to be preferred over the Pennsylvania System.

### 5. Pennsylvania System Versus the Auburn System

The Pennsylvania and Auburn prison systems received a lot of attention from states that were seeking to adopt a prison model. The popularity of these models went beyond international boundaries and countries in Europe and Asia began to adopt these models. Both system have their drawbacks and advantages. Many questioned the humaneness of solitary confinement of the Pennsylvania System while some had concern about contract labor undercutting the labor market in the Auburn System. Eventually it appears that the Auburn system's economic benefits prevailed.

Today the Auburn System exists in part. Inmates typically have 1–4 person cells. Inmate labor is still utilized. Discipline is still an important matter inside prison walls, however that may have more to do with correctional and inmate safety than reform.

## H. CONTEMPORARY CRIMINAL JUSTICE SYSTEM

As we have discovered our correctional system seems to mirror the attitudes and general attitude the public has not only about corrections but the entire justice system. These attitudes shape policy of correctional institutions, legislative initiatives, and court decisions. We see the philosophy and purpose behind punishment change and evolve. To be sure changes within corrections tend to take time and are generally not swift, but change in corrections is inevitable. These changes are best illustrated by the different correctional models or paradigms.

## 1.   Correctional Administration

Corrections has been a function of government since the **codification of law**. As you have learned in government and civics classes there are three branches of government. Each branch: executive, judicial, and legislative branch play key roles in correctional policy. However, typically the executive branch of government determine the day to day operations of both institutional corrections and community corrections. The legislative branch determines laws and requirements as well as providing resources for correctional departments in annual budgets. The courts act as a referee of sorts whereby they hear cases that can determine the legality of certain correctional practices or punishments. All three branches of government impact the administration of corrections significantly.

## 2.   Federal Correctional System

The administration of the federal correctional system is split among two entities. The first of which is the Federal Bureau of Prisons (BOP). It is part of the U.S. Department of Justice. The Department of Justice and subsequently the BOP is in the executive branch of government. The BOP is led by a director appointed by the U.S. Attorney General. The BOP is of course responsible for housing approximately 183,857 inmates sent to federal prison because the inmate was convicted of a federal crime[23].

The second part of federal corrections are administered through the judicial branch or the U.S. Courts System. The Administrative Office (AO) is responsible for establishing policy for Federal Probation and Pretrial Services. Supervising people on probation or on pre-trial supervision is only a part of the job. They also supervise inmates released from federal civilian and military prison.[24] The federal judicial branch is largely responsible for federal community corrections.

As we can see the federal correctional system is administered by two separate branches of government. Prisons are administered through the executive branch under the auspices of the BOP. Since BOP is under these auspices their policy and procedures are under subject to the change that mirrors the current political environment. The U.S. Courts system are largely responsible for community corrections for federal offenders. Policy and procedure are subject to the auspices of the court.

## 3.   State Correctional System

The administration of corrections is as varied as the 50 states in which they reside. However, one constant of the administration of corrections is the executive branch control of prisons and jails. Every state has a department of corrections, although the actual name "Department of Corrections" may vary. Jails are typically administered by the local elected sheriff. Regardless of prison or jail these institutions are under the auspices of either elected officials or those appointed by elected officials. Therefore the policy and procedure of jails and prisons are subject to change depending upon who is in office. To be sure incarcerative policy and procedure are relatively stable in many regards however the advent of programs like "faith mentors" or clemency for drug offenders implemented by members of the executive branch has important repercussions for corrections.

The executive, judicial, and legislative branches all have important impacts on American correctional policy. These three branches of government all have a connection to the current social environment of the time. We will see that corrections is a part of society, indeed a reflection of social control justified by the social climate. These are best illustrated by the "Hands Off Doctrine "and the "War on Drugs". Both of which have had lasting social and general correctional consequences.

## 4.   Hands Off Doctrine

The "Hands Off Doctrine" defined the relationship between federal courts and local, state, and federal correctional departments. This doctrine essentially meant that courts typically had no influence on the way corrections and especially prisons operated. That began to change in the 1960s as many different areas of society such as race and gender inequality were challenged[25]. The social environment of the time brought a recognition to the forefront that prison

Retrieved from Lib Congress

conditions were possibly too harsh or ineffective and a change needed to occur, much the same way the age of Enlightenment facilitated a social change in the concept of justice. The social atmosphere of the 1960s and 1970s in the U.S. fostered court involvement and thus change.

The "Hands Off Doctrine" stated that the federal government had no legal standing to intervene in the function of state institutions. However once extreme conditions of some prisons were exposed coupled with overall public sentiment that began to turn away from punitive correctional measures this doctrine. In the 1964 case *Cooper v. Pate* the U.S. Supreme Court established a legal precedent that helped set in motion the end of the "Hands Off Doctrine". That case held that prisoners had the right to have their grievances addressed under the Civil Rights Act of 1871. *Cooper v. Pate*, 378 U.S. 546 (1964) was just the beginning in a series of precedent setting cases which meant the federal government, namely Federal Courts became involved in many different correctional measures. Today the court hears many cases that deal with issues like the use of solitary confinement (see *Hudson v. McMillan*, 503 U.S. 1 (1992); *Williams v. Varner* 14–1469 and *Walker v. Farnan* 15–1390 (2017))[26], or inmates rights to practice religion (see *Africa v. Pennsylvania*, 662 F.2d 1025 (3rd Circuit 1981); *Dettmer v. Landon*, 799 F.2d 929 (4th Circuit 1986)).[27] These are just a few examples of court involvement concerning not only 8th Amendment issues of cruel and unusual punishment but also 1st Amendment issues such as freedom of religion or speech. Court involvement in corrections goes way beyond these examples.

## 5. War on Drugs

Perhaps no bigger executive policy decision has had such a profound impact on American criminal justice and certainly corrections than the "war on drugs". In June 1971, President Richard Nixon declared a "war on drugs" thereby committing vast federal resources to eliminating drug use. The focus of many law enforcement agencies became fixed on arresting and sending drug offenders, traffickers, and manufacturers to prison[28].

To date the "war on drugs" has cost approximately $1 trillion dollars. We spend about $80 billion dollars each year to incarcerate people in the U.S. about half of those inmates are serving a prison sentence for a drug related crime. Between 1980 and 2001, the number of people in state and federal prisons for drug related crime increased by 1,300%[29]. It is argued that building prisons has become big business and has provided many communities, especially rural communities, with a source of economic stability. The "war on drugs" has had widespread costs on not only corrections, but also carries social, economic, health, and political consequences.[30]

---

### Correctional Focus

In 2010, Congress passed the Fair Sentencing Act. This act among other things increased the quantity of crack cocaine a person must be found to be in possession of in order to trigger 5 and 10 year mandatory minimum federal prison sentences. In 2011, the U.S. Sentencing Commission amended federal sentencing guidelines stated in the Fair Sentencing Act to be retroactive. Thereby reversing what many scholars, legislators, and members of the public believe to be a biased law in which thousands of minorities were imprisoned at rates far higher than whites. Since the conditions in the act were now retroactive that meant those convicted of offenses that are now covered by this law must be applied to them. The Sentencing Commission estimated the average reduction of prison length to be 37 months. These people would have their prison time reduced which would lessen federal prison populations but then increase the number of people on terms of supervised release, in other words they would be placed on community corrections.[31]

---

## I. CONCLUSION

Corrections is certainly not unique in America however, we are unique because we use it more than any other country in the world. We were one of the first countries to implement the prison system on a large scale. Today there are more Americans in prison or on parole or probation than there are people in many states. The nature of corrections changes and evolves as society evolves concerning what constitutes justice. At times in our history justice was considered pay back or retribution against the offender. At other times there has been a more rehabilitative tone.

A relatively new way forward is the basing correctional practice on what the research tells us what works or what is effective and what doesn't work. The notion of using evidence or evidence-based practices has begun to emerge.

Sometimes the results surprise us and challenge what we think should work and what actually does work or is effective at reducing crime. These results and using empirical data to base policy and practice allow correctional measures to be more effective.

## Discussion Questions

1.  Why is corrections an important part of American society?

2.  What are the two different parts of corrections?

3.  Is the criminal justice system a true system? Why or why not.

4.  Why do you think the U.S. incarcerates more people per capita than any other country in the world?

5.  What role did the Enlightenment play in developing corrections?

6.  Explain the evolutionary nature of the early American prison system.

7.  What role do each of the three branches of government play in corrections?

8.  What is the "hands off" doctrine and how does it impact corrections?

9.  What is the "war on drugs" and how has it impacted corrections?

10. What do you think will be a major challenge that corrections will have to address in the near future?

## Student Exercises

1.  Research you own state department of corrections. How much money is budgeted to corrections in your state? How many people are in prison? On parole? On probation? What are the demographic characteristics of inmates in your state and how does that compare to the general population demographics.

2.  Identify and explain two substantial challenges in corrections in your city and then in your state. Do you think correctional challenges are unique in your area compared to your state; the country?

I Boot camp box.

Cullen, FT KA Blevins, Tager JS, and Gendreau (2005). The rise and fall of Boot camps: A case Study in common sense corrections. Journal of Offender rehabilitation 40 (3/4) 53–70.

And

Leary A. (2006). Boot camps losing favor nationally. St. Petersburg Fla Times. Retrieved May 8 2018, from Lexis Nexus Academic.

## Key Terms

**Codification of law**—the process collecting and arranging law into a code or system promulgated by legislative authority.

**Contract labor**—inmate labor leased to private business.

**Corporal punishment**—physical punishment intended to cause pain and act as a specific deterrent of future criminality.

**Executive branch**—one of the three branches of government in the U.S. The executive branch is tasked with implementing policy and enforcing the law.

**Hands Off Doctrine**—legal approach whereby the court system did not intervene with prison operation.

**Judicial branch**—one of the three branches of government in the U.S. The Judicial Branch is responsible for interpreting the law.

**Legal culpability**—being legally responsible and therefore liable for criminal prosecution and punishment.

**Legislative branch**—one of the three branches of government in the U.S. The Legislative Branch is responsible for making laws.

**Precedent**—a case or decision of the court considered an example or authority for similar cases.

**Restorative justice**—an approach toward criminal justice that seeks to repair harm done to the victim and community while utilizing rehabilitation measures for offenders.

**Warren Court**—a period of time (1957–1969) in the U.S. Supreme Court in which Chief Justice Earl Warren led the court. During this time the court ruled on a variety of progressive measures that expanded civil rights and liberties.

---

[1]   Kaeble, Danielle and Cowhig, Mary (2016). U.S. Correctional Populations 2016. Bureau of Justice Statistics. Washington D.C.

[2]   Kearney, Melissa; Harris, Benjamin; Jacome, Elsia; Parker, Lucie (2014). Ten Economic Facts about Crime and Incarceration in the U.S. The Hamilton project.

[3]   Kaeble, Danielle and Glaze, Lauren (2015). Correctional Populations in the US 2015. US DOJ Bureau of Justice Statistics.

[4]   Ibid.

[5]   Ibid.

[6]    US Census Bureau.

[7]    U.S. Courts.gov. Costs of Probation Supervision. Retrieved June 2 2018.

[8]    Kaeble, Danielle and Cowhig, Mary (2016). U.S. Correctional Populations 2016. Bureau of Justice Statistics. Washington D.C.

[9]    U.S. Courts.gov. Costs of Probation Supervision. Retrieved June 2 2018.

[10]    Ibid.

[11]    Ibid.

[12]    Macionis, John (2018). Sociology 15th edition. Pearson Publications.

[13]    Cullen, FT; Blevins K.A.; Trager, J.S.; Gendreau (2005). The Rise and Fall of Boot Camps: A case study in common-sense corrections. Journal of Offender Rehabilitation, 40 (3/4) pg. 53–70.

[14]    Leary, A. (2009). Boot Camps Losing Favor Nationally. St. Petersburg Times (FL).

[15]    Cullen, FT; Blevins K.A.; Trager, J.S.; Gendreau (2005). The Rise and Fall of Boot Camps: A case study in common-sense corrections. Journal of Offender Rehabilitation, 40 (3/4) pg. 53–70.

[16]    New World Encyclopedia. Age of Enlightenment. Retrieved June 7 2018.

[17]    New World Encyclopedia. Legal Precedent retrieved June 7, 2018.

[18]    BBC Website John Howard History. Retrieved June 8 2018.

[19]    Walmsley, Roy (2015). International Centre for Prison Studies. University of Essex.

[20]    LeRoy B. DePuy (1951). The Walnut Street Prison: Pennsylvania's First Prison Journals.psu.edu/phj/article.

[21]    Eastern State Prison. Smithsonian.com retrieved May 29th 2018.

[22]    Barnes, Harry Elmer (1921). The Historical Origin of the Prison System in America. Journal of Criminal Law and Criminology 12 (1). Northwestern University School of Law.

[23]    United States Bureau of Prisons webpage. Inmate Statistics. USBOP.gov retrieved June 1 2018.

[24]    US Courts.gov webpage. Probation and Pretrial Services retrieved June 1 2018.

[25]    Sigler, Robert T. and Shook, Chadwick L. (????). The Federal Judiciary and Corrections: Breaking the Hands Off Doctrine CJPR 7 3–4 pp. 245–254.

[26]    *Craig Williams v. Dorina Varner Secretary of Pennsylvania Dept. of Corrections* AND *Walker v. Michael Farnan Secretary Pennsylvania DOC*, 3rd Circuit Court of Appeals US Courts.

[27]    *Africa v. Pennsylvania*, 662 F.2d 1025, 1032 (3rd Circuit 1981). *Dettmer v. Landon*, 799 F.2d 929, 931–32 (4th Circuit 1986).

[28]    A Brief History of the war on drugs. Drug policy .org Retrieved June 2 2018.

[29]    Jensen, Eric; Gerber, Jurg; and Mosher, Clayton (2004). Social Consequences of the Drug War: The legacy of failed policy. Criminal Justice Review 15 (1) pp. 100–121.

[30]    US sentencing Commission: Frequently Asked Questions: 2011 retroactive crack cocaine guideline amendment—ussc.gov.

[31]    United States Bureau of Prisons webpage. Inmate Statistics. USBOP.gov retrieved June 1 2018.

## CHAPTER 2

# Evidence Based Practices and Criminological Theories for Corrections

## Chapter Objectives

- Discovering what evidence-based practices is.
- Understanding what research and the Scientific Method is.
- Connecting theory to correctional policy and practice.

## A. EVIDENCE BASED PRACTICES

When we use the term "evidence" in the criminal justice arena we tend to think of evidence or proof of a crime. We understand that police collect evidence such as fingerprints, witness statements, or DNA and that these pieces of evidence are used in court to prove that a suspect committed a crime or crimes. When we discuss **evidence-based practices** in corrections similar data collection takes place. However, instead of police collecting several different pieces of evidence or data researchers collect several pieces of data about how and why people commit crime or analyze data about how well a correctional program or policy curbs future crime. We use this data to inform correctional polices, to initiate new programs that show potential, or to end programs or policies that are not effective or at least as effective as we would like them to be. Often correctional administrators and legislators will focus on the costs of the program and compare it to the benefits. If the costs outweigh the benefits those involved in correctional decision making may choose alternative measures to show that what they are doing is supported by research. These polices are referred to as evidence-based practices.

## 1.   The Scientific Method

What is research? There may seem to be an obvious answer to that question. Yet, it's important to understand the question and the answer. Research certainly takes many forms and delving into research for papers and projects is an important part of the learning process. However, when we are looking at research in its relation to correctional polices or practices decision makers often consult with scholars that are well versed in the field of corrections and familiar with research techniques. The familiarity of corrections coupled with knowing how to collect and analyze data is critical to obtaining an accurate assessment of the area under study. Just as we want police to be highly competent when they collect and analyze data for courtroom purposes so do we want those that collect and analyze data that will impact correctional policy and practice to be competent in their work.

Those collecting and analyzing data use a standard approach known as the **Scientific Method**. The Scientific Method has five steps:

Step 1:   Ask a question(s) or identify a problem. We learn about the correctional problem by observing a problem/behavior/circumstance and then ask why there is an issue. We can make educated guesses as to why the problem exists and how to fix it but without a thorough examination our guesses about causes and solutions are just guesses. Identifying the problem is very important in the early stages of a study. One must be succinct in defining a problem. For instance if we want to investigate sex offender recidivism we want to identify what a sex offender is for a particular study and also what we define recidivism as. Recidivism can mean many things. For a particular study recidivism may be defined as being charged with a new sex offense yet still another study may define recidivism as being convicted of a new sex offense. Remember that being charged with a new offense doesn't necessarily lead to conviction therefor a succinct definition is very important to determine.

Step 2:   Reviewing the Literature. Here the review of the literature is the review of similar studies in the area. We would look at studies published in **academic journals** in order to gain a perspective of what research has already been done on the subject. Say for instance we continue with our study of sex offender recidivism. We would examine what other published studies were conducted on the subject. We may also want to see how these similar studies gathered and analyzed data to gain insight. The review of the literature helps the researcher become more informed on the topic under study and to develop a hypothesis.

Step 3:    Form a Hypothesis. At this step in the process the researcher(s) are well enough informed on the topic to develop a hypothesis, or educated guess to address the questions asked or problem identified in Step 1. This doesn't mean a solution to the problem or question has been found but that the hypothesis can actually be tested as true or false.

Step 4:    Collection of Data and analysis. The collection and analysis step is referred to as methodology. The researcher(s) gather the data in a specific fashion as to not taint or call into question their results. If the data is not gathered in an unbiased way the results become questionable and the study may not be accurate. The analysis of the data is as important as the collection of the data. Using the proper analysis tool for the type of data collected is extremely important. Analysis of data is typically split into two different categories. The first is **quantitative data**. Here we use numbers to determine and express results. The next is **qualitative data**. This type of analysis searches for themes or commonalities to draw a conclusion. Some studies will use a combination of quantitative and qualitative analysis. This is referred to as a mixed methods approach.

Step 5:    Conclusion. Once the data has been collected and analyzed the researchers can now address the problem identified in Step 1 and hypothesized about in Step 3. The hypothesis is either confirmed at this point or falsified. There may be certain aspects of the hypothesis that were true while another piece was determined to not to be accurate. In this step the researcher(s) also address the limitations of their study and areas that may need more investigation. The vast majority of **empirical study** addresses the focal point of the study but just as important opens up room for more questions and further study.[1]

Use of the Scientific Method is the standard for research by which many academic journals determine the accuracy of submitted research. The conclusions drawn by empirical data in research articles help determine evidence-based practices not only in corrections but a multitude of other areas as well. In fact articles that achieve this standard is the "evidence" in evidence-based practices. Thus just as police collect multiple pieces of evidence to identify a suspect to draw a conclusion so do those that use evidence-based practices collect empirical data to support or decline policy or practices.

## 2.    Connecting Research to Practice and Policy

Throughout correctional history there have been many different efforts, policies, and programs to stop people from continuing to commit crime. Some of these efforts have been successful and some have not only been unsuccessful but may have facilitated criminal behavior. The need to implement policies and programs that do what they are supposed to do (i.e. reduce criminal activity) has become a focus of correctional administrators and legislators alike.

Using research to determine correctional policy is not new. In 1974, Robert Martinson wrote an academic paper that impacted correctional policy for many decades and by some accounts helped advance a period of retribution which was a departure from a more rehabilitative philosophy adopted by corrections for well over a decade. Martinson reviewed 231 offender rehabilitation programs from over 30 years. He concluded that with few exceptions rehabilitative programs had very few appreciable effects on recidivism. The proclamation that "nothing works" when it comes to rehabilitation programs for offenders coupled with the retributive social atmosphere facilitated a movement toward more punitive sanctions that remains as a correctional staple today.[2]

Evidence-based practice in the criminal justice system is a partnership between research and practice. Many correctional departments have their own research units[3]. State and federal Sentencing Commissions study correctional sanctions and seek sentencing options are effective and reducing crime but also attempt to identify and eliminate bias in sentencing. Faculty at universities and colleges also conduct research on numerous correctional topics which once published or used otherwise can be developed and implemented into programs or polices that are more effective at reducing crime or identifying other outcomes.[4]

## Evidence-Based Practice in Action

### Sex Offender Buffer Zones

There have been numerous efforts to prevent convicted sex offenders from continuing to commit sex crimes. One of those policies has been to not allow sex offenders to reside within a certain distance from places where children tend to congregate such as pools, parks, playgrounds, and bus stops. These laws or restrictions are commonly referred to as "buffer zones". The purpose of these restriction zones is to prevent convicted sex offenders from preying on children by making it harder for offenders to inadvertently contact children or intentionally seek out children as the increased distance would hamper those efforts[5].

The intention of this law is to make it more difficult to sexually assault children. However, much of the research about sexual assault on children tells us that the vast majority (approximately 80% of child sexual assault perpetrators are known to the victim either through family connections or as acquaintances of the victim thus living in close proximity to places where children congregate is a moot point. Those that do sexually assault children and are not known to the victim tend to not select children from schools, pools, parks, or playgrounds[6]. This again calls into question the validity of buffer zones.

Buffer zones appear to be an effective measure to curb child sexual assault. However, the empirical data seems to tell us something very different. Many studies on buffer zones actually indicate that buffer zones can exacerbate sexual offending. The zones can be so restrictive that some towns and even cities are encompassed by overlapping buffer zones. This can mean reintegration into the community can be very difficult. Offenders can be prevented from living with families that support or even surveille them, they can find it difficult to get therapy and treatment services if removed from communities. Buffer zones can be counter-productive and even facilitate criminal behavior.

## B.  THE ROLE OF EVIDENCE-BASED PRACTICES IN CORRECTIONS

The role of evidence-based practices (EBP) is far reaching. EBP is used to examine diversion programs, probation practices, prison programs, and parole services. We will examine specific programs and practices in future chapters of this text. The role and importance EBP plays in every facet of corrections represents a major shift in correctional philosophy. Policies and practices are becoming judged by how efficient they are economically and how well they curb crime or perform whatever function the policy is intended to do. Often times if empirical data supports a measure it's replicated in other areas across the country. EBP can be used to evaluate current programs for effectiveness and if they are found to be ineffective or partially effective they are stopped or modified. The partnership between research and practice continues to grow and agencies like the National Institute of Corrections (NIC) has publications and training dedicated to enhancing this partnership.

> Weblink for NIC—
> https://nicic.gov

The role of EBP in corrections cannot be overstated. However, we need to remember that correctional policy does not solely reply on EBP. There are many factors that shape and influence correctional policy. Certainly, public opinion is a factor. For example, currently there are twenty-one states that have buffer zone laws that restrict where a sex offender can live in relation to where children congregate. However, the empirical data informs us that buffer zones are not an efficient means of curbing child sexual assault and may in fact facilitate offender by removing reintegration supports such as family, therapy, and employment. Yet, when faced with that information citizens still don't appear to be moved to repeal such legislation[7]. Empirical data that can question traditional thoughts and ideas about punishment can be difficult to digest. The public and the legislators that represent the public in these matters may not be receptive to change and progress in correctional policies or practice. Thus change is typically a slow deliberate process. American corrections will continue to change at its own pace. By educating the public and correctional professionals the pace of change can be affected.

## C.  CRIMINOLOGICAL THEORIES

The entire concept of corrections is based on social control. Societies find some behaviors so egregious that formal action needs to be taken. We base these corrective actions on criminological theories. In other words we theorize why people commit a crime and how to correct that behavior through formal or legal actions. These actions, sanctions, or corrective actions are rooted in theory.

There are a number of criminological theories that explain why people commit crime and how corrective measures can be taken to reduce crime. One should note that Criminology is a social science. As a social science it's inherently dynamic. Being able to represent alternative explanations for criminality is one of the characteristics that separate social science from natural science (i.e. chemistry or biology). Why people commit crime is as different as the people that commit crime thus there are various theories of crime. Employing various theories as an explanation why crimes occur addresses these variations. It's important to remember that there is no single "cause" for crime just as there is no single theory about correcting criminal behavior. Rather we can examine factors that facilitate crime or inhibit it. We see that solely applying criminal sanctions (i.e. probation or prison) from formal authorities has an effect on criminal behavior but just as importantly we should note the importance of informal social control that many criminological theories state. Thus discounting informal social control isn't advisable.

### 1.   Classical School and Rational Choice

Perhaps one of the most impactful theories concerning criminal behavior comes to us from the Classical School and thus the concept of Rational Choice. As we discovered in Chapter 1 Cesare Beccaria and Jeremy Bentham brought forward ideas and concepts that shaped our Bill of Rights. This theory is impactful far beyond that. Our criminal justice system is based on some of the major tenants of the Classical School and thus Rational Choice. The first is that people are self-interested and rational thinkers. If the person is deemed to be irrational to a certain point we don't hold the person criminally responsible (i.e. criminally insane). Also, we base our concept of punishment and therefore corrections on the premise that since people are self-interested they would chose to not commit a crime in order to avoid prison. The pain of imprisonment should outweigh the pleasure of the crime. A recent correctional era of "Just Desserts" adheres to this idea[8].

Rational Choice promotes the idea of specific and general deterrence. Specific deterrence concerns specifically deterring a person from committing a crime again. For example a released convict is supposed to remember the pains of imprisonment when in a situation where a crime may be committed and chose to not commit the crime. The threat of returning to prison in this case is supposed to be the deterrent. General deterrence is the threat of punishment if one is thinking about committing a crime. For instance a billboard along a highway may warn against a person driving drunk be explaining the penalties[9].

Deterrence relies on three concepts: severity of the punishment, certainty of being caught, and celerity or swiftness of the punishment[10]. The courts often determine the severity of the punishment during sentencing. However, inmates can also receive punishments administered by prison staff for violating rules while in prison. These punishments vary in severity from losing privileges such as watching television or having certain items in their cells to being removed from the general prison population and being placed in **administrative segregation**. Thereby making a prison sentence more or less comfortable. These potential measures employed by prison staff are supposed to deter inmates from negative activities while in prison. Being disciplined in prison can also affect **"good time"** and early release. These measures are used so the inmate will think about their actions and the possible consequences of their actions. They are supposed to be rational actors and will choose to avoid criminal behavior because the potential "pain" of losing privileges outweighs the potential pleasure of the criminal or unauthorized behavior. This is the rationale for punishment in that case.

Parole and probation officers ensure the person under community supervision is adhering to their conditions of release. The certainty of being caught for violating these terms increases when the officer is surveilling or checking on that person. Thus not only are the police there to deter crime but an officer assigned to the parolee or probationer is specifically watching them.

The swiftness or celerity of punishment varies. Whether in prison or in the community the offender is usually afforded a chance to rebut or challenge allegations of disciplinary infractions or technical violations. These can be addressed well after the event in question takes place. However, there are certain measures that community corrections officers can take in order to address probation violations. Some agencies allow officers to jail probationers for up to 48 hours for some technical violations in order to address the violation relatively quickly as opposed to waiting days or weeks for a court hearing.

Rational Choice theory impacts correctional policy and practice in a multitude of different ways. It is the purpose or rationale behind many correctional methods. We'll see in later chapters how EBP impacts those traditional ways of administering corrections.

## 2.   Biological and Psychological Theories

Biological and Psychological theories are often discussed together, however they are two different areas of study. They do both involve the decision making center of the body but biology has to do with the structure of the brain or the physical makeup. Psychology is about thinking, decisions, and processing information. Psychology is about the mind in that sense.

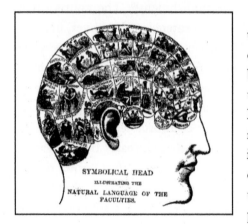

The philosophy of Positivism is the use of quantification, objectivity, and causality when studying different behaviors. One of the first people to use this approach to study crime was Cesare Lombroso (1835–1909). Lombroso, a medical doctor, studied physical features in an attempt to identify criminal features or outwardly identifiable characteristics that criminals might share. He also presented the notion that criminal behavior is hereditary and that certain groups of people committed criminal acts at higher rates than other groups because some groups of people were not as evolved as others. His work was widely accepted at the time, although it isn't seriously regarded today. Interestingly even though portions of his work were biased against groups of people a major contribution of this early work is the use of quantification and measures or the use of statistics that can reduce bias in research. Advanced statistical techniques of the time were also being used[11].

The role biology plays in corrections is growing. Large quantities of **psychotropic medications** are dispensed at jails and prisons every day. A regular condition of release for probation and parolees is to take the medication prescribed to them. These medications help to control brain chemistry and thus help prevent behavior that may turn violent as a result of failing to take the prescribed medications.

Psychology concerns decision making and thought processes. You may remember that Sigmund Freud (1856–1939) played a huge role in its early development. His use of psychoanalysis and theories of personality have been widely applied to the early study of criminal behavior. The use of psychoanalysis to explain or understand why someone committed a crime was just the beginning. The use of various therapies are utilized in corrections today. There are anger management groups, moral reconation therapy (MRT), and sex offender's therapy groups just to name a few. The validity and effectiveness of these therapies is as different as the therapy. Sometimes different therapies work better for males then females or different therapies can be more or less efficient for juveniles than adults. There is no one size fits all approach to therapy. We will discover in subsequent chapters how efficient or not some therapies are[12].

# D. SOCIOLOGICAL THEORIES

Sociological theories of crime involve social influences on criminal behavior. These influences can be at the macro level such as those that deal with culture or subcultural issues or economic structure and others are at the meso or micro level where social influence can help explain small group behavior. Here we will sample a few of these theories. We will review some of the main points of these theories. This is not an exhaustive review of criminological theory. We don't have time to review them at length, however it's important to see the connections between theory and correctional practice and policy. Remember these theories provide the basis or reasons behind the policy or practices. Once we understand theory we can conduct reviews and evaluations to determine "best practices" or evidence-based practices.

Social process theories are a category of sociological theories and just as the title "process" implies here the focus is on the process toward becoming criminal or identifying factors that facilitate criminal behavior and then addressing those factors in any number of different ways. One of those theories we'll discuss is Labeling theory whereby primary deviation takes place and the person is affixed a label. For instance an adolescent may be sanctioned formally for being truant and labeled a deviant. As a result of this **primary deviance** a label may be affixed to the juvenile. They may be made to attend an alternative school, and subsequently treated with less regard or avenues that don't involve intervention by the police or other formal authorities when trouble occurs. Their criminal behavior may escalate into **secondary deviancy**. Secondary deviance is usually more serious than the initial deviant act(s). The process involves the escalation and the self-identification by the deviant juvenile as being a deviant person.[13]

According to this theory of criminality we need to avoid affixing the label to the person. The stigma of the label provides a self-fulfilling prophecy of sorts whereby the offender identifies themselves as their given label (i.e. living up to their label as delinquent). The juvenile justice system and juvenile corrections attempts to avoid this label on many different levels. We will discuss **diversion** at length in Chapter 5, but this sanction is an attempt to divert the juvenile from the label and associated stigma of a delinquent or even felon.

Another social process theory is Differential Association. Edward Sutherland (1883–1950) was a sociologist at Indiana University when he presented his theory. The central concept of this theory relies on the idea that behavior is imitated in proportion to the intensity of the social closeness between people. There are two basic elements to this theory. The first is that the content of what's being leaned is important. This not only includes the specific techniques for committing the crime (i.e. how to break in to a car and start it) but also the motives and rational for criminal behavior (i.e. the person has insurance and insurance will pay for the car). The second is process. Process concerns how the learning of criminal behavior takes place. Here is where the context or reasons for committing crime is learned.

Sutherland presented his theory in nine clear propositions:

1. Criminal Behavior is learned.

2. Criminal behavior is learned in interaction with other persons in a process of communication.

3. The principal part of the learning of criminal behavior occurs with intimate groups.

4. When criminal behavior is learned the learning includes techniques for committing the crime and the specific motives, drives, and rationalizations, and attitudes.

5.  The specific direction of motives and drives is learned from perceptions of various aspects of the legal code as favorable or unfavorable.

6.  A person becomes a criminal when he or she perceives more favorable than unfavorable consequences to violating the law.

7.  Differential associations may vary in frequency, duration, priority, and intensity.

8.  The process of learning criminal behavior by association with criminal and anti-criminal patterns involves all of the mechanisms that are involved in any other learning process.

9.  Although criminal behavior expresses general needs and values, it is not excused by those general needs and values, because noncriminal behavior expresses the same needs and values.

The nine propositions can offer insight into why some people commit crime. Criminologists have pointed to proposition #6." A Person becomes delinquent because of an excess of definitions favorable to violation of the law over definitions unfavorable to law violations" as key to understanding this theory. Just how much of an "excess of definitions" is debatable but the point is that criminal behavior and attitudes toward crime are taught by people that matter to the offender more so than more conventional or legal behaviors are taught. Thus if criminal behavior can be taught new more legal behavior can be taught to replace motivations and rational for crime. In corrections we see a number of measures being deployed to teach conventional legal behavior. One of those Moral Reconation Therapy (MRT) is just one example. In MRT the offender is taught to challenge criminal thinking. Criminal or anti-social beliefs are confronted, attitudes and behaviors of current relationships are assessed, there is reinforcement of positive habits and behaviors, positive identity formation, enhancement of self-concepts, decrease in hedonism (self-interest) and development of tolerance, and finally development of higher stages of moral reasoning[14].

Other sociological theories operate in a different capacity. They seek to explain the impact of **social structure** and social pressures on groups of people. Perhaps one of the best known is Strain Theory. Strain Theory was developed by Robert Merton (1910–2003). Strain Theory posits that deviant behavior is a normal response to abnormal conditions and that people are socialized to act in certain ways and are therefore predictable. Strain theorists advise that society and culture cause strain as a result of social organization (i.e. hierarchy based on wealth or socio-economic status) and universal goals that are not as attainable for some versus others. Put another way if the societal goal is wealth the means of which to obtain that wealth is not evenly distributed. In our culture we tend to separate people based on wealth such as: middle class, upper class, or those at or below the poverty line. Merton's Strain theory recognizes that in some cultures success is defined by wealth and that most people want to be successful. Yet the avenues to obtain that wealth are not evenly distributed. For example someone with financial and emotional resources or support can afford to obtain a Bachelor's degree and therefore multiple legal doorways open to material successes via a career pathway in the job market. Others may not have the financial resources to afford a bachelor's degree or support to even attempt to earn one. For that person an option may be to make money through criminal means. Adaptations toward criminality are referred to by Strain Theorists as a state of anomie[15].

A correctional response to Strain Theory impacting crime would be to alleviate the strain. In the case of Merton's Strain Theory addressing economic the strain of those not able to attain the universal goal of wealth or material items is the focus. Since education is vital to economic success there are a number of job training programs for inmates. Also, allowing people to pursue Associates, Bachelors, and other degrees or certifications has been deemed vital in reducing criminal recidivating. There are also a number of efforts underway to remove criminal history questions from employment applications. This "ban the Box" movement has been adopted by many employers and allows those that may be passed over for employment a better chance at obtaining a job and a legal means to obtain financial goals.

Weblink—Ban the box Youtube video.

https://www.youtube.com/watch?v=ucSfbcTZ7O8

Another social structural theory of criminality has to do with people's criminal behavior and their environment. Social Disorganization is a criminological theory that suggests people that live in disorganized neighborhoods are at a greater risk of committing crimes as well as being a victim of crime. The theory of Social Disorganization developed from the Chicago School of thought. This line of thinking adheres to the concept that cities do not

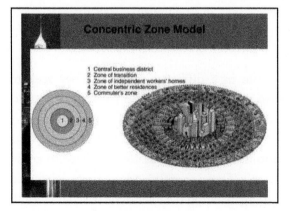

develop randomly. People live in certain areas and act accordingly based on social processes. Clifford Shaw and Henry McKay applied that Chicago School of thought to explain why certain neighborhoods of Chicago have higher crime rates that other areas. Their theoretical framework relied on the use of concentric zones. These zones radiated out from the city center. They discovered that the crime rate fell in each zone the further away from the center of the city.

A question emerged from the discovery, namely why did crime rates fall in zones further from the center? Shaw and McKay reasoned there was something about the social environment that facilitated crime in the city center that wasn't there in outer neighborhoods. Their hypothesis was that some neighborhoods are disorganized. What does a disorganized neighborhood look like? Primarily these areas lack **collective efficacy** where there is little or no community control or informal social control of neighborhood residents. There is little respect for traditional social rules and conventional norms of behavior. But why does that tend to occur in some neighborhoods? To answer that question we need to consider the historical context of the time when Shaw and McKay are conducting their research and forming their theory.

The Industrial Revolution took root near the end of the 18th Century. In the span of about 40 years nearly fourteen million immigrants poured into the country. The majority of these new Americans settled in and around large cities because that's where work could be found[16]. The result was a great melting pot of people of different ethnicities and backgrounds. Neighbors became transient and people were not invested in the interests of their community as a result. The lack of informal social control or collective efficacy was replaced to some extent with the introduction of gangs which could fill a gap in social control and therefore flourish. This new environment allows for a **subculture** to emerge. A subculture that prizes attitudes and beliefs that run counter to mainstream attitudes. These are best exemplified by Miller's Six Focal Concerns given below:

1.  Excitement—excitement is defined as causing trouble such as stealing a car and going on a joyride.

2.  Toughness—being physically tough is prized.

3.  Smartness—being street smart and knowing how to get over on someone else or scam, cheat, or trick another.

4.  Trouble—trouble is linked to #1 but being in trouble with police is embraced or seen as obtaining street credit.

5.  Autonomy—belief in individual independence, no need at all to rely on another. You live or die; sink or swim on your own merits.

6.   Fate—the belief that one is resigned to a certain way of life. This is the way life is.[17]

Social Disorganization Theory suggest that certain neighborhoods, regardless of the ethnic groups that occupy them at any given time are environments that facilitate crime. These neighborhoods lack collective efficacy as a result of people constantly moving from place to place, people perhaps not understanding or carry prejudices with them about other people from different cultures. In short the environment provides the context for the transmission of criminal behavior patterns and the failure or blocking of non-criminal learning.

We of course cannot legislate collective efficacy but there are programs or policies that can be used to foster it. Providing measures such as low interest loans for those wishing to buy a home is one way to promote permanency in the neighborhood and therefore reduce transiency. The creation of community is allowed to take root when people know their neighbors and become invested in their communities. The creation of low interest home loans is outside of the scope of correctional policy. However, promoting job training and education that allows a former inmate or current parolee to obtain employment which that inmate can in turn use when applying for a loan can be important. Although correctional measures or policy may not directly impact collective efficacy there are a number of different methods to obtain that result. Knowing that a neighborhood may be rather disorganized can be important to a parole/probation officer when confronted with someone on their caseload perhaps moving to such an area. The risk or re-offense or violating conditions of their release may be enhanced. Thus the officer made need to provide more resources to that offender.

We are only able to sample a few of the criminological theories in this chapter. This gives the student a good idea of the relationship between theory and practice. Theories of crime causation help those that work in the area of corrections to understand why people commit crime and potential ways of dealing with criminals. Here we see some of the evidence in evidence-based practice.

The solutions to preventing crime doesn't have to relate directly actions or sanctions taken against the offender for violating terms of release while in the community or simply warehousing inmates in prison. Solutions to preventing crime are often much more nuanced and can require actions outside of the normal criminal justice option of incarceration. Policies and practices outside of those traditional actions are becoming more commonplace as a result of adhering to a more evidence-based approach to corrections.

# E. CONCLUSION

Corrections is a constantly evolving field. A relatively new approach to correctional policy and programming is to rely much more on evidence-based practices to guide that policy and practice. This philosophical change to corrections is a slow process. The change comes from three separate influences. The first is social attitudes about corrections. Attitudes have changed from being retributive to one that's more reintegrate in nature. Second is the need for resources. Legislative bodies at the local, state, and federal level aren't as willing to fund programs or support policies that aren't efficient or effective. Finally, the empirical data can challenges current practices and policies as not being as effective or efficient as we thought in preventing crime or reintegrating offenders. Thus the implementation of policy and practice that's supported by data or research and that is evidence-based is becoming adopted. Once adopted they are usually replicated in other jurisdictions. Evidence-based practices uses criminological theory as an underpinning or rationale for implementation for correctional measures. These measures then evaluated to see what is effective and what isn't. The ultimate goal is to weed out those that are ineffective and support the measures that are effective.

## Discussion Questions

1. Explain what evidence-based practice (EBP) is.

2. What is he Scientific Method?

3. How is the Scientific Method important when considering the accuracy of research?

4. Why is it vitally important to define exactly what you are going to research?

5. What is literature review and how does it impact hypothesis development?

6. Explain the role of research in evidence-based practice.

7. Discuss the importance of Rational Choice Theory in correctional policy and practice.

8. What role if any do you think biology has on criminal behavior?

9. How do you think the social stigma of being a convicted felon impacts criminal behavior?

10. Discuss how social structure impacts criminality.

## Student Exercises

1.  Find a journal article that relates to corrections and:

    A.  Summarize it.

    B.  Explain how they collected and analyzed the data.

    C.  What conclusion(s) were drawn.

    D.  Can it be used to support some type of correctional policy or practice? Explain.

    E.  Cite the article using APA format.

2.  Research a single correctional policy or practice in the state where you live. Explain what the practice/policy is. Look for empirical data that is related to this policy/practice.

## Key Terms

**Academic journal**—a collection of empirical studies of other research published in various formats.

**Administrative segregation**—solitary confinement for inmates where there is very limited contact with inmates or staff.

**Collective efficacy**—the ability for community members to limit or control individual behavior; social cohesion.

**Diversion**—a sanction that does not involve a criminal conviction.

**Empirical study**—research that employs the use of the Scientific Method.

**Evidence-based practices (EBP)**—the use of what works or best practices based on empirical data.

**Good time**—time off a prison sentence granted to inmates for not receiving any or limited discipline.

**Primary deviance**—minor rule infractions of criminal behavior.

**Psychotropic medication**—medication prescribed by a medical doctor in order to affect moods or behavior.

**Qualitative data**—the use of non-quantifiable methods to evaluate data; finding themes or common characteristics among variables.

**Quantitative data**—the use of math and statistics to interpret data.

**Scientific Method**—principles and procedures for the systemic pursuit of knowledge involving the recognition and formulation of a problem, the collection of data through observation or experiment, the formulation of a hypothesis and drawing of a conclusion.

**Secondary deviance**—deviance that results after primary deviance has been reacted to by formal authorities, exemplified by an escalation in criminal behavior from primary deviance.

**Social structure**—the patterned social arrangements in society that are both emergent from and determinant of the actions of the individuals.

**Subculture**—a cultural group within a larger group whose moral, beliefs, and values differ slightly from the larger mainstream group.

---

[1]   Khanacademy.org 5 Steps to the Scientific Method. Retrieved 5-31-2018.

[2]   Martinson, Robert (1974). What Works? Questions and Answers about prison reform. The Public Interest 35 pg. 22–54.

[3]   King, Gary; Bresina, Dan; Glenna, Tianna; and Leich, Nicki (2013). Evidence Based Decision making from principle to practice. ICCA Conference Reno, NV 2013 from NIC website Google Search of Correctional Departments in the U.S.

[4]   Ibid.

[5]   Zgoba, Kristen M; Levenson, Jill; and McKee, Tracy (2008). Examining the Impact of Sex Offender Restrictions on Housing Availability. Criminal Justice Policy Review 20 (1).

[6]   Alexander, Ryan (2011). Pathways: Changes in Recruitment for Child Sexual Abuse and Life Course Events. Dissertation.

[7]   Levenson, Jill and Cotter, Leo (2005). Sex Offender Residency Restrictions: 1000 feet From Danger or One Step from Absurd. International Journal of Offender Therapy and Comparative Criminology 49 (2) 2005.

[8]   Williams and McShane (2014). Criminological Theory. Pearson Publishing.

[9]   Paternoster, Raymond (2010). How Much Do We really Know about Criminal Deterrence? The Journal of Criminal Law and Criminology 100 (3). Northwestern University School of Law.

[10]   Tomlinson, Kelli D. (2016). An Examination of Deterrence Theory: Where do we stand? Federal Probation: A Journal of Correctional Philosophy and Practice 80 (3).

[11]   Lanier, Mark and Henry, Stuart (1998). Essential Criminology. Westview Press. Boulder Colorado.

[12]   Martin, Randy; Mutchnik, Robert J.; Austin, Timothy (1990). Criminological Thought: Pioneers Past and Present. McMillian NY.

[13]   Becker, Howard (1963). Outsiders: Studies in the Sociology of Deviance New York Free Press.

[14]   Lizama, Jaslene; Mathews, Vikram; Reyes, Sean (2014). What Works? Short-term, in custody treatment programs. National Institute of Corrections.

[15]   Ibid.

[16]   The Industrial Revolution in the United States retrieved June 4th 2018 from the Library of Congress.

[17]   Miller, Walter B. (1968). Lower Class Culture as a Generating Milieu of Gang Delinquency. Journal of Social Issues 14 (3).

## CHAPTER 3

# Courts and Sentencing

**Chapter Objectives:**

- Understand the goals of sentencing and how they affect the criminal justice system.

- Assess the evolutionary nature of punishment.

- Evaluate the role Evidence-Based Practice plays in determining punishment.

- Define Sentencing models employed in the U.S. today.

- Understand the current issues in sentencing today.

## A. AMERICAN COURT PROCESS—THE DOORWAY TO CORRECTIONS

It's extremely difficult to understand corrections without first recognizing the role **sentencing** plays in corrections. Sentencing often represents the formal punishment for the offender. There are a wide range of punishments available to judges from fines or probation to the death penalty depending upon which **jurisdiction** the offender is sentenced in. Jurisdiction is important to understand for corrections students as this step in the court process determines the length and type of sentence.

Figure 3.1

Sentencing Outcomes for First Time Driving
Under the Influence (DUI) Offender

| South Dakota District (State) Court | Penalty: South Dakota Criminal Code 32–23–1= class "B" misdemeanor offender must serve 48 hours in jail but not more than 6 months |
|---|---|

| Federal Court | Penalty: 18 USC 3 = class "A" misdemeanor 48 hours in jail mandatory to 1 year in jail |
|---|---|

Depending on where a person gets arrested (jurisdiction) for the same offense there can be different punishment. For the crime of driving under the influence first offense the punishment is more severe in federal court than it is in Kansas State Court.

Corrections professionals must adapt to the flow of inmates that varies as courts sentence offenders to various types of sanctions. For instance in 2015, legislators in Utah adopted a policy that prioritizes prison space for serious and violent felony offenders. They also approved more resources for probation and parole supervision in an effort to decrease the number of technical violators thus reducing the prison population.

## Decriminalization in Utah

| | |
|---|---|
| H.B. 348 | Amends penalties (shortening) involving certain controlled substances. Expands the |
| 2015 | definition of "good time" for time served in jail. |
| S.B. 2 | Authorizes the state to hire more probation/parole officers |
| 2015 | |
| S.B. 3 | Makes supplemental appropriations for 2 fiscal years (FY '15 & '16) for probation and |
| 2015 | parole treatment programs |
| H.B. 2 | Makes appropriations for $1.5 million for FY '17 to counties for substance abuse |
| 2016 | treatment and mental health. Increases funds to hire 15 new adult probation/parole officers. $2 million to support data sharing efforts amongst counties and the state. |
| H.B. 3004 | Creates an administrative level of probation supervision that includes notification to the court of scheduled periodic reviews of compliance or non-compliance. Allows for modification of probation supervision along graduated sanctions and incentives developed by the sentencing commission. Permits earning of good time (incarceration time) for any jail time and completion of multiple programs. |

These sorts of measures impact not only the population or overall numbers of offenders in jail, prison, probation or parole but how long they stay incarcerated or on community corrections. So sentencing can determine the length of the sentence. These measures can have huge impacts on corrections. As we discovered earlier the U.S. incarcerates more people per capita than any other country in the world yet the crime rate continues to fall. How can that be one might ask? One of the reasons concerns sentence lengths and that we are holding people in jail more often when they are arrested for a crime and awaiting trial. According to the Bureau of Justice Statistics 93% of federal drug defendants adjudicated were subsequently convicted compared to 76% in 1981. The proportion of drug offenders sentenced to prison grew from 54% in 1988 to 80% during 2006. The average criminal sentence length for a drug case in federal court increased from 50.1 months in 1988 to 59.7 months in 2006 and for federal weapons cases the average prison sentence increased from 70.3 months to 87.2 months. Consider that in 2006, that U.S. Attorneys investigated 35, 210 drug cases alone.[1] Thus more and more people populate prisons and fewer are released. The same is true for jails. We will discuss jails at length in Chapter 4, but for now it's important to understand that jails and prisons are different. Jails are typically for short term incarceration. Jail populations have increased for a number of different reasons but when we consider sentencing many different crimes that didn't used to mandate jail time now mandate a jail sentence. Also more defendants are in jail awaiting trial. These are people that cannot pay their bail or were not granted bail usually due to the nature of the crime they are accused of or the risk of the defendant not showing up for trial.

Figure 3.2

Pretrial status of defendants charged with drug offenses, 1998–2004

| Pretrial status and type of release | 1998 | 2000 | 2004 |
|---|---|---|---|
| Total | 100% | 100% | 100% |
| Released | 68% | 64% | 60% |
| Financial total | 33% | 31% | 32% |
| Surety bond | 23 | 22 | 24 |
| Deposit bond | 5 | 7 | 7 |
| Full cash bond | 3 | 1 | 1 |
| Property bond | 2 | — | 1 |

| | | | |
|---|---|---|---|
| **Nonfinancial total** | 34% | 33% | 28% |
| **Emergency release** | — | — | — |
| **Detained** | 32% | 35% | 35% |

Note: Detail may not add to total because of rounding

—Less than 0.5%.

Source: BJS, Felony Defendants in Large Urban Counties, 2004, NCJ 221152, April 2008.

Sentencing acts as valve whereby the number of offenders involved in corrections can increase or decrease. It also can determine what sorts of programs a person is mandated to do.

For instance a person convicted of domestic violence will most likely be mandated to undergo some type of therapy such as anger management. The probation officer monitoring the offender may ask the judge to incarcerate the offender or revoke their release if they fail to attend this court ordered therapy. These types of sanctions can have major impacts on jails or prison populations. Court orders from sentencing also have huge impacts on the way probation and parole officers supervise offenders.

In this chapter we'll review how correctional populations are impacted by sentencing decisions. We will discuss the purpose of punishment. Recall from Chapter 2 there are various reasons why we carry out some punishments. We will review and look at multiple purposes of punishment. Some of those purposes become the dominant philosophy of corrections for a time. They can define a period of correctional history. For instance the notion of "Just Deserts" came to dominate correctional philosophy starting in the late 1970s and continues presently. However, the public and therefore legislatures are beginning to examine other purposes of punishment and question the status quo. The importance of research or evidence-based practices has begun to force changes in correctional policy and programs. Of course the matter of limited financial resources has forced many agencies to find different more efficient ways of handling offenders too. Corrections is an ever evolving field and currently there are many different philosophical changes occurring.

### Correctional Focus

It's unusual in Washington D.C. today where Republicans and Democrats can find something to agree about but it appears that one of those rare instances concerns sentencing reforms for federal crimes, specifically drug crimes. In February 2018, The Senate Judiciary Committee passed the Sentencing Reform and Corrections Act (SRCA) from the committee. The committee passed this bill with 16 yes votes and 5 no votes. It still has a very long way to go before or if it becomes law. If it does take effect it would have enormous effects on federal corrections. The bill would lessen mandatory minimum sentences. These set a minimum amount of prison time a judge can sentence a person too. Thus in some cases a judge cannot sentence a person to less prison time when they feel the crime warrants less prison time. It also makes the Fair Sentencing Act of 2010, which equivocates the amount of prison time for crack cocaine to powder cocaine. A measure that would release many people, specifically a number of minority inmates from prison **retroactive**. It also seeks to mandate the Federal Bureau of Prisons to put more emphasis on prisoner re-entry and education in order to reduce criminal recidivism.

The House of Representatives has a similar bill in their Judiciary Committee. President Donald Trump in his 2018 State of the Union address spoke about wanting prison reform, which is a relatively new perspective for Republican politicians. This stance is beginning to have more traction among Republican politicians. SRCA is not legislation and there are many that are skeptical it will become law. Whether it does or not this still shows that sentencing and correctional reform will take place in the future.

## B. GOALS OF SENTENCING

Providing formal punishment or corrections to those that violate the law is a form of social control. Punishments or the criminal sentence is supposed to serve a purpose. These punishments adopted by legislatures and then exercised by courts at sentencing provide utility or a reason for sentencing people to prison or placing them on probation or even handing down a fine for a speeding ticket. These formal actions serve many different purposes. However, there appears to be a dominant sentencing or correctional philosophy that often defines a period of time. This doesn't mean that other purposes of punishment wither away or are not relevant. No purpose for punishment is mutually exclusive. In other words just because an era of Just Desserts or revenge was the dominant correctional philosophy for a few decades doesn't mean there were no attempts at rehabilitation or that incapacitation was not employed. Instead these philosophies can complement each other as we will see.

Although it's important to understand each purpose for punishment it's also important to note the transitory nature of dominant correctional philosophies. Why the dominant philosophy changes is important to understand for the student of corrections because that helps us understand how corrections changes and

Web assignment—Each state has their criminal codes or statutes published online. Find a violent crime like robbery and determine what the punishment is for that crime. Find a property crime like theft and see what the punishments are for a property crime. Discuss with your classmates why the punishment is what is stated in the codes. Are the punishments too harsh or too lenient in your opinion?

evolves or what can prompt change. The social environment plays a big role in shaping the correctional philosophy. After all legislators are representatives of the people and as we covered in Chapters 1 and 2 the legislative branch of government makes laws. They determine which behaviors rise to the level of formal punishment and ones that do not. Judges determine the actual punishment at the time of sentencing but they operate within the parameters set by legislators. Legislators determine what the potential punishment is for each crime. The executive branch is also a representative of the people and that person appoints heads of agencies like a department of corrections or the Federal Bureau of Prisoners which they in turn set policy and are in charge of daily operations. Thus the social environment can have huge impacts and alter correctional philosophy.

There are five commonly recognized goals of sentencing: revenge/retribution, deterrence, incapacitation, rehabilitation, and restoration. Each of these rationale for punishment are legitimately criticized and each can prove to be effective. We will look at what each of these purposes are then we will investigate their faults and their effectiveness.

## 1. Revenge/Retribution

Revenge is certainly one of the oldest rationales for punishment. The notion of revenge as a purpose for punishment dates back to ancient Rome. The concept of **lex talionis** as a rationale for punishment was adopted It involves the punishment for the sake of punishment. Put a different way the only purpose revenge serves is to inflict some type of pain upon the offender. Today that "pain" is implicitly understood to be emotional "pain". Whereby the inmate is deprived of a host of freedoms and removal from society and family. However, revenge or retribution used to be carried out via inflicting physical pain upon the person. Any number of methods were used from whipping to the use of stocks or breaking of limbs.

The idea of "just desserts" is based on the concept of revenge. In the U.S. there is not a criminal sentence that directly intentionally inflicts pain upon the offender, even though some would say the death penalty violates this notion. "Just desserts" today holds those old notions of equivalent punishment for the crime compared to the harm caused on the victim, thus the term "just desserts". How do we know what type of punishment fits the crime? For instance students were asked earlier in this chapter to research the punishment for a violent and property crime. Do you all agree on the sentence for the crime of rape? Our idea of **justice** or fairness of punishment can change over time. Today, rape is more strictly enforced by police. Many states have more harsh punishment for rape then they had in the past. Our notion of fairness of punishment for the crime of rape has changed. This example is illustrated by the case in the web link.

Weblink—https://abcnews.go.com/US/california-judge-fights-recall-stanford-swimmers-sex-assault/story?id=55023577

www.alamy.com - HRP3CA

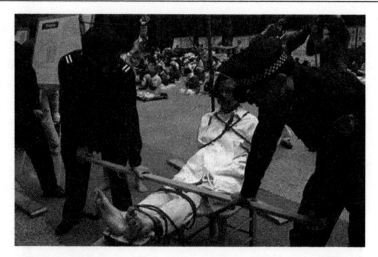

## 2.   Deterrence

The purpose of deterrence is to prevent crime. It acts as an ever present threat of punishment. Consider walking into a store and seeing a sign that reads, "Smile you're on Camera". Of course the intent is not meant literally. The sign acts as a notice to customers and potential thieves that people in the store are under surveillance. Remember in Chapter 2 we discussed the Criminological Theory of Rational Choice. Whereby rational people weigh the consequences of getting caught and punished for a crime versus the potential satisfaction of completing the crime. This thought process is known as hedonistic calculus. When we consider deterrence we are concerned with providing a consequence worthy or severe enough to deter us from crime.

The major tenets of deterrence are the certainty of punishment, the severity of punishment, and the swiftness of the application of punishment after the crime occurs. The idea is that without all of these components deterrence doesn't work or at least is minimally effective. Seeing the sign that tells us to, "smile your on camera" lets us know someone is watching what you are doing and provides a measure of certainty of getting caught if a person shoplifts an item. The sign is supposed to impact our hedonistic calculus and deter one from shoplifting there.

The logic appears to be sound. Who would steal something in plain view while security is watching? The issue relies on each of us developing that sense of calculation. There are any number of ways to rationalize stealing while allegedly being under surveillance. How do we know that someone is actually watching? Some may not care that someone is watching and still others may consider themselves too crafty or slick to get caught. The idea of surveillance is very important to deterrence.

The certainty of getting caught or being under surveillance has become a new market where billions of dollars a year are spent on not only cameras but other types of surveillance. Companies sell cameras that alert your mobile phone when someone rings your doorbell. Security companies sell a variety of detection devices to protect home and cars or other property from theft or damage because they increase the chance of getting caught. The certainty of punishment in the age of increased surveillance is an important part of deterrence. An extra set of eyes or someone like a probation or parole officer ensures someone is watching certain people that have already come under scrutiny. A person may figure in their hedonistic calculus that since they are already on probation shoplifting an item and getting caught may provide extra punishment versus a first time offender. Here the severity of punishment becomes relevant.

The severity of punishment is one more component of deterrence. How severely should we punish each crime? We don't incarcerate someone for 5 years because they shoplift a shirt, however there can be significant consequences. The severity of punishment are typically related to social attitudes about the crime. For instance we don't execute someone for stealing a horse or grapes today whereas once those were acceptable punishments.

Sentencing in criminal court is the handing down of punishment. Often the severity of punishment is determined by the type of crime committed. Shoplifting or theft can be considered a misdemeanor or if the amount of the stolen item is significant enough it can be considered a felony. The punishments for felonies and misdemeanors can be very different. Of course all punishments are relative to the jurisdictions in which they are prosecuted in. Thus the definition of felony theft in Georgia is different than it is in a neighboring state like Florida or a distant state like Hawaii. The punishments for offenses are different for each jurisdiction too.

The key is to find the right amount of severity of punishment to administer. List and Gneezy (2013) recount a study of a child daycare center in Haifa Israel. The center was having difficulty getting parents to pick up their children on time. In order to incentivize the prompt pickup of children a small fine was instituted. However the initiation of the fine had the reverse effect and more parents began to pick up their children later as opposed to the opposite more preferred result for the daycare. Upon further investigation parents started to pick their children up later because the fine was small enough that the "pain" of the fine was less than the inclination to arrive late (Gneezy, 2013). When the fine was significantly increased picking up children late significantly decreased. If we use that example and apply it to criminal justice then why aren't all punishments for criminal behavior very severe? The death penalty exists in 31 states and the federal government. Yet the death penalty doesn't seem to be much of a deterrent to committing murder. In fact in states like Texas the death penalty is administered more frequently than any other state in the nation. In 2015, Texas executed 13 people. The state of Missouri was second. They executed 6 people that year. Texas has executed 551 people since it was reinstated nationally in 1976. Virginia is second with 113, executions. Considering the possibility of being executed is highest in Texas you should expect their murder rate to be the lowest in the nation, however their ranked 24th (murder rates nationally by state, 2018).

The severity of punishment changes just as societies attitudes about punishment change. It appears the punishment for drug crimes are decreasing. Currently there are only 16 states in the U.S. that marijuana possession is fully illegal. Nine state and the District of Columbia have fully legalized recreational use. Canada has also legalized recreational use marijuana. A further 13 states have **decriminalized** recreational use significantly whereby possession amounts to small fines. A majority of Americans,61%, now support its legalization. It's quite possible that in the near future legalization will take place (A majority of Americans now support legal marijuana, 2018). Conversely we have increased the penalties for crimes like domestic violence and drunk driving to name a few. The solution lies in finding a tipping point where behavior is changed. That tipping point may not be prison, it may not be probation or a fine. This is the challenge for future corrections administrators.

The final component for deterrence is the swiftness of which punishment is applied after the crime has been committed. The idea is the offender must relate their punishment directly to the crime thus timing of the punishment is important. For example if a teen took the car without asking permission from their parents and their parents didn't apply the punishment until a month had passed the teen may think whatever punishment was rendered as unfair. The punishment may be lost because its' now out of historical context.

There have been significant attempts in probation and parole to apply swift punishments upon the discovery of a technical violation. Many agencies have the ability to incarcerate probationers or parolees for 48–72 hours as the result of a minor technical violation without a court or parole hearing. The effectiveness of these shock incarcerations are debatable but the purpose is to apply punishment swiftly.

Probation and parole officer officers may be able to apply sanctions with relative expedience. However, applying sanctions to crimes via sentencing is another matter entirely. The court process typically takes months from arrest to sentence and in some cases can take well over a year. The swiftness relies on many factors such as the offender taking a plea versus a court trial. An estimated 1.1 million people are convicted of felonies in state courts each year. 94% of those cases lead to convictions as a result of a plea bargain (Felony Sentences, 2018). The median time to resolve a case in federal criminal court is now 13 months. The weighted caseload for federal judges have climbed from an average of 600 civil and criminal cases a year in the late 1990s to over 1,000 (Thanawala, 2015). Typically the swiftness of which justice is applied is tempered by the court process and a backlog of criminal cases.

There are two types of deterrence, one is aimed at individuals and is referred to as **specific deterrence** the other is supposed to prevent crime in general and it referred to as **general deterrence**. These deterrent efforts share the common goal to prevent crime but how they accomplish that goal is separate. As we know the purpose or goal of incarceration is varied, but here the goal for those that have been to prison is to not return to it. The goal of specific deterrence is to prevent **recidivation**. The concept relies on the principles of Rational Choice again. Prison is supposed to be a place that people do not want to be. Therefore the "pain" of incarceration is supposed to outweigh the pleasure of crime. The offender, who has experienced this pain, should be deterred from committing future crimes as a result of their prison experience.

---

### Focus on Corrections

A report focusing on federal offender recidivation from the U.S. Sentencing Commission was released in 2016. It drew data from 25,400 former inmates who were either released outright from prison or on parole/probation. It found that 49% of inmates had been arrested again at least once within eight years of release. If we were to issue a grade based on that percentage we would find the result to be 51% success rate or using most grading scales an "F" would be recorded. However, we need to examine the data further. If we take a good look we would see that the re-arrest rate for new crimes to be 31.7%. Remember re-arrest for parole/probation can also mean re-arrest for technical violations which are not necessarily new criminal law violations. The grade received would still be 69.3% which on many grading scales is a grade of "D" (Hunt, 2018). Interestingly the report revealed that most re-offenses took place fairly quickly upon release, typically within the first 21 months after release. If prison as a specific deterrent had the desired effect should the recidivism rates be expected to be lower than 31%? If it is obtaining the goal for deterrence shouldn't an offender be less likely to commit an offense so soon after their release from prison, when memories of the "pain" of imprisonment is fresh in their minds?

---

There are a myriad of reasons for offender recidivation. If we had an answer to that problem then corrections would be much easier to implement. Specific deterrence does have value whether the deterrence is incarceration or a community corrections officer providing a measure of surveillance. Incarceration or any other measure doesn't appear to be a one-size fits all solution but rather one of many tools for corrections officials and the courts to employ.

General deterrence concerns deterring the general population from committing crime. The concept relies on a fear of being caught and punished. Much like specific deterrence which relies on the three components of deterrence: certainty of being caught; severity of punishment; and swiftness of punishment. Simply having police on the street and patrolling is supposed to satisfy this measure. Often we hear a call for more police to be on the street, thus we need to hire more police. This is an effort to ensure more surveillance of cities or areas of cities. A rational person and would be criminal would see that the chances of getting caught have substantially increased due to more police presence. Coupled with news reports, social media efforts, or other ways of spreading the word concerning more sever prison sentences even people who have not committed a crime should be deterred from potential criminal behavior.

## 3. Evidence-Based Practice in Deterrence: Felons with Firearms Recidivists

The issue of who can possess and firearm and where they can possess one has gained a lot of notoriety as of late. Even though there is a great debate on many issues surrounding firearm ownership and possession. In a recent survey 87% of Americans favored banning felons from owning guns (Hart, 2018). It is a federal crime for anyone convicted of a felony or misdemeanor crime of domestic violence in any court to own or possess firearms and even ammunition under 18 U.S.C. 922(g) (U.S. Code: Title 18, 2018).

In 2015, 5,391 people were convicted of violating 18 U.S.C. 922(g). Of course all of those convicted for this violation had a previous felony or domestic violence conviction. At least 25% of those people had the highest criminal history category (category VI), meaning at least one quarter of those convicted for this offense had an extensive criminal history. 5.6 % of those sentenced were sentenced under the Armed Career Criminal Act which carry very lengthy prison sentences. 96% of those convicted of this offense received prison time. The average length of sentence was 75 months. It is common place for offenders to be notified at sentencing and then again when placed on probation or on parole that they are prohibited from owning or possessing a firearm. There are also a number of media campaigns aimed at notifying the public that felons cannot have firearms. This campaign can act as a specific and general deterrent.

There were 67,742 cases reported to the U.S. Sentencing Commission in 2015. 5,391 cases involved convictions under U.S.C. 922(g). This means that approximately 8% of all the federal cases were felon with firearms or prohibited person's cases which is not a large percentage of overall cases, but it's a good example of proponents and critics of deterrence. The proponents may see that a small percentage (8%) of felons are convicted for gun/ammunition possession and thus because they either served time in prison or a period of probation they have learned their lesson and at least didn't own or possess a gun (United States Sentencing Commission, 2018). Critics may say this is a good example of deterrence not working. Well over 5, 000 people already conviction and committed a new crime by owning/possessing a gun or ammunition. Of those people many had substantial criminal histories and they were still not dissuaded from owning a gun.

Deterrence, both specific and general, has its benefits and its drawbacks. The purpose is to prevent crime from happening. We often envision that deterrence is the primary goal of corrections. Indeed a common goal is to prevent crime from occurring but are our current means to that goal as efficient as they could be? Are there different ways to deter crime besides prison, probation, or fines? As we know correctional practice is ever evolving. Deterrence can occur in many different ways. We continue to review what research (i.e. evidence) tells us is most effective and efficient. As a result evidence-based practice will most likely guide those practices.

## 4.  Incapacitation

The purpose of incapacitation is different than revenge or retribution. Incapacitation is simply incarcerating someone and removing them from society. Some have referred to as "warehousing people". This measure is used not to rehabilitate offenders or deter them from future criminal behavior. It is simply to remove the offender for a period of time. The reasoning for this removal is to ensure the offender will not continue to victimize others. The idea for incapacitation began to be utilized in the early 1990s. Where the public became aware of habitual offenders or career criminals. This portion of the offenders typically carry out multiple crimes for line periods of time as compared to the vast majority of offenders who age out of crime or commit one or very few crimes.

The notion of the career criminal is not new in the field of criminology. Criminologists such as Marvin Wolfgang studied a group of 9,945 males born in Philadelphia, PA in 1945. He and his group of researchers studied this same group of until they reached age 17. He found that about 33% of the group had some type of police contact during the 17 year study, but that only 6% of the of those that did have some type of police contact were responsible for well of half of the reported crimes. The Philadelphia Cohort Study was one of the first empirically based examples of the role career criminals play in the overall crime picture. Subsequent researchers such as Terrie Moffet (1993) have also concluded that a small group of chronic offenders seem to exist. She categorized offenders into two groups adolescent limited and life course persisters. Whereby adolescent limited offenders limit their offending to one or very few crimes during adolescence. Life-course persisters are a separate very small group of offenders that begin their criminal behavior in early adolescent and continue well into adulthood. Life-course persisters are also referred to have habitual offenders or career criminals.

When we look ahead to the establishment of incapacitory sentencing such as three-strike laws many point to the Richard Allen Davis case as the establishment for incapacitation types of sentences in the U.S. Davis had a long and violent criminal career. One June 27th 1993, Davis was paroled from prison after serving a 16 year sentence for kidnapping. Only three months later he kidnapped, sexually assault, then killed 12 year old Polly Klaas. Poly was taken from her bedroom in the middle of the night while having a slumber party. Davis later admitted to the crime and showed investigators where Polly's body was. He was subsequently sentenced to death and is currently on Death Row in California. The public outcry concerning the death of Poly led to the establishment of Three-strike laws in California. The purpose of this sentence is an effort to recognize who career criminals are. Once those people are identified, in this case by looking at their criminal history and determining the number of prior felony convictions they are sentenced to long periods of incarceration. In a sense the purpose of the Three-strike law is a guess that since the offender has committed felony crimes in the past they will continue to commit them in the future. Thus in order to support our guess we incarcerate people convicted of at least three felonies.

## 5. Evidence Based Practice in Incapacitation: Three-Strike Law

Today 26 six states and the federal government have laws that meet the general criteria as a Three-strikes Law. As we have discovered the sentencing purpose of incapacitation is to remove certain people from society and incarcerate them for long periods of time in order to avoid any possible new criminal behavior. In large part we have identified career criminals, habitual violators, or life course persistent people as those deemed to be a threat to continue criminal behavior.

When we examine evidence here the focus is simply on incapacitation. The purpose is not deterrence nor is it rehabilitation, not even revenge. Accordingly the focus will be on numbers of inmates incarcerated as a result of Three-strikes laws. Since one of the first states to adapt the three-strikes law was California we

> **Web assignment**—Does your state have a three-strikes law? If so explain how it works? How many people are in prison in your state due to this law? Are you in favor of this type of law? Discuss with the class.

will focus our attention there. California also has one of the largest prison populations in the country, approximately 202,000 inmates. The three-strikes law has had a great impact on those numbers.

In 1994, the California legislature and voters overwhelmingly approved the Three-strikes Law. This change in sentencing allowed offenders to be sentenced to a minimum of 25 years to life for people convicted of two prior serious felony offenses. The rationale for enacting this law was to "remove repeat felons from society for longer periods of time, thereby restricting their ability to commit additional crimes" (Brown, 2005). The three-strikes law not only extends the period of incarceration for a third felony offense it also extends prison time for a second felony offense. The second felony does not have to be a for a violent felony thus a wider net is cast that further increases the prison population. These offenders are often referred to as "second strikers". Under this provision offenders are sentenced to twice the length of the prison sentence that they would have received if they had no prior felony convictions. For example if the person had no serious felony offenses they might receive a 2 year prison term for burglary of a residence, but if they had a prior serious felony offense conviction they would receive a 4 year prison sentence for the same crime. Of course a third strike or third felony offense must result in a prison sentence of 25 years to life in prison.

Weblink—http://www.lao.ca.gov/Publications/Detail/1342

The implications to the California prison system have been enormous. Since this sentencing change has been enacted there over 80,000 people have had their sentence extended as "second strikers". The rise of the California prison population has been quite dramatic. Approximately 25,000 people have been incarcerated under the law. The California Auditor's Office estimates that it costs about $57,000 a year to incarcerate one person. Obviously the costs are quite burdensome (Miller, 2012).

The three-strikes law has been implemented in some form or fashion in 26 other states. California is not the only state to experience prison growth as a result of this law. This law and other similar laws illustrate incapacitation as its purpose is to simply identify those people that appear to be a continued risk via their prior criminal history. Once these people have been identified they are subject to long prison sentences. Three-strikes is often debated as a deterrent to crime or simply as punishment. This type of sentence may serve those purposes too however their effectiveness at accomplishing those goals is debatable. There is certainly very little debate on serving an incapacitative purpose.

The purpose of incapacitation is to simply keep people in prison. The goal here isn't to punish or rehabilitate but remove people for a period of time. Many consider the wider use of incapacitation is a signal that a new strategy of corrections may be emerging. The focus is centered on risk management or assessing people's risk potential. The is often referred to as **New Penology.** The objective is to identify individual risk levels and then manage that risk. If a person is deemed to be a risk to reoffend they receive a more severe sentence that another who doesn't present as much of a risk. Many different corrections agencies use actuarial techniques such as the Level of Service Inventory Revised (LSI-R) to asses' risk. The result of these tests can determine the length and type of sentence, release on bond, classification and prison designation, and level of risk for community corrections officers. The ramifications of the score are very consequential.

## 6.   Rehabilitation

The goal of rehabilitation is to modify a person's behavior so that it's more conventional or law-abiding. This can be done through a number of different methods, treatments, and therapies. Traditionally correctional treatment has been thought of as training inmates to do menial jobs or attending mental health therapy. Contemporary rehabilitation uses a more comprehensive approach. Judges at sentencing are starting to utilize more rehabilitative measures, which is actually reminiscent of the Medical Model era.

The Medical Model was the dominant sentencing philosophy after World War II until the early 1970s. The concept is much like what you would think of when going the doctor because of an illness. In this case instead of seeing a medical doctor to get a diagnosis and then a prescribed remedy the judge diagnosis the offender and then prescribes a remedy. The offender was seen as needing some type of remedy for their "illness" (i.e. criminal behavior). It relied on the notion the offender could be worked with and could be helped in order to be more compatible with society. In effect they could be rehabilitated through education, receiving job skills, going to mental health therapies, and even receiving medical attention. As a result sentencing models were indeterminate. Where an offender may receive an early release from prison based on their behavior in prison and by completing various education and/or treatments. This model began to fall out of favor gradually in the late 1960s into the 1970s as society changed their began to be more calls for more punitive sentences. Criminal Justice and corrections fell into the political spotlight whereas before it was largely left out of political debate. Martinson's critique, *Nothing Works*, of rehabilitative measures in corrections was published in 1974. When coupled with changing public attitudes about punishment the dominance of the Medical Model in sentencing and therefore in corrections too began to fade.

Today rehabilitation as a sentencing goal is beginning to pick up some traction. This again is due in no small part to changes in public attitude about how we deal with offenders, research, and a need from not only corrections but the criminal justice system to look toward evidence-based practices. There is more acceptance for measures that don't simply send people to jail or prison or if they are sent there to provide rehabilitation measures. To be sure the amount of money spent on rehabilitation in corrections is a small percentage of correctional budgets. When faced with budget shortfalls in corrections rehabilitation programs are typically the first to be cut. For instance the Florida Legislature left the corrections department with a $79 million deficit for the fiscal year 2018/19. In order to make up for this shortfall the secretary of corrections substantially decreased money for mental health treatment, transitional housing for inmates leaving prison, substance abuse services, therapeutic treatment, and basic education services (Klas, 2018).

## 7.  Evidence-Based Practice in Rehabilitation: Education

Weblink—https://www.rand.org/pubs/research_reports/RR266.html

The Rand Corporation (2013) conducted a comprehensive **meta-analysis** focusing on the effectiveness of education on recidivism rates of inmates. This comprehensive study revealed a number of findings that support educating inmates. Among the findings were:

— Education programs in prison reduced recidivism.

  o  Those that participated in programs had 43% lower odds of returning to prison than those you did not participate.

  o  The reduction rate dropped 13%.

— Correctional education improves the chances of becoming employed upon release.

  o  The odds of obtaining employment were 13% higher for those participating in education in prion than those who did not.

— Inmates exposed to computer assisted instruction learned better math and reading skills than those with did not have that aid.

— Providing education to inmates is more cost effective than a return to prison.

The study then recommended future studies to focus on the characteristics of effective programs. It also suggested more research grants to help researchers study the issue more in depth and a registry of educational evaluations in order to develop an evidence base for corrections.

Conclusion-Rehabilitation is a cornerstone in the field of corrections. When we look back at the purpose of the Walnut Street Jail or the Pennsylvania System the purpose is solidly entrenched in the idea of rehabilitation through work or other means. It remains as a purpose in sentencing. The access to rehabilitation programs varies widely. They are often the first items to be cut from budgets even when we know they can be effective as a means to reduce recidivism. The effort appears to be to look at long term solutions as opposed to expedient fixes. By looking at the "evidence" of what is effective at reducing recidivism like education programs legislators and corrections officials may begin to place more priority on these measures.

## 8. Restorative Justice and Reintegration

The use of restorative justice measures is relatively new as an overall sentencing goal. However the various aspects of it are not new to American criminal justice. Restorative justice relies on three basic principles. The top priority is to restore the victim, as much as possible, to their pre-crime state. **Mediation**, negotiation, and victim empowerment are common tools utilized to accomplish this aspect. The victim has the opportunity to

> **Student exercise**—Does your state have a "Victims Bill of Rights"? If so what are the codified rights of victims of crime in your state? Discuss with the class if you think these are beneficial. Is there anything else that can be done?

participate and be heard in many aspects of how they think the offender should be dealt with. The goal is not to punish or provide a measure of retribution against the offender. Judges and juries are allowed to consider victim impact statements given at the time of sentencing. Victim's rights have been established through legislative action. As a result victims have access to more information involving their case. They also can receive a variety of services depending upon which jurisdiction their case is in. Often times police agencies, prosecutors offices, and correctional departments will have professionals assigned specifically to be there for victims and families of victims of crime. These professionals can act a resource broker by suggesting various places to seek mental health treatment for emotional trauma, dealing with financial aspects of victims, and providing information about court proceedings and the status of each case. in Figure 3.3 below illustrates this approach.

Figure 3.3

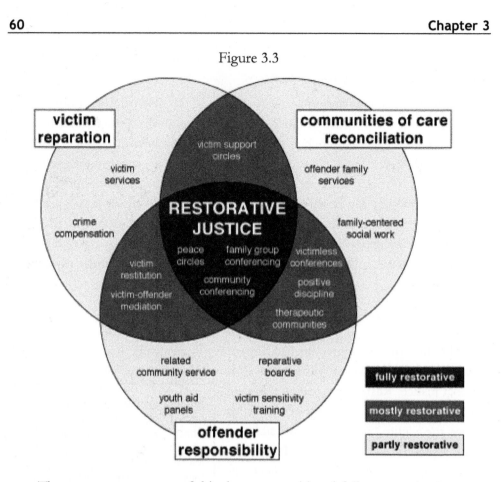

There are some aspects of this that are considered fully restorative in nature and some less comprehensive. Usually aspects of restorative justice are included into an overall sentencing philosophy like rehabilitation as these goals are seen as very compatible.

The emphasis for this goal is squarely centered on the victim but the restoration of the community is also important. The community is seen as a victim too. For example if a person is robbed the associated fear created in the community surrounding that event is addressed also. As result various community actions can occur such as community crime boards, marches where community members display solidarity and support. The involvement of police and the prosecutor's office are key for this to occur. Corrections professionals also play a role when the offender is either placed on probation, is an inmate in prison, or released on parole. These professionals are a conduit and source of information as the court and corrections system is complex and can be confusing to members of the general public.

The final component is offender accountability. Accountability is not measured by the severity of the punishment but rather the offender's involvement in making amends with the victim and the community. Offenders can be required to contact their victim, if the victim is willing. These contacts can be written or sometimes individual meetings with a victim or their family members. Typically an offender will receive instruction prior to meeting or contacting a victim or their family. This preparation can take quite some time. Victims too receive counseling prior to meeting. The court process is adversarial. An environment of removing oneself from responsibility can certainly occur. An offender can remove themselves from experiencing the consequences of their actions. The goal in restorative justice in this aspect allows the offender to connect their actions to the victims.

Reentry fits in with restorative justice. The focus for reintegration is an acknowledgment that there is a transition period for inmates coming back to the community. Consider for example a first year college student getting off a bus at a large university and being expected to find housing, find the right classes, and to just generally be successful in that environment with no help at all. Luckily that's not the case at many universities large and small. Transitioning to a new environment takes time. It takes time to find a job, find a place to live, to navigate where things are yet often times what we have done with offenders leaving prison is to do just that in addition to complying with any number of directives for a parole officer that might require extra duties.

Reentry back into the community is usually started before a person leaves prison. They begin to make living arrangements and often need approval from a parole officer to reside with people and at places before they leave prison. Job prospects are also considered as well. The overwhelming majority of inmates, approximately 95% (NRRC Facts and Trends, 2018), are released back into the community many serve multiple years in prison. Some do not have family to support them both financially and emotionally. In these instances reintegration efforts like a **halfway house** or residential reentry center (RRC) can at least provide some type of structure and well as a resource for employment and treatment services. In cases where an inmate does not have a place to live halfway houses offer a place to reside while employment or other living arrangements are made.

## 9. Evidence-Based Practice in Restorative Justice: Offender Employment

One of the most important factors for an offender the stay out of prison is the ability to obtain employment, especially employment in a job or a career they find satisfying. Approximately 70 million people in the U.S. have a criminal record, that's roughly one in three working age Americans. Having a criminal record in addition to not possessing a skill set or educational background can be a further obstacle to employment, or at least employment where benefits like health insurance and financial compensation at beyond minimum wage.

Many employers are reluctant to hire people with a criminal record. Some types of employment restrict people with criminal histories from gaining the necessary license to work in certain fields. Other employers do not want to take the chance of hiring someone with a criminal history as they fear litigation for any number of different reasons. Often employers won't grant interviews to people who divulge criminal convictions on employment applications. Even though research suggests employees with criminal histories perform job duties as well as those without criminal histories (THE FEDERAL INTERAGENCY REENTRY COUNCIL A Record of Progress and a Roadmap for the Future employment, 2018). Initiatives such as "ban the box" have been implemented in a number of different states. This initiative does not allow employers to ask job candidates about criminal history information on employment applications. Many businesses such as Coca-Cola, American Airlines, Googles, and Koch Industries to name a few launched the "Fair Chance Business Pledge" whereby these major companies made substantial commitments to provide people with criminal histories a fair chance at employment (THE FEDERAL INTERAGENCY REENTRY COUNCIL A Record of Progress and a Roadmap for the Future employment, 2018). The Small Business Administration and a number of other federal agencies are developing or have developed ways to remove the stigma and increase the chances for those people with criminal histories to start businesses by securing loans or other avenues to operate in the economy.

Reintegration occurs through a number of different avenues. There are over 2 million people in American Prisons or jails. Over 95% of them will eventually be released. Employment is an important factor in their success. Corrections officials both in institutions and those in community corrections play a very important role in reintegration.

## C.  SENTENCING OPTIONS

There are a number of sentencing options for judges. What is considered as "just" punishment is relative to historical context and of course within the confines of the law. The public may think the vast majority of criminal offenders are sent to prison, but the data tells us something different. The U.S. does incarcerate more people per capita than any other nation in the world 2.3 million people in 2018.

Prison inmates only represent about 25% of the total number of offenders in our criminal justice system. We reviewed the financial cost in earlier chapters and when we consider that cost along with other negative consequences of imprisonment sentencing options other than incarceration are being utilized more often.

Many jurisdictions use a continuum of **sanctions** when considering how to punish a person for a specific type of crime (i.e. infraction, misdemeanor, felony). The level or amount of punishment at which the criminal behavior is associated with is prescribed amount of punishment by legislators. These punishments are gradient. In other words the level of punishment is supposed to increase as the seriousness of the crime increases. For instance theft can either be a misdemeanor or a felony depending how much the stolen item(s) are worth. A misdemeanor theft conviction can result in a short period of probation which can be supervised or not. On the other hand a felony theft conviction may result in a prison sentence, large fine or a long period of strictly supervised probation. It is the responsibility of the prosecuting attorney to decide what to charge the person with (i.e. misdemeanor theft or felony) and then the responsibility of the judge to levy the sanctions available to him or her at the time of sentencing.

The level of punishment handed down at sentencing is commensurate with what the law allows but it also serves other purposes too. When considering incarceration alternatives to sending someone to prison are considered because prison is expensive and sending someone to prison instead of allowing them to remain in the community can actually be counter-productive not only to the offender but society as well. Treatment options can be very limited in prison. As we have discovered treatment and therapy programs are usually the first items to be reduced or cut from correctional budgets. Thus the options are more numerous in the community. Offenders deemed to not present as much of a risk as others may benefit more from treatment or educational avenues that are not presented to them in prison.

## 1. Fines

We have noted there are three different levels of illegal behavior: infractions, misdemeanors, and felonies. The vast majority of Americans will commit some type of illegal behavior in their lives, many won't get caught for all of these behaviors. Most people that drive

Weblink—The Environmental Protection Agency (EPA) has a criminal enforcement branch. See the following link for cases and associated fines.

https://www.epa.gov/enforcement/2017-major-criminal-cases

will receive a ticket for violating a traffic law such as speeding (1 in 5 Americans got a ticket in past 5 years, 2018). The vast majority of these infractions are dealt with by fining the guilty party. Fines are also used as punishment in criminal cases. Fines are spate from restitution. Remember that fines are a penalty levied against someone or a company. Restitution is repaying the victim of a crime as a result of injury or damage. Thus if a person vandalizes a car they would have to pay restitution to the car owner for the damage. A fine is money paid by the offender to some government entity. The logic is manifest in Rational Choice Theory: a fine, especially the potential of a large fine is supposed to deter unwanted behavior.

## 2.   Probation and Diversion

Probation is used more to resolve criminal cases (i.e. misdemeanors and felonies) than any other method. Probation is meant for cases that don't rise to the level of needing to incarcerate someone yet still holding them accountable to a higher degree than a fine. Probation as a sentencing method has a fixed time period otherwise known as a term such as six months or a year. The range of probation can be much longer than a year depending on the latitude the judge has at sentencing. When a person is placed on probation they have to abide by the conditions the court sets out. If those conditions are violated then the offender may be sent to jail or prison. It's important to note that probation is not parole. Probation is an opportunity for the offender to remain in the community and upon completion of the term of probation they are released from probation conditions.

Diversion is an option that is typically exercised by prosecutors. Some types of crime are eligible for diversion as determined by local ordinances or state laws. A diversion is used to divert the person from further prosecution and thereby avoid a criminal conviction. The purpose is to relieve the person accused of the crime from stigma that surrounds a criminal conviction while at the same time holding them accountable for the crime. These are being utilized more in a variety of ways such as drug courts and for driving offenses like driving under the influence (DUI).

## 3.   Incarceration

When the public thinks about sentencing their attention is easily drawn toward high profile cases in the news where people receive long prison sentences and even death sentences. Students of corrections understand these cases do not represent the vast majority of cases they will have to deal with when in the workforce. To be certain there are plenty of prisons and plenty of inmates.

Jail is typically the first place of confinement for those beginning incarceration after sentencing if they are **remanded** to custody. If they have been sentenced to prison they will be held in jail until they are transferred to prison. Some people are sentenced to a period of incarceration and them given a day and time to report to prison. This happens in federal cases more frequently than state criminal cases. Whether or not to take someone immediately into custody is at the discretion of the judge. A jail term is quite possible for people convicted of a misdemeanor offense. In some jurisdictions a short jail term is mandatory for crimes like driving under the influence. In other misdemeanor cases a person can be sentenced to a range of time but usually not longer than a year.

In cases that involve felony conviction where the sentence is a year or longer the offender is sent to a prison. Prisons are meant for long term incarceration. They have a number of different features and services that jails do not. The nature of the amount of time a person will remain in custody determines what sort of features and services a prison has that jails do not. For example some prisons house certain types of inmates. The Federal Correctional Faculty in Springfield, MO houses federal inmates with medical issues. Judges may suggest where a person is sent to prison but it is up to the correctional administration under which the custody of the offender has been given who determines classification and designation.

# D. SENTENCING MODELS

A model for sentencing is essentially a strategy for imposing punishment. This strategy guides judges concerning the parameters in which they can sentence a person. The model is usually throughout the jurisdiction thus in the state of Texas the sentencing model is indeterminate and Illinois uses a determinate sentencing structure. The Federal government uses a determinate sentencing structure. Thus if a person is convicted of a federal crime regardless of the state in which they were convicted a determinate sentencing structure is used. Today 33 states use primarily an indeterminate sentencing structure the other 17 states, the District of Columbia and the U.S. government use a determinate model (Lawrence, 2018).

Sentencing models just like many other aspects of corrections are subject to change. The **flat sentence** was the predominate sentencing model for much of the 19th century. Flat sentences imply just as it sounds. For instance under a flat sentence model when a judge pronounced a sentence of 5 years in prison it meant the person was going to serve 5 years in prison. The preeminence of the model began to change as prison space dwindled and public sentiment about how to treat inmates began to change (Ditton, 2018).

## 1. Indeterminate Sentence

An indeterminate sentencing model allows for a lot of discretion concerning how much time a person will actually spend in prison. When this model is used the judge sets a minimum and maximum length of sentence. For instance a person may be sentenced for a 5–10 year sentence. This means they must serve no less than 5 years and no more than 10 years total in prison. When an indeterminate sentencing model is used there is the possibility of parole for the inmate. Only inmates sentenced under this model can truly be paroled from prison.

The purpose of an indeterminate sentence is to allow the inmate to improve their chances of early release. If we look at the 5–10 years sentence as an example the inmate can present themselves to a parole board after serving a 5 years in prison and potentially be paroled. The chances of parole are of course greater if the inmate has completed programs like education and/or substance abuse treatment. Their chances are better for parole if they have not received any discipline reports in prison. The hope is that a person will seek reform and manage behavior in prison if there is reward for it.

Under this model corrections officials have a tremendous impact on an inmate's release from prison. Prison officials can influence a parole board's decision by allowing or not allowing an inmate access to programs which may be beneficial to the inmate and impress parole board members. Correctional officer's decision to officially write a disciplinary report versus another method of correction can also be impactful. A parole officer's decision to seek revocation can also have serious consequences for a parolee's return to prison. If we use the 5–10 example again we can see of a parolee's supervision is revoked they could potentially serve another 5 years in prison.

The indeterminate sentencing model was and continues to be utilized in the majority of states. However, it became criticized in the 1970s by people on both ends of the political spectrum. During this time criminal justice and especially how we punish people became part of the political environment. Conservatives saw indeterminate sentencing as a way to circumvent punishment and the early release for offenders wasn't palatable. People with more liberal thoughts saw indeterminate sentencing as a way to discriminate against minorities. Thus even though both sides were criticizing this model for different reasons they felt there was a need for change.

## 2. Determinate Sentence

A determinate sentencing model specifies a certain amount of time that an offender will spend in prison. The sentence is usually fixed in months. As an example a person may receive 54 months in prison. Determinate sentencing is different from a flat sentence because in a determinate sentencing model an inmate may earn good time. Good time is earned several different ways deepening upon the jurisdiction. Thus even though the offender may be sentenced to serve 54 months in prison they could potentially earn an earlier release. Earning good time or not earning it is specifically stated in each jurisdiction therefore a parole board does not review inmates for early release. Good time computations are done by correctional officials. The time off earned for good behavior is typically 15%. Therefore if a person is sentenced to 54 months in prison and they earn all their goodtime credit (15%) they would actually serve approximately 46 months instead of 54.

An inmate does not receive parole in a determinate sentencing model. Since the term of incarceration is fixed and a correctional administrator determines good time there is no parole for an inmate. However, inmates can still fall under community supervision. This is referred to as a term of supervised release or post-release supervision. It is much easier to still use the term parole instead of post-release supervision and that a "parole" officer supervises offenders in the community but the system for release if very different. The mechanism of early release here is simply time served. An inmate may be released directly into the community and under supervision from administrative segregation or solitary confinement. They can also be released into the community after having been a model inmate. The amount of time a person has to spend on post-release supervision is also determined at the time of sentence. A person may have to spend 54 months in prison followed by a 24 month period of post-release supervision. If an offender violates their conditions of release they can be made to serve a period of time in prison for that violation. These are usually 60–90 days. The amount of time is dependent upon the jurisdiction.

The purpose of using a determinate model was to accommodate both arguments that were critical of indeterminate sentencing. It accommodating those calling for tougher sentences by fixing a period of time to a specific crime while considering a person's criminal history. This model attempted to satisfy those calling for a more **crime control** method of justice by not allowing or limiting early release. It also

> **Student exercise**—Which sentencing model does your state utilize. Try to find the guidelines used in your state. Discuss the positives and drawbacks for indeterminate and determinate sentencing models

addresses those wanting to incapacitate offenders by affixing a specific period of time in prison for a crime and not allowing release until the sentence is complete. It also was an attempt to address the discretion of parole board. It essentially eliminated the need for them under this model therefore the mechanism of release is not discretionary but simply dependent upon time served in prison.

## 3.   Sentencing Guidelines

Sentencing guidelines aid judges and other court employees such as probation officers when deciding a criminal sentence, especially where determinate models are used. Probation officers are often tasked with writing a **pre-sentence investigation report.** This is a detailed report concerning many aspects of the offender's life and the crime(s) for which the offender has been convicted of. These reports help the judge decide on the proper guideline to use when sentencing.

The use of guidelines have become a point of contention. There are a number of U.S. Supreme Court cases and the use of guidelines which has established legal precedent on the matter of a judge's discretion Whether or not to strictly abide by the guidelines. Three important cases have influenced this matter. In *Apprendi v. New Jersey*, 530 U.S. 466 (2000) the Supreme Court ruled that the sentencing judge could not aggravate or increase a sentence solely on their own accord. In *Blakely v. Washington*, 542 U.S. 296 (2004) ruled that no criminal sentence in state courts can be enhanced beyond what is set in the guideline unless the defendant waives the right to a jury. In 2005, the case of *United States v. Booker*, 543 U.S. 220 (2005) summarily ruled that federal sentencing guidelines were not mandatory but advisory. This ruling made it much easier for judges to have more discretion when considering sentencing.

## 4.   Mandatory Minimum Sentences

Mandatory minimum sentences refer to a sentence wherein if a person is convicted of particular crimes the judge has no discretion at sentencing and must affix the sentence established by law. As early as 1994, every state had adopted some type of mandatory sentencing law. These laws began to be legislated more as the public outcry over particularly heinous crimes such as the 1993, kidnapping, sexual assault, and murder of 12 year old Polly Klass prompted Three-Strikes Laws and more recently the 2005, case of kidnapping, sexual assault and

Weblink—Jessica Lunsford was kidnapped, sexually assaulted and then killed by previously convicted sex offender open the weblink to learn more.

http://offenderwatchinitiative.org /Resources/Jessicas-Law

murder of 9 year of Jessica Lunsford in Florida by a man previously convicted of sexually assaulting young girls spurred Jessica's Law. This law allows for a minimum sentence of 25 years in prison for the rape of a child under the age of 12.

The purpose of mandatory minimum laws are twofold. First they are supposed to serve as a general deterrent to those that may attempt this crime. The other is specific those that once released, as in the case of those with "two strikes" the next time a law is broken the consequences will be that much more sever. The other goal is simple incapacitation. Those that are convicted of certain offenses that are considered under minimum mandatory statues will be incarcerated for long periods of time.

# E. ISSUES IN SENTENCING

The sentence handed down by the court is where corrections begins. The impacts of a sentence, especially overall sentencing strategies, can change the field of corrections. These strategies not only impact families of victims and offenders but society as well. The following are contemporary issues:

- Sentence disparity for minorities.

- Truth in Sentencing.

- Finding equity in sentencing.

## 1. Sentence Disparity

African-Americans represent only about 13% of the overall U.S. population. Yet, 40% of those incarcerated black. Latinos represent 16% of the overall population but 19% of those incarcerated are Latino. When we compare that slice of the minority population to the proportion of white Americans we see that the overall 64% of the U.S. population is white and 39% of those incarcerated are white.

> **Student exercise**—What is the demographic makeup of your states prison population? Compare the proportion of racial groups in prison to the general population in your state.

There is a distinct likelihood that a black male born after the year 2000, will be incarcerated at some time in their lives. When the current rates of incarceration are calculated about 1 in 3 black males will serve prison time at some point. 1 in 6 Latinos males will end up in prison. This is compared to 1 in every 17 white males. Females we see the same pattern as 1 in 111 white females will go to prison compared to 1 in 18 black women and 1 in 45 Latina females (Hagler, 2018).

The "war on drugs" has impacted minorities far greater than whites. Whites and minorities use drugs at the same rate yet 72% of those in federal prison for drug trafficking are minorities. In 2010, the U.S. Sentencing Commission, which is responsible for setting the punishments for federal law, recommended a change for the punishment and threshold amounts for crack cocaine. On July 28th 2010 U.S. Congress passed a change to the law that changed the mandatory minimum sentence and increased the threshold amount for crack possession which used to trigger long prison sentences. The disproportionality of crack laws versus powder cocaine laws were seen by many as unfair to minorities as minorities were more likely to traffic and/or possess crack than powder cocaine (The new crack law, 2018).

The reasons for sentencing disparity are myriad. They go far beyond outright racism, but to discount racism would be neglectful of the truth. The reasons relate to a host of social inequalities from a lack of education and opportunity in the job market to social ills that plague communities. Legislation is important to reconciling this but so are those that work in the correctional system.

## 2. Truth in Sentencing

Prior to the correctional changes that began in the 1970s inmates would often serve one fourth or less of the prison time they were sentenced. The public began to clamor for punishments that were more in line with what a judge would sentence an offender to. Subsequently there was shift toward, **truth in sentencing.** This took much of the discretion of prison officials away concerning early release. There was a focus on violent offenders to spend more of their sentence in prison. The federal government incentivized states toward a truth in sentencing approach. The Violent Crime Control Act of 1994, included a provision that would give states more federal money if they made offenders serve at least 85% of their prison sentence. This is the reason that we see many states allow 15% good time credit.

## 3. Equity in Sentencing

Finding a balance of prison time for the crime committed can be tough to settle upon. You may think one type of punishment is fit for the crime of burglary yet your classmate may think of a different punishment. It is this difference of thought about punishment makes the establishment of a sentencing commission

Weblink—The following is the weblink to the U.S. Sentencing Commission. They help determine sentencing practices in the Federal Court System.

https://www.ussc.gov/

pertinent. 21 states, the District of Columbia and the federal government have sentencing commissions. Sentencing commissions are made of court and correctional professionals. In some states they also include members of the general public and law enforcement. Their job is to collect statistics about sentencing in their jurisdiction, detect crime and sentencing trends, calculate sentences and suggest sentences to law making bodies.

# F. CONCLUSION

Sentencing is the gateway for corrections. The criminal sentence determines the type of sentence (i.e. probation or incarceration) but also other conditions the offender must meet. The models of sentencing and the purposes will change and those in corrections will adapt to those changes. Correctional professionals do not sit idly by as these changes impact their field. By examining what the research tells us about how punishment works, rehabilitation, deterrence, reintegration, and incapacitation professionals can influence and tailor best practices.

## Discussion Questions

1. What role does sentencing play in corrections?

2. What is jurisdiction and how can it impact sentencing?

3. Explain how the goals of sentencing are not mutually exclusive.

4. Pick 1 of the 5 goals of sentencing and explain it.

5. Which goal of sentencing do you think is the most effective at reducing recidivism? Explain your answer.

6. What is the difference between specific and general deterrence?

7. Discuss why it's important to find a balance of punishment for crime.

8. Explain what a determinate and an indeterminate sentencing model are.

9. Discuss which sentencing model do you think is most effective at reducing future crime.

10. Which issue in corrections do you think is the most important and explain why you think that.

## Student Exercises

1. Every state has a yearly report. Find the yearly report for your state's department of corrections and:

   A. Report the total correctional population.

      a.    Institutional population.

      b.    Community corrections population.

    B.    What are the demographics of the correctional population?

      a.    % race.

      b.    Age make up.

      c.    1 other interesting statistic.

    C.    What is a current correctional issue in your state?

2.    Find a journal article that relates to sentencing in the U.S. It can deal with any number of issues within sentencing such as sentencing disparity, the effectiveness of specific deterrence, etc. and discuss what the article is about and the author's conclusion.

## Key Terms

**Decriminalized**—to lessen punishment or criminal sanction.

**Felony**—a category of crime considered to be the most serious types of crime. Terms of incarceration are typically more than one year and are served in state or federal prisons.

**Flat sentence**—a sentencing model where a specific amount of time is to be served which allows little or no variation.

**General deterrence**—method of deterrence in which the goal is to prevent members of the general public from committing crime due to the threat of punishment.

**Halfway house**—a structured living environment where offender have access to a number of different services.

**Jurisdiction**—the legal authority a court has in a criminal case.

**Justice**—protecting the rights of people and punishing wrongs using fairness.

**Lex talionis**—the ancient Roman concept of punishment that relies on the notion of revenge upon the offender that is equivalent to the offender's harm upon the victim; an eye for an eye.

**Mediation**—intervention in a dispute.

**Meta-analysis**—a statistical approach to gather the results from multiple studies on a certain topic in an effort to provide comprehensive conclusions.

**Misdemeanor**—a category of crime that is seen as less serious than a felony. Terms of incarceration are less than one year and served in a local jail.

**New penology**—criminal justice policies that focus on risk management and assessing certain people's risk level and thus assigning different levels of punishment.

**Pre-sentence report**—a detailed biographical report of a person convicted of a crime which helps the judge determine the proper sentence.

**Recidivation**—a criminal offender continuing to commit crime.

**Remanded**—take someone immediately into custody.

**Retroactive**—a legislative measure that changes the legal consequences such as a criminal sentence before the law was enacted.

**Sanctions**—different types of punishment.

**Sentencing**—once a defendant is convicted or pleads guilty the judge pronounces a sentence or punishment upon the offender.

**Specific deterrence**—method of deterrence in which the goal is to prevent the offender from committing future crimes.

**Three-strikes law**—an offender that has been previously convicted of at least 3 felony crimes who is sentenced to long periods of incarceration such as 25 years to life imprisonment. The types of felony and prison length vary by jurisdiction.

**Truth in sentencing**—a sentencing mandate which requires an offender to serve the vast majority of their sentence before they become eligible for release.

---

[1]  Bonczar, Tomas P.; Hughes, Timothy A. (2011). National Corrections Reporting Program: Sentence Length of State Prisoners. Bureau of Justice Statistics. Washington DC.

## CHAPTER 4

# Jails and Detention Facilities

**Chapter Objectives**

- Describe how jail has evolved.

- Explain the process of detention.

- Discuss the role of jails today.

- Identify who is in jail today.

- Discuss contemporary issues within American jails today.

## A. INTRODUCTION

What's the difference between prison and jail? We often hear people confuse the two terms. They both mean incarceration of some sort yet there are stark differences between the two. We will discuss those differences and find out who is in American jails today and why they are there. We will look at the evolving role that jail plays in corrections today. The purpose of jail has grown more complex than simply holding someone in custody while they await the outcome of criminal charges. The challenges of jail staff and administrators face today are daunting. Not only are jails becoming increasingly overcrowded but recruiting for correctional officer positions and other staff has become very difficult. Jails play a crucial part in the correctional system. Everyone arrested is taken to jail yet most people may never end up in prison. This taste of incarceration can provide deterrent value for many while for others it represents a long road ahead.

## B. BRIEF HISTORY OF AMERICAN JAILS

We have adopted many aspects of law and corrections from England. The concept of using a jail is one of those adaptations. The jail or "gaol" as they were called in England started out as a place of simple detention whereby the purpose was to keep someone until the outcome of the charges were rectified. The preferred method of actually carrying out justice or some form of punishment from the time of the first jail was built in 1066 A.D. until the middle 1800s was corporal punishment and the idea of using jail as a punishment was not often considered.

The Tower of London is largely regarded as the first jail. The Tower is one of many structures built in 1066 A.D. by William the Conqueror. The original purpose of the tower and surrounding buildings was to provide defense as a fortress. However, the White Tower, was soon utilized as a holding area for those awaiting trial, execution, or some other form of corporal punishment. As the rule of law began to be respected and considered a normal part of society the use of the gaol became widespread not only in England but much of Europe (Encyclopedia Britannica, 2018).

The use of the jail in early America served much the same purpose as it did in England. Those charged with crimes were confined in large rooms. There was no classification system and inmates with serious crimes were housed with inmates charged with minor crimes. There also was no distinction between adults and juveniles or men and women. Needless to say violence and abuse between inmates was a common occurrence.

Jails were a normal fixture in early American towns and cities. Jamestown, VA is regarded as the first settlement in America and it had a jail. Any settlement of size had a jail. Often a jail was one of the first public buildings erected in growing towns (Lynch, 2018).

Early jails in American and Europe required inmates to pay for subsistence. Families or other supporters would have to bring food items or other amenities or buy they could buy these items from jailers. Jailers often supplemented their incomes from the sales of such items. In some instances jailers would require a fee just to be housed in jail. This payment system often resulted in several different abuses perpetrated by jailers upon inmates. Coupled with inmates abusing each other and general neglect by authorities jails in America and Europe were wretched places.

The Enlightenment period brought many reforms in criminal justice. We discussed these briefly in Chapters 1 and 2 of this text. It's important to remember the contributions of these reformers. One such reformer, John Howard from England, was instrumental in addressing abuses and neglect of jail inmates. As a result of his work and the general social milieu of the time changes in the way jail inmates were housed and the purposes of the jail were reexamined and realigned (BBC America, 2018).

This new wave of thought allowed jails to be regarded as a form of punishment instead of always relying on corporal punishment. Also the way inmates were treated began to change and the potential for abuse diminished slightly as inmates no longer had to rely solely on supporter for food and clothing. Thus jails started to receive more public funds to care for inmates. The purpose as just a holding facility changed too. In Chapter 2 of this text we discussed the Walnut Street jail and the new purpose of jail which ultimately became the initiative for these establishment of prisons. This evolution from simply a holding facility to a place of correction ushered in the advent of prison. It altered how we punish people from simply punishing the body to punishment of the soul.

## C.  CONTEMPORARY JAIL IN AMERICA

Jails are different from prison. They are administered at the local level, usually the county level. An elected sheriff is routinely the chief administrator of the jail. Alternatively, prisons are administered at the state level and the chief administrator, secretary of corrections, is appointed by a governor. Jails are fairly transient in nature and inmates are often incarcerated for a couple of hours or days. There are on average 721, 300 inmates in American jails every day (Minton, 2016). Compare that to an average of 1.51 million state and federal prisoners and we see that jail inmates make up a small, yet very important portion of the incarcerated population. Some jails can hold as many inmates as an entire state prison system. For instance the Los Angeles County Jail has 19,185 inmates and cost over $700 million

Weblink—The following website contains detailed information about the jail inmate population in the U.S.

https://www.bjs.gov/content/pub/pdf/ji15.pdf

annually to operate. It had 2,690 inmates beyond its capacity in 2015 (Hare, 2018). Compare that to New Mexico and we see that their state prison system has roughly 7,000 inmates (Prison Policy Initiative, 2018). Smaller rural areas do not have jails and send people arrested in their jurisdiction to neighboring communities in order to house them.

## Summary of America's Jail Population

- An estimated 721,300 inmates were confined in county and city jails on an average day in 2015, down from the peak of 776,600 inmates on an average day in 2008.

- In 2015, there were 10.9 million admissions to jails, continuing a steady decline since 2008.

- The number of admissions to jail in 2015 was nearly 15 times the size of average daily population in 2015.

- The adult jail incarceration rate declined from a peak of 340 per 100,000 in 2006 through 2008 to about 300 per 100,000 each year since 2013.

- The juvenile population in local jails continued to decline in 2015, to fewer than 4,000—down from a peak of about 7,600 juveniles in 2010.

- About 68% of jail inmates in 2015 were held for a felony offense, and the remaining 32% were held for either misdemeanor (27%) or other offenses (5%).

- The rated capacity in jails reached 904,900 beds at yearend 2015, up by nearly 47,000 beds since 2010. Local jail jurisdictions employed an estimated 213,300 full-time staff at yearend 2015 of which most (79%) were correctional officers.

Source: Bureau of Justice Statistics Report, *Jail Inmates in 2015*. Todd D. Minton and Zhen Zeng.

Today jails in America not only hold people awaiting trial they are tasked with many other duties and house people for a number of different reasons. Jails are often the first stop after an arrest. However, jails also receive inmates from prison to help relieve overcrowding in prisons, they receive people awaiting processing on federal immigration holds, they can also receive people as inmates as transfers from court appearances and other types of holds.

The nature of a jail is to hold someone for a short period of time (usually less than 1 year). Many people spend only hours in jail and then are released after a bond is set. Yet for some the wait can be longer. For instance in study of West Virginia Jails found that a person spends an average of 29 days in jail while awaiting trial. Many have begun to question holding someone in jail while they await trial. One must remember that simply because one is arrested and charged with a crime does not mean a conviction is certain. As such reducing the number of people awaiting trial is a concern for jail professionals, especially where holding juveniles is concerned.

Jails have increasingly had to hold and deal with inmates who have a variety of mental health issues. People with severe mental health issues are three times more likely to be held in jail than in a mental health facility (Ortiz, 2018). As a result it has become imperative that jail staff know how to identify and deal with people who have these issues.

A large percentage of inmates also enter jail with substance abuse issues. As many as two thirds of people entering jail have a substance abuse dependency issue (Karberg, 2002) This presents a challenge for jail staff who often deal act a detoxification centers. Whereby inmates come in off the street and act erratically while being booked into jail. Later many inmates suffer withdrawal symptoms that represent a challenge to jail medical staff. Inmates with these issues have to be monitored carefully and treated. This can be an extra burden especially when a jail is short staffed. It also represents potential civil legal liability.

Jails are also dealing with a large number of inmates with health problems. As a result jails can spend a large portion of their budgets on medication and other medical treatments. The cost of healthcare varies widely from jurisdiction to jurisdiction. That said the average amount of money spent on inmates for healthcare across the country was $5,720 (Pew Charitable Trust, 2017). A jail can spend anywhere from 9–30% of its entire budget on healthcare alone (Bird, 2018). Jail staff can also spend a large portion of their shift transporting inmates to and from medical appointments. The Los Angeles County jail recently requested hiring 160 more deputies and support staff for the purpose of improving medical and mental health in the jail.

## Corrections in Action

The Los Angeles County Jail has an average daily population of over 17,000 inmates. It operates several facilities throughout Los Angeles County. It spends millions of dollars each year on healthcare. Rikers Island is the county jail for New York City. It has an average daily population of 9, 183 inmates (New York

City Department of Corrections, 2018). It also spends millions of dollars each year for healthcare.

Sherriff Jim McDonnell recently asked the L.A. County Commission for 160 new deputies not for purposes directly related to security or concerning new programs in order to reduce recidivism but rather to ensure inmates are receiving healthcare services. These new deputies will transport inmates to and from medical appointments plus the additional support staff for the deputies. In fiscal year 2017, deputies made nearly 6,000 trips to and from medical providers. Deputies make evaluations of inmates in front of their cells as opposed to private areas (City News Service, 2018).

The City of New York's county jail is well known throughout the country, Riker's Island. The City of New York recently ended its contract for health services, Corizon Health Inc. The for profit company has had a history of issues providing healthcare to inmates. The cities Department of Investigation found that Corizon has had several disciplinary problems and failed to follow basic background investigation protocol when hiring employees. The company had hired staff with criminal convictions that included murder and kidnapping. The investigators found that Corizon had several missteps that most likely lead to the deaths of two inmates. There are well over 800,000 inmate contacts each year with inmates on Rikers Island. Staff also took inmates to 78,499 clinic visits in 2016 (New York City Department of Corrections, 2018).

Rikers Island administration and staff are taking measures to address the healthcare challenge. Fully 42% of inmates at Rikers Island have mental health issues. Staff are trained to identify and spot not only mental health concerns but physical health concerns. They have implemented the PACE and Clinical Awareness to Punitive Segregation Program (CAPS). Detoxification and mental health treatment are preventative in nature which cut down on acute and emergency situations that require off site care. They have also partnered with agencies like the New York City Health Department, Department of Health and Mental Hygiene, and various local social services (New York City Department of Corrections, 2018).

Large and small jails share many of the same concerns healthcare and mental health care are just one of those. The fiscal costs of that care is enormous and has had a ripple effect on other program ability to be effective or even be implemented. There is also a cost for the corrections officers that work with inmates. Not only can this be dangerous work for many different reasons but working with increasing numbers of inmates with mental health issues compounds the danger not only to officers but to other inmates and the inmates with mental health issues. Officers also dal with dangers presented from communicable diseases. These too are areas of concern for jail staff.

# D. THE PROCESS

How do jail inmates become inmates? The process varies by jurisdiction however, there are some general process that most jurisdictions follow. The process typically begins with some type of police contact that results in an arrest. Entry into the jail does not always begin that way. For instance a person can be sentenced to jail time in court and ordered to report to the local jail on a time and day specified by the judge.

## 1. Arrest or Reporting to Jail

In order for an arrest to occur there must be probable cause that a crime occurred. Police identify the suspect and take that person into custody. Once that is done they are taken to the county jail. Upon entering the jail grounds the person is driven into the **sally port** area. This is a general reception area where the police drive the person into a secure location such as a garage type structure. At this point the **custody** of the inmate is transferred from the police to the jail staff. The person arrested is searched again in order to ensure the safety of jail staff end prevent **contraband** from entering the jail.

The transporting officer usually briefs the jail staff about any security or safety concerns the inmate presents as well as any information such as mental health issues, possible substances ingested by the person, or other relevant information. At this point the inmate and jail staff enter the booking area.

## 2. Booking

Many people may be familiar with the term "booking". This is a process within the jail process. The first step often involves identify the person. This is done through a couple of different ways. The inmate can provide a name, sometimes they don't and sometimes false information is given. Inmates are fingerprinted to verify information given. In some jurisdictions a cheek swab for

DNA is completed. This can be done for people arrested for felony offenses or in some cases for any arrest. A series of photos are also taken.

Once identifying information is completed the inmate is seen or evaluated by medical staff of jail staff with training in the area of physical and mental health. Inmates are asked a series of questions covering physical and mental concerns to substance use or medication needs. Suicide issues are also addressed during the evaluation period. Health and mental health care providers may be contacted for follow-up concerns however, obtaining information from outside sources ca be very difficult due to privacy concerns.

Inmates are then taken to holding cells while awaiting further processing or depending upon the jail many inmates sit in a common area and await release for assignment to a **pod**. Jurisdictions decide release based on many different factors such as the seriousness of the crime, past orders of the courts, state and local laws, and jail capacity. Often crimes that are viewed as petty such as public intoxication may mandate that a person not be considered intoxicated anymore prior to release. This may necessitate a person blowing into a breathalyzer and when a certain blood alcohol level is reached the person can be released while they await a court date. Other crimes such as domestic violence require mandatory jail time prior to release. Again, depending upon the jurisdiction no **bail** may be set until the inmate is seen by a judge. The judge determines the type, amount, and conditions of bail.

## 3.   Classification

If the inmate is awaiting a bail hearing or is otherwise going to be detained for a period of time more than a day they will receive a classification. The purpose for classification serves is twofold. First by identifying any security or health issues each inmate represents staff safety is ensured. Staff also know what risks and needs the inmate has. The second is for inmate safety. If the inmate presents security concerns they may be housed in a different part of the jail. The inmate may need special care which can then be afforded the inmate.

## 4. Release from Custody

Release from custody can happen in several different ways. Forts the police or prosecuting attorney can drop the charges which got the person in jail initially. Another road to release is bail. Bail is essentially an insurance policy which seeks to ensure the person if released from jail will report to subsequent court hearings. Often people are released on bail by simply promising to report to future court dates. This is referred to as release on your own recognizance. Other types of bail require a person to give up money to meet bail. These monetary thresholds have been criticized for years and it's also address in our Bill of Rights, specifically the 8th Amendment which not only prevent cruel and unusual punishment for crime but that, "excessive bail shall not be required".

> **Class exercise**—Discuss with your classmates the criticisms of bail. Is it fair to people with little or no financial resources to remain in jail when someone with money can bail out of jail?

### TYPES OF BOND (Cohen, 2007)

**Own Recognizance (OR Bond)**—This is purely a promise to return to court for future court dates.

**Own Recognizance Cash Deposit (ORCD)**—A percentage of the total bond is proffered to the court. For example if the bond is set at $10,000 ORCD the person may have to pay the court $1,000. In the event the person does not show up for court the balance of the bond may be sought (i.e. an additional $9,000).

**Cash**—The entire amount of the bond is due. For example if bail is set at $10,000 cash the person must proffer all $10,000 in order to be released while awaiting trial.

**Professional surety**—This requires the use of a bail **bondsman**. The judge sets a bail which the bonding agent proffers to the court on behalf of the inmate. The inmate pays the bondsperson a set amount for this "loan". If the person awaiting trial fails to show up the bondsperson forfeits the money they proffered to the court. For example the judge may set the bond at $10,000 Professional surety. The bondsperson would proffer the $10,000 to the court. The service provided by the bondsman will cost the inmate a set amount of money which is not refunded to the inmate regardless the outcome of court proceedings.

When a bond is preferred to the court the money is collected by the jail. At the end of the court proceedings the money is given back to the defendant regardless of conviction or not. Typically court costs and fines will be deducted from bail proffered.

Inmates are released from jail for a number of different reasons than simply bonding out of jail. Often people are released because criminal charges have been dropped. During an examination of misdemeanor arrests in Cook County Illinois (i.e. Chicago) it was discovered that 8 out of 10 misdemeanor arrests resulted in the charges being dropped. That rate is well beyond the national average which is approximately 20% of arrests leading to (Cohen, 2007). Still others will serve out their sentence in jail. Typically a person will serve no longer than one year on jail.

## E.  WHAT IS A JAIL?

Exactly what is a jail? What makes a jail a jail and how is it substantially different than prison? We often here the term "jail" and "prison" used interchangeably. They are similar considering they both serve to incarcerate people. However, there are many ways in which they differ. Their administration is different than prison. The type of inmates may be similar to prison but the reasons for holding people vary widely. If we look back at history, for example the Walnut Street Jail in Philadelphia, we can trace the origins of the prisons back to jails. Jails are unique places they represent the entrance into corrections.

Jail today does not have to mean what we typically think of as a strongly constructed building with gates and razor wire. Jails certainly still have those characteristics but jail encompasses different avenues of confinement like weekend programs in minimum security facilities, electronic monitoring or house arrest. People are considered "inmates" confined to their homes. Many jails have day reporting centers. Here people are mandated to attend education or therapy of many different varieties. There are work programs supervised by jail staff whereby jail staff supervise work crews. Still other jails have therapeutic communities and outpatient services. Although jails certainly exist as we commonly think of them they have has evolved to meet the non-incarcerative needs of the community.

## 1. Administration

The administration of jails are conducted at the local level. They are usually managed by an elected sheriff and it is their responsibility is to determine policy, hiring procedures, and budgetary matters just to name a few duties. Sheriff's departments are split into two main branches, one serves a law enforcement purpose and deputies patrol and make arrests just like city police. The second branch serves a correctional purpose as a deputy/correctional officer. In many

> **Class exercise**—Familiarize yourself with the local jail. Arrange a tour of your local jail OR have jail staff visit class.
>
> What are some issues your local jail staff are concerned about?
>
> What is the demographic makeup of inmates? Of staff?
>
> What is the typical day of a jail deputy like?
>
> What are jail administration looking for in employee prospects?

jurisdictions people wanting to work in the law enforcement or patrol branch start as deputies working at the jail. This allows the deputy to encounter and deal with inmates in a controlled environment.

Jails are funded at the county level of government. The sheriff is responsible for overseeing day-to-day operations but county commissioners determine how much money and resources are devoted to the jail. The control of financial resources impacts how a jail is managed. For instance the average salary for a correctional officer at a jail is between $24,000 and $36,000. In California the average jumps to $66,720 per year (Payscale.com, 2018). The amount of compensation for correctional deputies can impact the pool of employable prospects. The job of a correctional deputy is demanding on many different levels and compensation can attract or deter job candidates.

The availability of resources can impact what programs like education and substance abuse treatment are available to inmates. In some jurisdictions resources in jails are more plentiful when compared to other jails. Put another way not all jails are equal and some jails offer a number of different rehabilitative measures that others simply cannot afford. For example Johnson County Kansas, in the Kansas City Metropolitan area, is one of the wealthiest counties in the country per capita (US Census Bureau, 2018). As a result their jail has a number of different opportunities for substance abuse treatment, mental health treatment, a residential center, and work release program. Inmates are charged $1 per day to participate in a Therapeutic Community for substance abusers (Roth and Davis LLC, 2018).

The local sheriff determines how a jail operates. That person determines what programs to implement or not. She/he determines employment and retention of staff. The county commission determines how much money to budget to the jail. That body can determine how the money is to be spent and therefore also has a say in jail programs, staff salary, or hiring more staff. The local management of a jail allows a community to confront certain crime issues that may be unique to that community. For instance many communities, especially rural communities, are experiencing more inmates that have an opioid dependence. As a result jails may need to devote more resources toward dealing with that specific issue.

## 2.  Custody Level

Once it's determined that an inmate will be incarcerated for a period of time jail staff need to determine where to house the inmate. This is often done using several different ways to analyze the risk an inmate may present to other staff or inmates and also the inmate's needs, such as health needs, dietary needs, or mental health needs. Prisons initially began to classify inmates and then house and care for them accordingly. Jails large and small have also adopted this practice. Many jails rely on "objective classification". This relies on a narrow set of legal factors such as the severity level of offense as charged, prior convictions also personal characteristics like age of the inmate, employment, and health/mental health history. These items are incorporated into a checklist used by staff to assess several factors relating to risk and the needs of the inmate.

Jails were relatively slow to adopt classification because the nature of a jail has been to confine people for a short period of time therefore classification of inmates was not seen as an effective use of time. One National Institute of Corrections report advises, "Currently most jail Indeed, many people are in jail for 72 hours or less thus classification can be futile since release from jail is forthcoming. In addition large jails that hold thousands of inmates experience massive inmate **turnover**. Large inmate turnover negates the reason for classification.

The following have been identified as barriers for inmate classification:

- Overall shortage of jail personnel.
- Lack of appreciation for the role and benefits of the detention operation to larger departments.
- Insufficient number of staff trained to perform classification activities.
- Staff apathy with regard to classification.
- General budgetary constraints.

Today the overwhelming majority of jails utilize some type of classification system. The primary responsibility jails have are to provide a secure environment for staff and inmates. By classifying inmates either with risk issues and separating them from other inmates is one way to accomplish safety. Also by identifying and treating inmates with special concerns such as mental health or communicable diseases further protect staff and inmate but identify those that may need treatment and resources.

## F.  WHO IS IN JAIL?

The average daily population (ADP) in American jails is approximately 721,300 inmates. This number is a fraction of the over 10 million jail admissions each year in the U.S. That sounds like an incredible number, and it is, but that doesn't mean 10 million individuals enter the jail each year (Minton T. a., 2015). Unfortunately, some people may be arrested several times during the course of a year and have several admissions to the same jail.

It's important to understand who is in prison and why they are there. In this section we will discuss some of the "why" aspects but for now the focus is on "who". Certainly individuals are in jail for any myriad of reasons but if we examine groups of people we can spot trends. Identifying rates of incarceration for groups such as young minority males can help to focus resources. We can identify groups that are entering jail such as those with mental health issues and target alternatives to jail that not only reduce the jail population but get those that need care other than incarceration the assistance they need.

The number of people in jail is actually in decline. It's been in decline since 2008. There are many reasons for this decline. Jails also see rates seasonally fluctuate. The year-end total is about 4% lower than the mid-year total (Minton T. D., 2016). This is not a trivial number. By spotting this trend jail staff and administrators can target resources and triage priorities.

### 1.   National Demographics

Unlike prisons nationally jails have an excess of bed space capacity. Approximately 47,000 jail beds are empty on any given day. Only 17% of

American jails were operating at or above their capacity (Minton T. D., 2016). This availability has given jails some room to create a source of revenue by allowing inmates from other jurisdictions or prisons to reside at their jail for a fee. This new development has allowed for some jails to have cells occupied for a price. It has also changed the demographic makeup of many jails. Jails are beginning to house more state and federal prisoners for a fee.

Jails incarcerate people arrested for felony and misdemeanor offenses. Over two thirds (68%) of jail inmates are incarcerated for a felony charge and awaiting trial or pending transfer to another facility. 27% of jail inmates are incarcerated for a misdemeanor and 5% are listed as other offenses (Minton T. D., 2016). The number of jail inmates awaiting trial has grown since the year 2000. Although the number of jail inmates is decreasing the number of people incarcerated and awaiting trial has been increasing. This may be troubling to some as being incarcerated while not being convicted of a crime seems counter to the idea of innocent until proven guilty. Yet, others may be perplexed about those that are arrested for a crime being released and continuing to commit a crime, especially a heinous crime. Grappling with this issue is one that's beyond the scope for jail administrators and staff since its legislators and judges that determine many release procedures. However, jail professionals are often consulted by these representatives.

Males make up an overwhelming majority of the jail population. They still make up about 86% of the total jail inmate population. However, female inmate number in jail have been increasing since the year 2000. There has been a 3% increase in the jail population since 2000 (Minton T. D., 2016). This does seem like a small overall percentage but jail space that once was devoted to males must now be devoted to females. Jail staff also has to abide by different jail procedures for female inmates. For strip searches female staff must do the search and considering a general shortage of jail staff finding female staff can be difficult.

Minorities are overrepresented in jail. Although white inmates make up the majority of inmate racial groups at 48.3% of the ADP, black/African American inmates make up 35.1% of the ADP. Black/African-American were incarcerated at a rate 3.5 times higher than whites XXX Zhen ONLY. Consider that black/African Americans make up only about 13.4% of the entire U.S. population and whites make up 76.6% of the population. If we look at Hispanic or Latino representation in jail we see that the number of Hispanic/Latino inmates is fairly representative of the general population: 18.1% general population and 14.3% in jail population is Hispanic/Latino (Minton T. D., 2016). There are a number reasons for the over representation of black/African Americans in jail and then ultimately prison. **Cumulative disadvantage** is one of those facilitators. Specifically if we focus on pretrial detention and the ability to proffer the amount of bond set we see that black/African Americans have one of the highest poverty rates of any racial group in America (US Census Bureau, 2018). There are of course many other factors that range from overt discrimination to subtle reasons like poor access to education and therefore limited **life chances**.

Considering jail staff demographics is also important. There are approximately 226,300 people employed in local jails across the country. 80% of those employees have jobs that are related to **direct supervision**. The other 20% perform jobs in administration and support (Minton T. D., 2016). Jails administrators are striving to make their employees more representative of the community. Males are predominantly working as correctional officers. In fact male correctional officers outnumber females approximately 2:1 (Minton T. D., 2016). Women of any racial background are very under-represented. That said we must remember that 85% of jail inmates are males.

Diversity in jail staff is very important. Diversity allows jail staff and inmates to relate to each other better as well as jail staff to inter-relate to each other. Jail staff from a variety of backgrounds allows other jail staff to learn from each other on a professional level. A diversified jail staff can ease tensions between inmates and staff as inmates may view staff as more relatable. There are a number of different benefits of diversity.

> **Class exercise**—What is the demographic make-up of jail staff in your local jail? Discuss with classmates the importance of diversity in jail staff. Also how can jail administrators attract people from a variety of backgrounds.

## 2. Immigration

Jails are housing more people on immigration federal immigration **holds**. Many jails have entered agreements with the federal agency, Immigration and Customs Enforcement (ICE), to hold people either arrested for a criminal offense and who are undocumented immigrants or people detained by ICE for entering the country as an undocumented immigrant. The Immigration and Nationality Act was implemented in 1996, allows state and local police to arrest undocumented immigrants who have committed a crime (Immigration and Customs Enforcement, 2018). This act also broadens police powers for agencies that sign agreements with ICE in order to aid federal agencies in enforcing immigration laws, which fall under federal jurisdiction. Undocumented immigrants detained not only by federal authorities but also local police are ultimately taken to jail for detention and processing. Jails along the border can fill up as a result. Still other jails hundreds of miles away from the border can be tasked to handle ICE detention overflow. Chase County Kansas is one example.

## Focus on Corrections

Chase County Kansas is near the geographic center of the state. It's approximately 130 miles southwest of Kansas City, KS. This rural county has a population of 2,683 people (US Census Bureau, 2018). It's one of the last places you might expect would house a large amount of undocumented immigrants.

The Chase County Jail received substantial remodeling and upgrades in 2002, due to the prospect of housing illegal immigrants for a substantial fee from federal authorities. In 2008, Immigration and Customs Enforcement (ICE) began housing their detainees at the jail when Chase County Officials reached an agreement with federal authorities to be begin housing ICE detainees. The jail has capacity to house 148 inmates. Only 1 in 10 of the inmates are local residents the other 90% of those inmates are being held either on an ICE hold or by the U.S. Marshalls Office (TRAC Immigration, 2008).

Chase County Jail is only 1 of 1,528 facilities that house people under ICE detention. The jail in Chase County was ranked in the top 27% nationwide in the number of detainees leaving ICE detention. In 2008, 840 people had been detained in this jail alone. The vast majority of the inmates were from Mexico, 78.6%. The second most were from Guatemala at 6.2% (TRAC Immigration, 2008).

The Jail administrator, Dow Wilson said in a 2017, interview with a local news station the county receives "hundreds of thousands of dollars each year" from the federal government to house these inmates KWCH interview (Pedraza, 2018). These funds pay for all the jails costs. This frees up money to be used elsewhere in the county budget. While other rural counties struggle to pay bills Chase County does not. Other counties in Kansas have followed this model. There are an average of 53 ICE inmates at the Chase County Jail (Office of Detention Oversight Compliance Inspection DHS, 2017).

We spend about $2 billion each year to house undocumented immigrants. It costs ICE facilities and contract facilities like the Chase County jail approximately$134 per day to house 1 inmate. ICE estimates the average detention is 44 days. The Department of Homeland Security estimates that

51,379 people will be held in detention each day for fiscal year 2018 (Urbi, 2018).

Immigration holds in county jails are just one of many reasons people are held in jail. Several other inmates are on holds with federal agencies. The U.S. Marshalls Service (USMS) provides transport services for federal inmates awaiting court proceedings. As a result they contract with several local jails to hold federal inmates. The U.S. Marshalls service spends about $1.3 billion for housing and subsistence of detainees. The average daily population of inmates in Marshall's Service custody in 2017, was 55,338. A little less than half of those inmates were in custody due to immigration holds. 35,208 of those inmates were held in local jails. The USMS paid jails $82.22 per day to house those inmates. The USMS has seen a significant rise in immigration detainees due to the implementation of the zero tolerance policies. The Southwest Border Region has been identified as having the most significant impact on the USMS detention population. Only 19% of USMS detainees are housed in federal facilities the rest are housed in local jails or private facilities (US Marshalls Service FY 2017 Performance Budget, 2017).

## G. PURPOSE OF JAILS

The main purpose of jail is to hold a person immediately after arrest. The person may be able to bond out of jail and thus be released or they may be held pending court proceedings. However, jails have evolved and now confine people for a number of different purposes.

Jails are used by probation and parole agencies to incarcerate those under community supervision either as a sanction or short term punishment or pending revocation hearings. Many probation/parole agencies can arrest and hold people as a result of a violation of release. These sanctions are typically short (i.e. 48 hrs). When a person is arrested for a violation of release that involves revocation the parolee/probationer may be in jails for days or weeks awaiting a revocation hearing. Often times a bond is set for probationers but not for parolees.

Jails also serve as temporary confinement for those with mental illness and are awaiting placement to a mental health facility. States have facilities and hospitals dedicated to serve those with mental illness. The bed space at these places can be limited. Those with a mental illness and that have either been charged with or convicted of a crime may have to stay at a jail until a space at one of these facilities opens up.

Jails also hold people for the military. Sometimes those in military service are arrested either for committing a crime under a local or state statute. Those under the military can also be confined for violating the Uniform Code of Military Justice (UCMJ) which contains crimes and misdeeds not found in state and local statutes. Military personnel are often transferred from jails to military installations for processing under UCMJ.

Jails can act as a transfer hub. As we have seen for immigration cases several different agencies use jails as detention centers while inmates await court proceedings in jurisdictions outside of the one the jail is located. The U.S. Marshalls Service acts as a transport service bringing inmates to and from Federal Court. Often someone in federal custody will stay in a local jail until they can be transported to a federal facility. Jails may hold someone who has a warrant or a hold in another local jurisdiction as well. The transient nature of a jail allows it to serve as a hub for transporting inmates very well.

Jails not only act as a short term incarceration for arrest and bonding out or transfer. They also act as long term incarceration places. Someone sentenced to serve jail time for a misdemeanor conviction will serve their time at a county jail. A misdemeanor sentence can be a couple days or months. As a result of some inmates staying for long periods of time jails have adopted programs often found in prisons. Since the inmate may be incarcerated at the jail for a long period of time programs like education, job training, or substance abuse therapies can be available.

Jails are evolving more and being seen as places that do not just detain people but act as a place where inmates and those under some type of community supervision receive a number of services. Jails can be used as day reporting centers. People go to educational classes, received mental health and substance abuse therapy amongst other services. The jail in this sense acts as a resource broker that provides services beyond confinement.

## 1.  Private Jails

Jailing an individual has traditionally been a governmental function. The police act on behalf of the government arrest a person. The person is taken to jail where jails are administered by a locally elected government official, namely a sheriff. This has begun to change a bit. As the number of inmates in jail increased during the late 1980s and through the early 2000 jails could not keep pace or hold the number of people that police were arresting. The drug war fueled many of these arrests (Mauer, 2007). As a result of this need private jails began to emerge.

Privatization of prisons and jails were pushed by President Reagan in the mid-1980s. Private prisons promised increased business-like efficiency. It was attractive because local officials saw it as a cost saving measure. New Jails are extremely expensive to build some estimates put the cost at between $60,000 and $100,000 for a single new bed space. Forgoing that cost for local governments became very attractive. Private prisons were also appealing because they offered potential accountability. Private businesses could be fined or lose the contract to provide services if they were found to be deficient. The business would also deal with the human resources aspect thus hiring, firing, and litigation may be avoided by the county government (FindLaw, 2018). The benefits of private jails is appealing in many ways. However, there are also critics of privatization.

The privatization of jails has be criticized. There seems to be an inherent social conflict of interest with businesses making a profit from incarcerating people (FindLaw, 2018). Some have used the term "prison industrial complex". The term implies a wide ranging business plan that influences public sentiment and therefore law. The benefit to business would be impact law to send more people to jail. Harsher laws create more people being arrested and therefore more demand for bed space. Some companies have occupancy guarantees with governments. This guarantees the company will receive a certain number of inmates in order to remain profitable (Austin, 2001).

Incarcerating people has become very profitable. Core Civic formerly known as Corrections Corporation of America is a publically traded company on the New York Stock Exchange just like Apple or the Ford Motor Company. They operate 125 facilities thought the country. The total revenue for Core Civic during the last four months of 2017, was $440.6 million dollars (Core Civic, 2018). A competitor GEO Group operates 71 facilities with 75,365 beds in the U.S. They also operate internationally. During the last 4 months of 2017, GEO's revenue was reported at $569 million. This was up from 2016's fourth quarter which was $566.6 million (Geo Group, 2018).

Private jails and prisons are not new to American corrections. California's San Quentin Prison opened in 1852, as a for profit institution (FindLaw, 2018). Today the scale and influence private prisons and jail corporations have are tremendous. Companies like Civic Core and GEO hire lobbyists to represent their interests to law makers. They spend millions of dollars in this area. Private prisons have benefits as well as negatives. It appears that privatization will continue to be apart of American corrections for years to come.

# H. JUVENILE DETENTION

The juvenile justice system is a separate system than the adult one. There are several similarities between the two but it very important to note that the juvenile

**Weblink**—Go to the following url to examine other characteristics of juvenile offenders:

https://www.ojjdp.gov/ojstatbb/ snapshots/DataSnapshot_JCS2015.pdf

system is a separate system. The overall philosophy is centered on rehabilitation of the juvenile, unlike the adult system which focus' is on retribution. One example is referring to juvenile detention as detention instead of jail. Detention centers are not meant to necessity resemble jails. They are secure places with locked doors and high fences but appearances as well as more substantive things like education are not just offered but mandated for inmates.

The number of juvenile cases and thus detention numbers have decreased sharply since 1997. Since 1997, juvenile delinquency cases across the country decline by 53% (Office of Juvenile Justice and delinquency Prevention, 2018). Interestingly although the total number of new juvenile cases has declined sharply the number of females arrested has increased slightly from approximately 500,000 in 1985 for about 750,000 in 2015 (Office of Juvenile Justice and delinquency Prevention, 2018). There are a number of different programs, policies, and avenues that do not end with a juvenile behind bars. When a juvenile ended up in detention it was usually due to an offense where another person was assaulted or injured. 78% of juvenile residential facilities, jails and long term care both secure and not, were not at capacity (Office Juvenile Justice and Delinquency Program, 2016). This is s stark contrast to adult correctional facilities.

There are 1,772 facilities that house over 45,000 juvenile offenders (Office Juvenile Justice and Delinquency Program, 2016). These are not all jails. In fact 55% of these residential facilities are private facilities. There has been a concerted movement amongst juvenile detention centers to find alternatives to jail due to while they await **adjudication.** Only 15% of those arrested and awaiting adjudication are still in detention after 90 days (OJJDP Stat Handbook).

Juveniles in custody, especially a secure place like juvenile detention, are decreasing and this population will most likely continue to decrease as more alternatives to incarceration are utilized. The idea of locking up juveniles is beginning to wane. The public appears to be changing (Pew Charitable Trust, 2014). It's also very expensive to detain a juvenile in detention. The average cost to incarcerate a juvenile is $407.58 per day. That equates to $148,767 per juvenile per year (Justice Policy, 2014). The combination of changing public attitudes and limited resources will continue to impact juvenile detention.

# I. CONTEMPORARY ISSUES FOR AMERICAN JAILS

There are a number of contemporary issues for American jails. We cannot address them all here. We will examine a few of those, such as the increasing burden jails shoulder in relation to physical health and mental healthcare. The ability and struggle jails have to recruit and retain staff in a challenging environment has become one of the most pertinent issues for jail administrators to encounter. Jail violence is also a concern not only for inmates, but staff. Finally we'll briefly examine the relatively new role jails play in reentry of inmates back into the community.

## 1. Healthcare and Mental Health

Healthcare for inmates is a major concern for jail administrators as they seek to pay for increasing healthcare costs for inmates. Typically jails spend any were from 9–30% of their entire budgets in healthcare (Schaenman, Davies, Jordan, & Chakraborty, 2013). Jail staff cannot just take an inmate to the local hospital and drop the patient off. Inmates are in the custody of the jail therefore it becomes the jail's responsibility to take care of the needs of the inmate. Several jails with medium to very large populations contract with healthcare providers. These providers provide services in jails as much as possible. Indeed, many jails have what we may associate as a clinic or even more long term type care.

The U.S. Supreme Court case *Estelle v. Gamble* set legal precedent that jails and prisons must provide the same amount of healthcare that a non-incarcerated person would receive. Another reason for treating inmates while in jail concerns public health both inside and outside of jails. Communicable diseases are easily spread in the respectively tight confines of jail. Jails are also typically used for short term confinement. The purpose of jail is to confine not as a place where diseases may be more effectively transmitted. People interested in the public good view jail as an opportunity to positively affect public health by treating diseases before they become widespread or epidemic (Schaenman, Davies, Jordan, & Chakraborty, 2013). Also, jails can identify people in need of mental health services instead of jail.

In a joint report from the Treatment Advocacy Center and the National Sherriff's Association they advised that American jails were becoming our "new Asylums" ((Torrey, et al., 2014)p.6). The number of people in jail with a serious mental illness exceeds the number of seriously mentally ill people 10 times over. The report also contends that most of those inmates currently in jail with a serious mental illness would not have to be there except for the deinstitutionalization movement which has led to closing state run and privately subsidized psychiatric hospitals all over the country.

Mentally ill people are more likely to be abused or taken advantage of by fellow inmates. Correctional officers can mistake mental health issues for aggressive behavior and instead of getting the mental health treatment that's necessary they can instead be punished or physically treated by staff. If treatment is not received while in jail an inmate once released can end up with more severe complications and issues than when they entered jail (Torrey, et al., 2014).

There are a number of complications that arise due to mentally ill inmates being incarcerated rather than in psychiatric facility. Jails can become overcrowded as a result of those with mental health issues being incarcerated. Mental health inmates can present behavior issues. Correctional officers may not be able to spot of the nuances or outward symptoms of mental illness. Inmates with mental health issues can receive treatment such as being placed in **administrative segregation,** which can exacerbate illness. Those that are not recognized by staff with mental health issues present a greater danger to themselves. Those with mental health issues present a higher risk of suicide. Finally, crime such as acts of violence, can be a symptom of a larger mental health issue. When the person does not get the appropriate treatment while in jail they get released and again get arrested by police thus we see recidivating.

In 44 of 50 states and the District of Columbia a single jail or prison houses more people with a serious mental health issue than the largest remaining state psychiatric hospital. Resources have gone to criminal justice and other resources at the expense of entities like state psychiatric hospitals. The Treatment Advocacy Center and National Sherriff's Association 2014, concluded several different ways to solve the problem of mentally ill people remaining in jail:

- Reform mental illness treatment laws and practices in the community to eliminate barriers to treatment for individuals too ill to recognize they need care, so they receive help before they are so disordered they commit acts that result in their arrest.

- Reform jail and prison treatment laws so inmates with mental illness can receive appropriate and necessary treatment just as inmates with medical conditions receive appropriate and necessary medical treatment.

- Implement and promote jail diversion programs such as mental health courts.

- Use court-ordered outpatient treatment (assisted outpatient treatment/AOT) to provide the support at-risk individuals need to live safely and successfully in the community.

- Encourage cost studies to compare the true cost of housing individuals with serious mental illness in prisons and jails to the cost of appropriately treating them in the community.

- Establish careful intake screening to identify medication needs, suicide danger, and other risks associated with mental illness.

- Institute mandatory release planning to provide community support and foster recovery.

- Provide appropriate mental illness treatment for inmates with serious psychiatric illness.

Source: Treatment Advocacy Center and National Sheriff's Association Joint Report April 8, 2014.

## 2. Recruiting and Retaining Staff

Recruiting and retaining jail staff can be a major challenge for jail administrators. As the baby boomer generation continues to retire and leave the correctional workforce a new pool of officers isn't replacing them as quickly as necessary. Considering the relatively low wages and difficult working conditions those that would have once considered working in jail just aren't there. Correctional officers have to tackle numerous situations and deal with inmates from varied backgrounds and in various states of health both physical and mental. The transient nature of jail typically does not allow for officers to develop a rapport with inmates. Officers often have to triage inmates and provide help to inmates with any of a host of issues. Since jail correctional officers deal with people recently incarcerated understanding how to deal with people under the influence of any number of substances is part of the job. A career as a correctional officer may be one of the most difficult duties in criminal justice.

Jail correctional officers are dealing a population of inmates that reflect the results of any number of public policy decisions such as homelessness, unemployment, mental health, physical health, and substance abuse (Stinchcomb, McCampbell, & Leip, 2009). Jails have acted as the resource of last resort as arrest is the primary intervention for these and many more issues. As a result of this "catch all" status correctional officers are now tasked with a number of responsibilities.

The challenge to retain jail correctional officers is difficult. As we previously discovered a large part of the overall American workforce is in the process of retiring. This creates two distinct problems. The first is trying to fill the void in numbers of correctional staff. Many agencies are operating well below staffing levels that they should be operating at. This creates a problem in and of itself. Those employees that remain must work more shifts to cover job vacancies. This creates a high degree of officer "burnout" which results in even more officers leaving. This cycle of overwork leading to burnout and more vacancies can seriously disrupt jail operations. The second problem is one of "brain drain". Officers with years of experience are valuable in many ways as they understand jail operations implicitly. Not having a seasoned veteran to learn from can impair training.

There are many opportunities in the labor market that offer better pay and less stress. The result is a shrinking pool of qualified candidates. Working conditions in jail along with increased economic opportunity. A "talent war" of sorts has developed for some job markets. Corrections appears to be one of those (Partnership for Public Service, National Academy of Public Administration & New York Times Job Market, 2005).

## 3. Jail Violence

The average daily population of American jails hovers around 700,000 inmates. The rate of violence varies greatly among these facilities. Larger jails experience greater rates of violence than small jails (cite). The reasons for violence in jails varies as much as the inmates that reside there. However, there are several ways in which jails can reduce violence.

The architectural design of jails can create opportunities for assault. Some jails' design make it difficult for officers to monitor inmate behavior. Inmates can easily learn the "blindspots" in a facility. These areas are not only dangerous for inmates but staff alike.

The nature or code of silence make it difficult more inmates and staff to report inmate assaults. Jail culture is dissimilar to mainstream culture. Reporting and assault, especially a sexual assault by an inmate is not only less than desirable reporting an assault to jail staff can actually increase the threat level experienced by a person.

The nature of people entering jail has also changed the threat levels to inmates and staff. In the past jail inmates sentenced to a jail sentence (i.e. less than 1 year) were low level less dangerous offenders. Today more people are in jail for violent crimes (ref Zhen). Even though the "victim class" doesn't tend to stay in jail for long there are non-violent inmates housed with violent inmates which can increase victimization.

The criminal justice system does little deterrent effect on inmates who sexually assault other inmates. Even though a very small number (approximately 2%—Rantala, Romona (2018). Sexual Victimization Reported by Adult Correctional Authorities, 2012–2015. Bureau of Justice Statistics Washington DC) of jail inmates are sexually assaulted by other inmates there appears to be little consequence. Reporting sexual assault as an inmate has numerous explicit and hidden barriers.

The Prison Rape Elimination Act (PREA) was passed by Congress in 2003. This was an effort to better understand sexual assault in jails and prisons. One guiding purpose of the act was to address sexual assault in jails and prisons and of course help eliminate it. When looking at the statistics we see that a very small number of jail inmates report being assaulted. Reporting sexual assault is a difficult thing to do for many inmates.

## J.   RESEARCH AND EVIDENCE-BASED POLICY/PRACTICE

Programming and offender therapy in jail used to be viewed with great skepticism. However that view is changing as more jails are offering a host of different programs to address inmate's needs and ultimately reduce risk of recidivism. There is not room here to address all of these but we'll examine one program.

## 1.   Allegheny County Pennsylvania Reentry Specialist Program

In 2010 and 2011, criminal justice and human services personnel in Allegheny County Pennsylvania worked together under the Bureau of Justice Assistance's **Second Chance Act**. The goal was to launch two programs aimed at reducing recidivism. The first was a Reentry Specialist Program. The program sought to reduce recidivism by improving offender reentry from the local jail to the community. The jail would work with local professionals in various human services fields to ensure continued care received while in jail through the transition back to the community.

The program was targeted for a select group of inmates. Male and female inmates with sentences 6 months or longer and were going to return to the local community upon release. Inmates who were determined to be at a medium or high risk to reoffend were targeted for this program. Risk was determined based on many factors like: current age, age at first offense, and number of prior offenses.

The program had 2 phases. The first phase included providing jail inmates with various programming (education, training, and healthcare) for 5 months. The second phase was to provide the same inmates with continuing aftercare in the community. The continuation of care beyond the "captive audience" of being an inmate was key. The program attempted to reduce recidivism by:

1.   Using a structured risk/needs assessment, referring inmates to a cognitive-restructuring program (called Thinking for a Change), and transferring them to the jail's Reentry Pod. The Reentry Pod was designed to give inmates greater access to reentry services and program staff.

2.   Coordinating services in jail and in the community by assigning a Reentry Specialist to work with the inmate. The Reentry Specialist provided case-management services such as designing transition plans and providing basic support for up to 12 months post-release.

3.   Improving educational outcomes through literacy classes, GED classes, peer tutoring, adult basic education, and pre-apprenticeship training both pre- and post-release.

4.   Improving employment outcomes through an employment program that typically began with the Urban League's Reentry Assistance Management Program (RAMP), which is a 22-hour, job

readiness program. The program matched inmate interests and skills to various job options, taught important communication and problem-solving skills, and guided inmates through the job search process.

5.  Reducing substance abuse through prevention programs, including cognitive-based therapy, gender-specific treatment, and relapse prevention.

6.  Enhancing housing opportunities through access to Goodwill's HARBOR project, which provides eligible ex-offenders with housing and supportive services.

7.  Supporting healthy family functioning and relationships through parenting classes, relationship classes, and structured visits between inmates and their children. Additionally, the program included a family support specialist who worked with inmates and their families to prepare them for the inmate's release.

8.  Increasing post-release compliance through the program's Probation Officer (PO). The PO conducted additional risk/needs assessments and used them to modify the Offender Supervision Plans, which were then provided to the inmate's supervising PO and ensured that housing plans were in place, and that the inmate and supervising PO received information about the date and location of their first meeting.

Source: Willison, Janeen Buck, Sam G. Bieler, and KiDeuk Kim. 2014. *Evaluation of the Allegheny County Jail Collaborative Reentry Programs*. Washington, D.C.: Urban Institute.

Researchers from the Urban Institute evaluated the program. The researchers reviewed all aspects of the reentry program and came up with some encouraging results concerning offender recidivism. They found that only 10% of the reentry participants were rearrested compared to 34% rearrests rates for the control group (National Institute of Justice, 2016). Programs like these look promising. Understanding that just because someone is released from jail doesn't mean they are "cured" or learned their lesson. Rather it's an opportunity to identify people with issues that need correction or help simply beyond locking them up and then releasing them back to the same environment with the same lack of coping skills that result in arrest initially.

# K. CONCLUSION

Jails are a very important part of corrections. For the vast majority of people involved with the criminal justice system their first experience of corrections is at a jail. The purpose of a jail has evolved from simply detaining people while they await trial. Indeed, there are many efforts to reduce the time people wait in jail for their case to be decided. Interestingly, while jails are trying to keep the population of those awaiting court dispositions down they are tasked with a variety of new duties. Some of these are to identify people that have health and mental health issues, they act has detention centers for agencies beyond their localities, and they provide services that extend into the community.

## Discussion Questions

1. What are some differences between jail and prison?

2. Why were jails one of the first public buildings erected in early American towns and cities?

3. What are some purposes of jail beyond simply housing people until their court proceedings are finished?

4. What is classification in jail and why is it important?

5. What is a bond? What is so controversial about criminal bonds?

6. What are some issues that jail correction officers face?

7. Why do jail administrators have a difficult time recruiting and retaining employees?

8. Explain why private jails are being utilized more.

9. How is juvenile detention different than adult jail?

10. What is 1 contemporary issue faced by American jails today? What's your solution to the issue?

## Student Exercises

1. What programs, is any are offered at your local jail? Discuss with people that facilitate these programs and discover if they are effective at accomplishing whatever their goal is.

2. What is the demographic makeup of your local jail? What are most inmates currently incarcerated for (i.e. awaiting trial or as a sentence). What are the issues your local jail are experiencing?

# Key Terms

**Adjudication**—the final disposition of a juvenile court case.

**Administrative segregation**—separating inmates from the general inmate population by housing them in an individual cell. Often times inmates will have very limited human contact and very few amenities.

**Bail**—the release from jail of a person pending trial. There are many types of bail.

**Bondsman**—a person or business that provides money to people charged with a crime in order to satisfy a bond.

**Civil legal liability**—the legal ability to hold someone civilly liable through filing a lawsuit. Often the remedy in civil cases is monetary compensation.

**Contraband**—illegal or restricted items in jail.

**Control group**—a group that was not offered the "treatment".

**Cumulative disadvantage**—a systemic tendency for people or groups of people to be disadvantaged socially and economically which facilitates social ills such as crime and/or health issues.

**Custody**—assuming control and responsibility for a inmate.

**Direct supervision**—Correctional Officers whose main duty is to supervise, control, direct, and care for inmates.

**Hold**—an order to detain a person in custody.

**Life chances**—opportunities people or a group of people have to improve their quality of life.

**Pod**—living area of the jail. Inmates usually slept in areas with several people assigned to a cell. Several cells make up a pod which share a common area.

**Prison Rape Elimination Act**—act of Congress whereby jails, state prisons, and federal correctional facilities report sexual assault statistics and participate in training to help reduce sexual assault in correctional facilities.

**Resource broker**—an entity that services to provide avenues for other to receive services.

**Sally port**—area of the jail, usually a secure garage, where police transfer custody of a person to jail staff.

**Second Chance Act**—a Congressional Act of Congress in which the federal government provides financial and other support to local, state, and non-profit groups that work to prevent offender recidivism.

**Turnover**—inmates entering and leaving jail.

## CHAPTER 5

# Diversion, Pretrial, and Probation

**Chapter Objectives**

- Define what diversion, pretrial, and probation is and its function within the larger criminal justice system.

- Understand the roles of a probation officer.

- Compare the different ways probation is administered in the U.S.

- Compare and contrast how the history of probation affects current probation practices.

- Identify the current issues within diversion, pretrial, and probation today.

## A. DIVERSION AND PROBATION

Unbeknownst to most Americans the most frequently used type of criminal sanction is probation. It's utilized far more than jail or prison is. Probation and parole often are used to mean the same thing. It's true that both probationers and parolees are supervised in the community. Each are released conditionally but probation and parole are quite different. A person may be granted probation after sentencing and the released back into the community usually with **conditions** that must be abided by. They are supervised by a probation officer who is tasked with verifying a person is following the conditions provided by the court. If the probationer is found to be in violation of their conditions of release then the probationer might be sent to jail or prison. A person under parole supervision is released from prison or jail after serving a period of incarceration. Their release is conditional too and if found to be in violation of release conditions a parolees can be sent back to prison or jail.

Today there are approximately 3.6 million people on probation in the U.S. The number of probationers has actually been in decline since 2008. It decreased by 2% from 2008 to 2016 (Kaeble, 2016). This may seem like a small decrease in percentage but it represents an overall correctional trend in decreasing numbers of people involved in the correctional system.

Diversion is another way to hold people accountable for criminal actions while keeping them in the community. Placement on diversion does not result in a criminal conviction unlike probation. Diversion is diverting a person from continued prosecution in order to prevent a criminal conviction. Today there are a number of diversionary courts and programs with prosecuting attorney offices'. Statutory pretrial diversion is very well established and it exists in 48 states and the District of Columbia. The Federal Courts also allow for pretrial diversion. Diversion exists under the assumption that people charged with certain offenses (usually minor offenses) do not benefit from formal prosecution and criminal sentencing. Processing through the criminal justice system may in fact be detrimental for some. Diversion is another venue to address criminal behavior without having to spend resources on someone who ultimately would not benefit from criminal prosecution and where the interest of justice are not served.

## B. DIVERSION

Across the U.S. criminal justice agencies and the entire system are dealing with people that have substance abuse or mental health issues. The criminal justice system status quo is also being challenged by those seeking more efficient means to not only dispense justice but to prevent future criminality. The combination of ever increasing numbers of people with substance abuse and/or mental health issues along with increased public demand for results have opened up the opportunity for many different **diversion** programs. There appears to be strong public support from the public and legislators as well as correctional professionals for community based alternative beyond traditional probation (Center for Health and Justice TACS, 2013). There is a strong effort to seek more effective and less expensive ways to hold people accountable for criminal actions and reduce recidivism policies such as justice reinvestment offer approaches that eschew former get-tough on crime policies. Evidence-based practices and data driven results have generated some interest.

Diversion can occur in any one of the following three phases. The first is at the street level law enforcement phase. Where the local police or county sheriff oversee the diversion. It is perhaps the least formal of the three phases and typically doesn't involve involvement in a program the person has to complete but more often the police officer will act as a **resource broker** or provide crisis intervention. The second phase involves a prosecuting attorney's office. Oversight is through that office or through probation. A person on diversion through this venue will most likely participate in a formal program, such as a drug treatment program. The final phase is through a specialized court, such as a drug court or mental health court. Oversight is through a court whose task is specific to a certain type of offender or offense. For instance drug courts usually handle cases where a person has been charged with simple drug possession and therefore the person may have a substance abuse issue that can be better handled through a court better equipped to handle these specific types of cases. Court specialization offers some benefits such as the court is becoming familiar with the nuances of drug use, drug user, treatments, and the most efficient ways to handle this sort of case. Judges, attorneys, probation officers, and other court staff are familiar with various treatments available and treatment personnel in turn become better acquainted with court personnel.

Typical oversight, diversion, and practices of
the 3 justice system phases of diversion

|  | **Law Enforcement** | **Pretrial/ Prosecution** | **Specialty Court** |
|---|---|---|---|
| *Oversight:* | -Local police | -State/District Atty. | -Court |
|  | -Sheriff | Pretrial Services via *Court or probation* |  |
| *Diversion Goal:* | -Street level safety | -Reduce docket pressure | -Reduce recidivism |
|  | -Reduce pressure on jail | -Reduce court and jail expenses | -Supervision with rehabilitation best practices |
|  | -Identify treatment needs of individuals that motivate crime | -Maximize prosecution resources for more serious cases |  |
|  |  | -Identify treatment needs of individuals that motivate crime |  |

| *Diversion Practices:* | -Street level crisis intervention | -Deferred prosecution | -Deferred adjudication/ sentencing |
|---|---|---|---|
| | -Co-location with or immediate diversion to behavioral health services | -Referral to community services | -Multidisciplinary staffing |
| | | -Individualized conditions for success-failure | -Referral to community services |
| | | -Justice supervision (for more serious Crimes) | -Justice accountability |
| | | | -Clear rewards/sanction |

Source: A National Survey of Criminal Justice Diversion Programs and Initiatives (2013). Center for Justice and Health at TASC.

Which crimes are eligible for diversion depend on the jurisdiction where the crime was committed. Some jurisdictions allow for diversion based on state statute. Others depend on the policy of the prosecutor's office. Participation in diversionary programs are generally voluntary. They can continue with their case until its outcome, however the accused person may miss their opportunity to be granted access to diversion. There are several factors that determine eligibility for diversion as each jurisdiction is different but generally criteria that make a person ineligible are:

— prior criminal history

— being charged with a serious offense (some felony crime are still eligible for diversion)

— a person be unwilling to accept treatment or abide by a diversion program

The prosecutors charging the crime typically determines eligibility for diversion. The accused person often times will sign a "diversion agreement" whereby they agree to abide by the terms of the diversion program. In this agreement the accused usually **stipulates** to the criminal charges. If they violate these terms the prosecuting attorney's office will resume criminal charges and considering the accused signed the stipulation to the charges a conviction is relatively certain.

> **Student exercise**—Contact your local prosecutor's office or investigate via the web and see what sorts of diversion program exist in your community. Discuss with your classmates.

The number and types of diversion programs have grown in the last 25 years. Diversions are handled on a case by case basis. Types of crimes like driving under the influence or domestic abuse can be handled by specialty diversionary courts or departments that specialize in those specific cases. Others can handle specific offenders that can be charged with a host of various crimes. Today there are 39 states that have diversion programs that specifically address substance abuse. These courts are generally for people charged with possessing small amounts of controlled substances for personal use or for alcohol related offenses. There are presently 24 states that have diversion courts for people with mental health needs (National Conference of state legislatures, 2018). There are many courts that deal with specific offenders regardless of the crime. Teen courts are utilized in some places, whereby teenagers charged with minor offenses such as shoplifting or vandalism can have their case diverted. There are many veterans that leave military service who may end up with criminal charges and in some cases there are veteran's courts which take into account issues that are unique to veterans.

The outcome for someone granted diversion can be positive or negative. Diversion programs have a beginning and an end date. If the person meets all of the requirements of the diversion agreement they can be successfully discharged from their respective program. Successful completion means the pending charges are dismissed and there is no criminal conviction. People placed on diversion may violate the terms of their agreement. This may not result in an unsuccessful discharge from diversion but if it does the person will most likely resume prosecution and since most diversion agreements include a stipulation to the charges a criminal conviction is eminent and whatever criminal sanction would ensue in addition to a criminal record.

There are benefits and criticisms of diversion. The benefits are twofold. The first benefit is for the person accused. If they successfully complete diversion they do not have a criminal record as far as that charge is concerned. They also get to stay in the community and potentially remain employed, receive the benefit of the mandated diversion program and be supported by family. The prosecutor conserves their resources and is able to devote those resources to more serious cases. It frees up not only money but staff. Lastly the interest of justice for the community occurs. The person accused of the crime is held to account for their actions and the offender receives some measure of rehabilitation which is supposed to curb recidivism.

# C. PROBATION IN AMERICA

**Probation** is one of the most utilized criminal sanctions in the U.S. Approximately 3.6 million people were on probation supervision in 2016. There are far more people on probation than parole (874,800 in 2016) and prison (1,526,600 in 2016). That said, the probation population has actually been in decline since 2008. It's declined about 2% each year since 2008 (Kaeble, Probation and Parole in the United States, 2016, 2018). This decline mirrors the overall correctional population decline that began the same year.

Recall that probation supervision begins after a person has been convicted of a crime. The judge may allow the person to be placed on probation or placement may be mandated by law. Probation is an alternative to incarceration. The defendant now offender is granted probation provided they abide by conditions of supervision. Conditions of release are meant to restrict what an offender can do. They also are put in place to incentivize rehabilitation too. Probation is largely viewed as an opportunity for the offender to remain in the community while attempting to strive toward rehabilitation. Below are the standard conditions of probation the U.S. Probation for the Eastern District of New York:

While the defendant is on probation pursuant to this judgment, the defendant:

| | |
|----|---|
| 1) | shall not commit another federal, state or local crime; |
| 2) | shall not leave the judicial district without the permission of the court or probation officer; |
| 3) | shall report to the probation officer as directed by the court or probation officer and shall submit a truthful and complete written report within the first five days of each month; |
| 4) | shall answer truthfully all inquiries by the probation officer and follow the instructions of the probation officer; |
| 5) | shall support his or her dependents and meet other family responsibilities; |
| 6) | shall work regularly at a lawful occupation unless excused by the probation officer for schooling, training, or other acceptable reasons; |

| 7) | shall notify the probation officer within ten days of any change in residence or employment, or if such prior notification is not possible, then within five days after said change; |
|---|---|
| 8) | shall refrain from excessive use of alcohol and shall not purchase, possess, use, distribute, or administer any narcotic or other controlled substance, or any paraphernalia related to such substances, except as prescribed by a physician; |
| 9) | shall not frequent places where controlled substances are illegally sold, used, distributed, or administered; |
| 10) | shall not associate with any persons engaged in criminal activity, and shall not associate with any person convicted of a felony unless granted permission to do so by the probation officer; |
| 11) | shall permit a probation officer to visit him or her at any time at home or elsewhere and shall permit confiscation of any contraband observed in plain view by the probation officer; |
| 12) | shall notify the probation officer within seventy-two hours of being arrested or questioned by a law enforcement officer; |
| 13) | shall not enter into any agreement to act as an informer or a special agent of a law enforcement agency without the permission of the court; |
| 14) | as directed by the probation officer, shall notify third parties of risks that may be occasioned by defendant's criminal record or personal history or characteristics, and shall permit the probation officer to make such notifications and to confirm the defendant's compliance with such notification requirement; |
| 15) | shall pay any fine or obligation imposed by this judgment; |
| 16) | shall not possess a firearm or destructive device. |

(Eastern District of New York U.S. Probation, 2018).

Of course the person responsible for making sure the offender is following the conditions is the probation officer. They try to balance community safety with the needs and rehabilitation of the offender. Their duties are considerable and they have to deal with first time offenders as well as career criminals.

Probation is also viewed as a fair an appropriate sentence. Many are in agreement that not all criminal behavior merits incarceration but nor does it mean that the crime should go unpunished. Deciding who is granted to probation can be difficult as some on probation continue to commit crime while others do not.

If the sentencing model is determinate granting or not granting probation is pre-determined. Deciding who is placed on probation is a subject of great debate and will most likely continue to be.

---

### Corrections in Action

Ethan Couch of Burleson, TX was 16 years old when he crashed his car in 2013. He and a group of friends stole beer from a store and went to his parent's house for a party. After consuming a large quantity of alcohol he and some friends went for a drive. Shortly after leaving he caused an accident that left 4 people dead and a passenger in his car was also left paralyzed and brain damaged. His blood alcohol level was .24. This is three times the legal limit in Texas.

He eventually plead guilty to 4 counts of manslaughter in juvenile court. The judge sentenced Ethan to 10 years probation. The prosecution asked for a 20 year prison sentence. Many in the community were outraged at the sentence. Some claimed that Ethan received special treatment because his family was wealthy. His defense team and a psychologist claimed he couldn't know right from wrong because his family was wealthy and indulged his every whim. The case quickly gained national attention and he became known as the "affluenze teen".

In December 2015, a video surfaced of Ethan at a party drinking alcohol, which was a violation of his probation. Shortly after the airing of this video Ethan and his mother Tonya went missing. They were captured 2 weeks after they went missing in Puerto Vallarta Mexico.

Ethan spent 720 days in jail for absconding probation. He was placed back on probation. Tarrant County Texas Sheriff Dee Anderson said Mr. Couch had created "0" issues while in jail and that, Ethan Couch is not the same person he was when he came to jail". (Victor, 2018)

---

The "affluenze teen" being placed on probation is an example of a possible placement error. However, many people that end up on probation are successful. They complete their term of supervision with no or very little violations. Many also complete treatment and education programs that positively benefit not only the offender but ultimately society as a whole. These stories typically go unnoticed.

The goals of probation vary to reflect social values. Therefore probation goals can be punitive or rehabilitative. They tend not to be solely one or the other but lean toward either being punishment and enforcement oriented or more rehabilitative. During the Crime Control Era of the middle 1980s up until approximately the middle 2000s probation agencies largely oriented themselves toward more surveillance and enforcement. Today that seems to be changing in many ways. There are more alternatives to incarceration and **intermediate sanctions** aimed at addressing condition violations without using incarceration. Regardless of leaning toward punishment or rehabilitation there are constant goals in many probation agencies:

> Weblink—The American Probation and Parole Association (APPA) is an organization that's dedicated to providing a number of different services to the community corrections arena. Visit the web site at:
>
> http://www.appa-net.org/eweb/

1.  Community safety is the first priority. Even though many agencies do not view themselves as enforcement agencies their duty is to protect the public.

2.  Promote rehabilitative measures. Rehabilitating offenders not only helps the offender but also the community. Additionally rehabilitation improves community safety.

3.  Victims of crime have rights that deserve protecting. Prosecution and punishment of the offender is a part of the responsibility of the criminal justice system as is the recognition that the victim is another part. Just as the offender uses resources of the criminal justice system so too is the victim deserving of such resources.

4.  Probation's duty is to carry out the will of the court. Any conditions, sanctions, or orders the court may impose, it is the duty of the probation office to carry out. (APPA cite)

These are general goals of probation. How each agency reaches these goals are unique to the jurisdiction. A probation agency philosophy is a combination of many things such as the philosophy of the administration, individual leadership, the community, and the offenders under their care.

# D. HISTORY OF AMERICAN PROBATION

Probation has a long history in American corrections. It started out as an effort to reform those involved in the criminal justice system through means other than incarceration. The initial rehabilitative spirit is still one of the major tenets of the profession. However, as with much of corrections it has evolved tremendously, especially in the last 50 years. It's important to look back at where it originated and why it originated. This informs us as much about contemporary probation as it provides an answer to why or how we conduct probation as we do.

Probation developed in the middle part of the 19th century. It was first utilized in Boston Massachusetts in 1830, as a more humane way to hold people criminally accountable yet not punish them to the extent of incarceration. The fact that probation was established during this time period and in an urban location should not be ignored. The establishment of probation or any correctional measure is not happenstance. If we consider the historical context of the time it becomes easier to see why probation was an acceptable alternative. If you recall the establishment of America's first professional police force was in New York, NY 1829. There was a growing social acceptance of authorities exerting **formal social control**. This acceptance was largely due to the urbanization that was taking place as a result of the Industrial Revolution. People were being drawn from rural areas in American and especially from other countries to cities like Boston, New York, Philadelphia with the hope of finding regular work which required little to no skills or education. Cities began to swell with people and as a result crime rates too began to rise. Just as there was a need to keep order via a police force so to be there a need to provide court remedies or corrections to those convicted of crimes. Incarcerating everyone convicted of a crime is not feasible nor was it seen by many people, especially those with social influence, as just. In other words not every crime should result in jail or prison. The combination of a social environment favorable to a less punitive measure than prison and a recognized need for formal social control to hold those people that did break the laws of the day accountable allowed for a corrective measure like probation to be utilized.

Not long after first being used in 1830, John Augustus became interested in courts and probation in particular. Augustus, a wealthy shoemaker, was a member of the Washington Total Abstinence Society. Wealthy people being a member of a society or club whose purpose was to impact society was a frequent pursuit. This organization was committed to helping individuals abstain from drinking alcohol. In 1841, Augustus began posting bail in certain cases. Prior to providing bail Augustus would **vet** candidates for release. He gave preference to first time offenders also a person's demeanor, past experiences, and potential current influences informed his decision He would have those charged with crimes released under his supervision. Upon their release those released would have to abide by certain conditions and if they did not they would be remanded into custody. He helped offenders with employment, education, and housing. Augustus did this work voluntarily. From 1841 until his death in 1859 Augusts supervised almost 2,000 adults and thousands more children (Free dictionary, 2018).

Initially Augusts was more of a pre-trial supervisor than probation officer. He did make contributions to an area that eventually would become known as probation. He is largely regarded as the father of American probation. Today the focus on rehabilitation instead of punishment is still an overarching philosophy of probation. Although the vetting process for placement on probation is more complex than Augustus used he is still credited with that as well as probations close relationship with the court.

Probation continued not only in Boston courts, but was adopted in many other metropolitan courts. However, those providing probation services were volunteers. In 1878, the Massachusetts legislature created the first state statute authorizing probation, but only in Suffolk County (Boston). The opportunity for offender to be placed on probation was extended to rural areas and small towns in 1880. The caveat here was that mayors would appoint probation officers and placement on probation was voluntary. The initial weal implementation of probation and the new concept meant that few cities utilized probation. There was criticism that mayors appointed probation officers based on political affiliation. Again backed by social pressure in 1891, the power to appoint probation officers and utilize probation was transferred to the court which bowed far less to political pressure (New York City Probation, 2018).

It took many decades for probation to become accepted as an alternative to imprisonment. The practice of probation started in the northeast and was slowly adopted across the U.S. In 1925, President Calvin Coolidge signed the National Probation Act, which authorized every federal district court to appoint salaried probation officers. It took 2 years after the act was signed before 8 federal districts hired their first probation officers. The juvenile justice movement of the late 1800s helped accelerate its use. The early juvenile's court approach of rehabilitating offenders was very much in line with the rehabilitative nature of probation. Thus as juvenile courts became established so did probation as a way to deal with juvenile offenders become more acceptable. It wasn't until 1956, until probation was available for adults in all 50 states.

# E. PRE-TRIAL

Many probation agencies compartmentalize services between probation and pre-trial services. **Pre-trial** services are tasked at times by judges to provide pretrial supervision of a person involved in the court process. When a person has been arrested and charged with a crime(s) they may obtain bail. When the bail is originally set or at any time during the court process the judge overseeing the case may wish to have the person's release supervised by a pre-trial officer. The judge will determine the conditions of the bond. Some typical pre-trial release conditions are:

— Electronic monitoring and abiding by conditions of the electronic monitor such as time restrictions/movement.

— Refraining from using illegal substances or alcohol.

— Not to suffer any further arrests.

— Weapons prohibition.

— Reporting for court dates.

— Restricting associations with others.

• Cite state National Conference State Legislators (National Conference of State Legislatures, 2018)

The pre-trial officer ensures the conditions of the bond as set by the judge are followed. In the event that they are not followed the pre-trial officer will notify the judge. Typically a bond revocation hearing takes place where the prosecution may ask for the person's bond to be revoked. If the bond is revoked the person may is subject to incarceration until their case is adjudicated. The defense may refute the allegations of the bond conditions violation in the hearing. It's ultimately the judge's decision whether to revoke the bond and issue a new one, revoke the bond and place the person in jail, or dismiss the allegations of the bond violation.

---

### Corrections in Action

Paul Manafort, a former campaign chairperson, in President Donald Trump's 2016 presidential election campaign was arrested in October 2017, for a number of crimes including money laundering and making false statements to investigators. After his arrest he was released on $10 million bail and placed under house arrest. While on bail and under pretrial supervision Mr. Manafort was charged with witness tampering concerning the case he was released on.

During the bail revocation hearing Judge Amy Jackson decided that Mr. Manafort could not be trusted to abide by the law. Mr. Manafort was directed by another federal judge in a separate criminal case not to contact witnesses in that case or the current case, which he apparently violated. His initial bond was revoked and he was remanded into custody while his case is adjudicated.

Mr. Manafort had previously been warned by the judge about his conduct and lack of adhering to the conditions of the bond before the most recent violations were brought to her knowledge. In Aug. of 2018, Mr. Manafort was convicted of a number of felonies in the case for which his bond was revoked. The sentencing phase of the trial won't occur until early in 2019. He does however face new charges and a separate trial in September 2018 (LaFraniere, 2018).

Once the case against the person placed under bond supervision is adjudicated or if the case is dropped by the prosecution they are released from the conditions of bond. In cases where a person abided by the conditions of bond and they are convicted their actions while under bond supervision may be beneficial for determining release on probation or incarceration.

# F. PROBATION SUPERVISION

Probation supervision occurs after the person has been placed under probation supervision by the sentencing judge. The judge will advise the offender how long their term of supervision is and of their conditions of supervision. The conditions of supervision provide the offender and the probation officer the "rules". Below are the **standard conditions** of probation for adult felons in Florida:

- Report to the probation supervisor as directed by the court.
- Allow the probation officer to visit the probationer's home, place of employment, or other places.
- Remain gainfully employed in a suitable job.
- Stay within a specific area, such as within county or state limits.
- Do not break any new laws.
- Make restitution to any parties who were harmed by the crime.
- Financially support one's dependents.
- Do not associate with any people who are engaged in criminal activities.
- Willingly submit to random drug and/or alcohol testing.
- Do not possess, own, or carry any firearms.

- Do not use any controlled substances unless they were lawfully prescribed by a doctor.

  - The terms and conditions of probation are found under Section 948.03 of the Florida Statutes.

Jurisdictions have standard conditions of probation but judges will often times require **special conditions** unique to the offender. These special conditions can help the offender and the probation officer to address specific issues the offender may have or to provide another measure of public security. A probation officer's primary duty is to ensure the person placed on supervision is following these rules. If the offender doesn't follow the conditions several different types of sanctions can be employed or the probation officer may wish to ask the judge to revoke a person's probation which can possibly end up in incarceration.

After sentencing the probationer meets with their assigned probation officer. The officer and the probationer review the conditions of probation and any other requirements or forms the agency may have. At this point or at some point very early in the term of supervision a **risk/needs assessment** is completed. There are a number of different types of assessments that agencies use. The purpose of these assessments is to determine what level of risk a probationer may present to reoffend or to violate conditions of probation. This of course is the, "risk" portion of the risk and needs instrument. The "needs" portion helps an officer determine what needs a person may need in order to lessen the risk and also to improve their overall well-being. The results often determine how the probationer will be supervised. For instance if a probationer received a score that puts them at a "high" risk to reoffend the probation officer will meet with them more often to ensure compliance. The "high" risk probationer may be required to enter and complete different programs in order to address risky behaviors. If a violation is detected a "high" risk probationer may have their supervision revoked sooner than someone with a lower risk level. Thus the "risk/needs" level associated with probationer can have quite important consequences. (pic of R/N instrument)

In order to ensure the offender is adhering to the conditions probation officers perform many duties. Office appointments are one way to address issues, prevent potential issues, and provide resources for rehabilitative efforts. Many jurisdictions require probation officers to conduct home contacts at offender's homes. These can take place at any hour of the day and the offender may or may not know ahead of time that a probation officer is coming to conduct a contact. Home contacts can be very beneficial to ensure compliance with the conditions of probation as well as allow the probation officer to detect any warning signs of potential condition violations or criminal behavior. These contacts also present a challenge for probation officers. Officers are meeting with offenders in their homes and can present a host of dangers. As a result many probation officers are armed, carry police communication devices, and wear bullet proof vests (pic of probation officer home visit). (APPA states that allow to carry and not).

**Caseloads** for probation officers can reach beyond a hundred. Ensuring probationer is following their conditions can be taxing. Officers are trained in a number of areas such as mental health, dealing with gang members and other violent offenders, sex offenders, and substance abusers. Many agencies have officers that specialize in supervising certain types of offenders. The purpose of **specialization** is to ensure cases are handled more effectively and efficiently. Officers with a specialized caseload becomes familiar with the various therapies, such as sex offender therapy. This familiarity allows officers to communicate with therapists and probationers more effectively. Specialization also allows the officer to spot warning signs a probationer may be exhibiting that a less informed officer may miss. Thus officer can efficiently provide resources or counter measures to prevent conditions violations or criminal behavior.

## 1.  Role of the Probation Officer

The question of whether or not to arm probation officers has been debated since agencies began to arm officers in the 1980s. The debate concerns the primary role probation. Some see a probation officer's role as it was originally intended as that of an advocate of the probationer. The role was largely predicated on the probation officer finding or providing resources to help probationers rehabilitate and therefore discontinue criminal behavior. Today some see the role of the probation officer as more of an enforcement oriented role. The primary purpose is to surveille and detect **technical violations** or criminal actions of the probationer.

Many officers today are tasked with providing resources or providing different strategies to prevent probationers from future criminal behavior as well as making more prosocial decisions in general. A number of different initiatives are being used by probation officers such as Moral Reconation Therapy (MRT). MRT is a systemic cognitive behavioral strategy used by probation officers to improve a probationer's self-image, promote a prosocial self-identity and facilitate the development of moral reasoning. The basic idea is to instill a recognition in them concerning the social ills they add to by committing crime. MRT groups are facilitated by probation officers and require officers complete training in this area prior to facilitating groups.

Probation officers also act in more enforcement oriented roles. A condition of probation that is more prevalent today than it was twenty years ago concerns probation officers searching probationer's homes or other possessions such as vehicles etc. A standard condition of probation in many jurisdictions allows probation officers to search a probationer's home or other possessions without a search warrant. Probation officers must have reasonable suspicion prior to searching but the requirement to search does not have to reach the same threshold that a search warrant for the police must reach. Each jurisdiction that allows search without a warrant has their own procedure for such.

> **Class exercise**—Designate a student in class to contact the probation office in your area and inquire about their search protocol.

When a probationer is found to be in violation of their terms of probation a number of tactics can be used instead of seeking revocation. Intermediate sanctions can be used to address technical violations of probation without having to seek revocation. The purpose of using these sanctions are to address probationer behavior that does not rise to the level of seeking revocation. Below are some examples of intermediate sanctions:

- House arrest.

- Electronic monitoring.

- Increasing the number of probationer contacts.

- Use of day reporting.

- Short jail holds.

There are a number of different sanctions that agencies use in order to gain probationer compliance with conditions. Sanctions are typically used on a gradient scale. In other words minor violations illicit minor sanctions and more serious violations can mean more severe sanctions. The hope is to reduce the number of probation revocations and thus prison inmate populations while at the same time holding probationers accountable.

## 2. Revocation

At some point during the probationer's term of supervision the probation officer may request that probation be revoked. Typically the probation officer will have to write a renovation report and request the probationer either be arrest via a warrant or summoned to court for a revocation hearing. A judge presides over the hearing and the judge determines if the probation should be revoked. If the probationer stipulates to the allegations the probation officer made in their revocation report the judge can impose the original sentence that was suspended or the judge can impose further sanctions that don't require incarceration. If the probationer does not wish to stipulate they have a right to a lawyer (See *Gagnon v. Scarpelli*, 411 U.S. 778 (1973)) represent them in the revocation hearing. Probation is represented in court by the prosecuting attorney. Each side can submit evidence and cross examine witnesses during the hearing. Since the probation officer requested the revocation they will most likely have to testify in court. The purpose of the hearing is to determine if there is probable cause that violations of probation were violated. This is a far lower legal threshold than a court trial to determine guilt or innocence. Upon adjudication of the hearing the judge may impose the original sentence or the judge may impose additional sanctions that do not result in incarceration.

Many probation agencies seek to reach a balance between providing advocacy and enforcement. The original intent of probation officers was to provide probationers resources so that they might rehabilitate and discontinue criminal behavior. Today officers are also tasked with providing more enforcement oriented measures directed at improving community safety and ensuring court conditions are being satisfied. Achieving this balance can be tenuous.

Probation officers today require training in a variety of areas. Many are tasked with caseloads where probationers represent a host of different challenges from mental health issues, medical health issues, violent criminal behavior, and substance abuse problems. Their roles vary from advocacy to enforcement. These roles can be difficult transition from. This career though challenging has many rewards too.

# G. ADMINISTRATION OF PROBATION

The **administration** of probation is jurisdictionally dependent. Probation can be administered at the county level like in Oregon and Texas. It can be under the auspices of the state executive branch such as Oklahoma. In those states their state department of corrections administers probation. In still other jurisdictions such as the U.S. Federal court system and states like Alabama probation is administered by the judicial branch of government. Even within states probation can be administered by both the judicial and executive branch. In Kansas Court Services oversees many misdemeanor and some less serious felony probation cases. Court Services is within the judicial branch of government and it receives funding and directives through the Kansas Supreme Court. Community Corrections or Intensive Supervised Probation (ISP) is

> **Student Exercise**—Find out who administers probation in your area.

administered through Kansas department of Corrections which is under the executive branch. ISP receives its funding and directives through the state department of corrections, however human resources and certain other duties are administered at the county level. The administration of probation can be simple or complex depending upon the jurisdiction.

---

### Corrections in Action

The Community Corrections Act was first developed and instituted through the state legislature in Minnesota in 1973. This act allowed local entities such as county governments to receive state monies in order to directly supervise probationers in the community. The reason for this act concerned a combination of prison overcrowding and a call from the public for more effectively correctional measures. The result was this community corrections legislation which allows localities like counties to prioritize policies that fir better with that community. Instead of a state agency whose policies cover the entire state local or targeted correctional measures were to be implemented. These address specific community concerns that may not be a concern elsewhere in the state (Schoen, 1978).

---

Why does it matter which branch of government or other entity administers probation? The agency responsible for administering probation can dictate the overall philosophy of probation in the given jurisdiction. Those in the executive branch are appointed by a government official, usually a governor. These officials may wish to implement a more enforcement or alternatively advocacy oriented philosophy about how probation is administered. These philosophies can change policy and practices that can have important effects for community corrections and the criminal justice system in general considering there are many more people under probation supervision than in prison or jail.

## H. RESEARCH AND EVIDENCE-BASED POLICY/PRACTICE

Is probation an effective measure of reducing recidivism? Probation is supposed to act as a specific deterrent to future criminal behavior. People are placed on probation because their offense may not warrant incarceration yet does require some type of punishment. The terms of probation act in an effort to restrict what a person is allowed to do thereby providing a measure of punishment. People placed on probation are under closer surveillance and scrutiny because they have a probation officer monitoring them. Finally punishment is supposed to be swifter considering a probation officer can detect and react to violations in a rather quick manner.

The Bureau of Justice Statistics collects information pertaining to probation cases nationwide. We see that 1,928, 687 exited adult probation in the U.S. in 2016. Of that number 971,498 (50.4%) people successfully completed their term of supervision. 64,177 (3.3%) people were incarcerated with a new sentence obtained while on probation and 98,698 (5.1%) people were incarcerated as a result of violating their probation (Kaeble, Probation and Parole in the United States, 2016). Thus approximately 8.4% of adult probationers were incarcerated. These statistics are limited as 307,978 (16%) of probationers exited probation as "unknown or not reported". Yet, another 262,418 (13.6%) probationers were listed as "other unsatisfactory". Even though the data may be incomplete in a number of areas we see that relatively few (3.3%) appear to be committing new crimes while on probation.

## I.   REDUCED PROBATION CASELOAD IN EVIDENCE-BASED SETTING

This program seeks to intensify the effectiveness of probation supervision by reducing the caseload size of probation officers that deal with high risk offenders. The purpose of this project is to utilize evidence-based tools and risk assessment in conjunction with smaller caseloads. A more "hands-on" monitoring and greater scrutiny of rehabilitative efforts and involvement in treatment are the means to improve recidivism goals.

The officers with smaller caseloads are more available and thus more responsive to adherence to rehabilitee efforts like treatment and education. This availability allows the officer to address risks before they result in criminal behavior or technical violations that require court action such as revocation.

The agency patriating (Polk County Iowa, Des Moines) in the program in Iowa implemented the following:

- Risk/needs assessments.

- Specialized caseloads for domestic violence, sex offenders, and those with mental health issues.

- Concentrated services/treatment for probationers that received a risk score of "medium" or "high".

- Considered Responsivity (cognitive-behavior programs).

- Comprehensive case management.

The probation officers were tasked with identifying those probationers who were deemed most at risk to reoffend on dynamic (changing factors) such as drug use. A risk/need/responsivity (RNR) model was used whereby he core principals of:

Risk—Level of service should be matched to the level of the offender. High risk offender receive more services.

Need—Targeting criminogenic needs like substance abuse and/or pro criminal attitudes.

Responsivity—The ability of the probation officer to learn the style of the offender and then determine how services should be applied.

The results of the study yielded some interesting results considering targeting high risk offenders. Probationers in receiving these heightened services were arrested less often than peer not receiving services. Those receiving treatment after 36 months of follow-up reduced the likelihood of recidivism by 47% for property crime. It also resulted in 20% less violent crime (National Institute of Justice, 2012).

# J.  CONCLUSION

Probation is the most utilized direct correctional measure in the U.S. There are almost 4 million people under probation supervision. These numbers appear to be decreasing slightly. However, as more effective community based programs are established the efficacy of probation as a correctional measure is supported. The rising costs of incarceration appear to be motivating legislators and correctional officials to use their resources wisely. Programs and policies that are evidence-based will continue to gain traction.

Probation agencies will continue to seek a balance between providing resources to probationers and providing a measure to community safety. One focus does not negate the other, rather the two notions seem to be symbiotic. If the probationer receives and then follows the directives of probation officer who have the proper resources at their disposal the chances of continued criminal activity by the probationer decreases. However, resources are limited and it can be difficult to use limited resources for probationers instead of other places.

## Discussion Questions

1.  How is probation different than parole?

2.  Explain what diversion is.

3. Discuss what each of the 3 phases of diversion are.

4. What are the advantages of diversion and what are the criticisms?

5. Explain what intermediate sanctions are.

6. In your own words explain what the goals of probation agencies are.

7. What impact does early probation have on contemporary probation?

8. What is pre-trial supervision?

9. What do you think are some stressors that probation officers experience?

10. Explain some of the conflicts between advocacy and strict condition enforcement. IS there room for middle ground between the two philosophies?

## Student Exercise

1. Look up the U.S. Supreme Court case *United States v. Knights*, 534 U.S. 112 (2001). Explain what the case was about and what the court decided. How did this case change probation supervision?

## Key Terms

**Administration**—the entity responsible for the management and dispensation of probation services in a jurisdiction.

**Caseload**—the number of people assigned to a specific probation officer.

**Conditions**—term that a person placed on community supervision must abide by.

**Diversion**—programs that provide accountability and rehabilitative resources to those charged with criminal offenses but avoid further prosecution upon completion of program requirements.

**Formal social control**—external sanctions enforced through governmental actions.

**Intensive Supervised Probation**—an agency tasked with supervising those probationers deemed to represent a risk to the community that warrants intense supervision. Caseloads are typically fewer than non-intensive probationers.

**Intermediate sanctions**—sanctions administered against a probationer for violating the conditions of their release that are non-incarcerative.

**Pre-trial services**—an entity, often within a probation agency, tasked with supervising people released from custody and pending further prosecution and adjudication.

**Probation**—a correctional measure whereby a person is granted release into the community upon conviction . Release is based on the probationer adhering to specific conditions by a judge at the time of sentencing.

**Resource broker**—person that provides information used by others to seek out assistance.

**Revocation**—a probation officer may seek the revocation of a probationers release usually for violating the terms of release.

**Risk/needs assessment**—an instrument used by probation officers to determine the level of risk to reoffend or to be unsuccessful in probation and a gage of how many resources a probationer may need.

**Special conditions**—the conditions of release on probation that are unique to the probationer.

**Specialization**—caseloads assigned to a probation officer that share a common offender characteristic such as offense (i.e. sex offense) or proclivity (i.e. mental health issue).

**Standard conditions**—the conditions of release all probationers within a jurisdiction must abide by.

**Stipulates**—agreeing to the charge.

**Technical violations**—violations of the terms of probation that are not criminal law violations.

**Vet**—the process of examining a person's fitness and applicability for probation.

## CHAPTER 6

# Prison

**Chapter Objectives**

- Examine the history of prisons in American and compare and contrast past to present.

- What do contemporary prisons look like and what issues do they face.

- Summarize the different security levels of prisons and inmate custody levels and the impact on how a prison is managed.

- Articulate the problems that Security Threat Groups represent.

- Recognize the role of private prisons today.

## A. HISTORY OF PRISON IN AMERICA

There have been a host of different correctional measures employed throughout not only American history but across the globe. Perhaps one of the most ubiquitous measures have been the use of physical punishments up to and including various methods of corporal punishment and ways to execute people. Cultures across the globe have continued to evolve and in many ways and continue to use less physically retributive punishment to punishments more oriented to incarcerate people. Certainly the conditions in which people are incarcerated vary as greatly as countries vary. The predominant approach to deal with those that violate the law are to incarcerate them.

When considering the evolutionary nature of punishment prisons especially have changed how they incarcerate people and the nature in which they dispense corrections. Incarcerating people for long terms of confinement instead of execution or corporal punishments developed in America. The transition from only using jails to hold someone in order to punish them to prison as a punishment illustrated a cultural change in the way we view justice.

If you recall earlier in the textbook we reviewed how the Walnut Street Jail eventually morphed into the first **penitentiary**, Eastern State Prison. The purpose behind the establishment of this prison was to incarcerate large numbers of people and utilize similar correctional measures utilized at the Walnut Street Jail such as solitary confinement, strictly limited communications between inmates, and instruction which focused on labor and moral development (i.e. Pennsylvania System). Parts of this system where then adopted but other aspects modified to create the Auburn System which allowed inmates to work together more often during the day and eventually sleep in multiple occupancy cells too. Today most systems have a congregate type of system. However, more voices are advocating a slow return to solitary confinement. The advent of the **Supermax prison** is one such example.

The transition from Pennsylvania to Auburn System and then perhaps sliding back into a version of the solitary type prison system is a microcosm of the nature of prison. Many speculate how prisons will be run in the future as technology allows for more surveillance and less need of human correctional officers to supervise inmates. A futuristic return to a more solitary type of prison is not too far-fetched.

What is certain are the ways in which prisons were used as a correctional measure. Prisons confine inmate movement no matter which time period we discuss. However, the manner in which corrections is dispensed has changed over time. The goals have varied from retribution to rehabilitation. The methods to achieve these goals have also changed. As we review these eras note what the goals are and how each era attempted to reach those goals. Another important aspect to consider are what propelled those changes. Understanding what facilitates change is essential in forecasting the future and to spur change.

Today the thought or idea of what a prison is and what happens inside has been captured by various forms of media. There are TV series dedicated to exploring certain prisons across the U.S. Dramas about women in prison is currently very popular. All of these inform the public about prison. Some are based in reality while others focus on different aspects. All however tell a story and inform the public that there is a large segment of the American population involved with the criminal justice system.

## B.  AMERICAN PRISON ERAS

There are nine largely recognized eras in prison development. Each era has fixed dates. These dates should signal an approximate time when considering prison development and not a fixed point in time. Also students should consider that changes in one area did not mean immediate change in other parts of the country.

## 1.  Penitentiary Era (1790–1829)

The American Prison system emerged during this time period. The Walnut Street Jail in Philadelphia, PA was built in 1773. One of the wings of the jail was devoted to housing inmates in solitary confinement while instructing them on moral development. This concept was later modeled by the first American prison which was established at the Eastern State Prison located Philadelphia, PA in 1829 (Free Legal Encyclopedia, 2018). Thereafter large prisons which housed hundreds of inmates were built in the Northeastern part of the U.S. Today there are 1,719 state prisons and 102 federal prisons located in every state. They house over 2.3 million Americans (Bureau of Justice Statistics, 2018).

## 2.  Mass Prison Era (1825–1876)

The concept of building massive prisons became rapidly popular through the 1820s even through the civil war. Crime rates increased as newly developed police forces in major metropolitan areas began to arrest and process more people through the criminal justice system. Naturally people convicted of crimes had to be sent somewhere. Thus prisons like Sing Sing Prison in Ossining New York were built in 1826, to alleviate overcrowding at Newgate Prison where you recall the Auburn system was introduced (Encyclopedia Britannica 2018). The building was not limited to the northeast part of the U.S. as territories became states one of the first public buildings erected were prisons. Lansing Prison in Kansas was built by inmates and opened in 1868 (Kansas Department of Corrections, 2018). San Quentin Prison near San Francisco CA was built in 1854. Those prisons like Sing Sing prison are still in operation today (Britannica 2018).

## 3.  Reformatory Era (1876–1890)

Perhaps one of the shortest eras in prison development was the Reform era. The era just like others were a reflection of public sentiment about how prisoners should be treated. It was elocutionary from the previous eras because the focus concerned changing people's behavior though more nuanced approaches than solitary confinement or limited human contact. This era's focus was rehabilitative. Indeterminate sentences were utilized in order to encourage behavior changes. Education that was not aimed at learning a specific trade but more academic in nature was allowed. Reformatories for men and women sprang up during this time.

## 4.  Industrial Era (1890–1935)

The Industrial era was a response to the burgeoning need for workers to occupy jobs in America's growing factories and transportation needs. As a result inmates were viewed as a very good source of cheap labor. Using inmate labor was not new but the use of it defined this era. Inmates were **contracted** to complete jobs for private business. Prisons sold labor to the highest bidder. Public works projects such as building roads or bridges were often built through prison contracts. Inmates also worked in textile manufacturing as well as other jobs which required low skill levels.

Leasing convicts became prevalent in the Southern U.S. after the Civil War. It was seen as a potential replacement for the slave labor lost after the Civil War. This labor not only brought money into the prison to help pay for its cost but also provided cheap labor for the contractor. As one might imagine there were numerous abuses that occurred through this type of lease system as inmates were housed, fed, and disciplined by contractors.

Inmates were also used by the states in which they were incarcerated for state labor purposes. They built furniture and of course manufactured licenses plates for the increasing numbers of cars being used. Sales of products inmates made were only available for state use. Building or manufacturing these products saved states large sums of money.

During the 1920s and into the 1930 labor unions became a major political force. Inmate labor was seen as unfair competition to labor as inmates certainly worked at little cost. As a result Congress passed the Hawes-Cooper Act in 1929, and the Ashurst-Sumners Act in 1935. This federal legislation eliminated the interstate transportation of goods made in prison. This legislation virtually ended the Industrial prion era. Today inmates answer phones as customer service representatives, fight wildfires, and in packing and shipping (CBS). They are often paid at or less than minimum wage. We will return to inmate labor in Chapter 10 of this text.

## 5.  Punitive Era (1935–1945)

The availability of using inmates for prison labor quickly evaporated after federal legislation made transporting goods across stateliness illegal. The public view of inmates also began to change from more rehabilitative programs to more punitive incarceration. World War II started in 1939, and the U.S. became involved in December 1941. People that caused trouble or broke the law were viewed very poorly by society as not being productive members a nation that was about to go to war and then later involved in war. The opening of Alcatraz Prison in San Francisco Harbor best illustrates this era. Its major purpose was simply to isolate and incarcerate inmates. Rehabilitative measures were not employed at all.

## 6. Treatment Era (1945–1967)

The treatment era was a complete reversal of the punitive prison era. World War II had ended and many had experienced the horrors it brought. As a result the American public viewed inmates as fixable again. Inmates needed not only reform in the fashion of learning a trade or education but due to many changes and advancements in psychology inmates were often seen as "sick".

What became known as the **medical model** was used. Inmates were seen to be in need of some type of treatment whether psychiatric treatment or substance abuse treatment or that they lacked social skills and coping mechanisms. Inmates were perceived as having an illness which precipitated criminal behavior. The judge took the role as a medical doctor. Just like a doctor would prescribe some type of medical treatment the judge at sentencing would provide a legal remedy.

## 7. Community-Based Era (1967–1980)

The community-based era of corrections reflected popular sentiment in America about how we felt about the purpose of punishment. President Lyndon Johnson (president 1963–1969) established many social welfare projects among these efforts was the *President's Commission on Law Enforcement and Administration of Justice.* The final report titled, "The Challenge of Crime in a Free Society" called for sweeping changes for law

> Weblink—https://www.ncjrs.gov/pdffiles1/nij/42.pdf

enforcement, courts, and corrections. The Commission called for more offenders to receive community corrections as an alternative to prison. The use of probation and parole should receive more resources to impact criminal behavior. The report also encouraged the use of **halfway houses** as an alternative to prison (President Johnson Crime Commission, 1967). This report in combination with more social acceptance concerning community corrections forced corrections agencies across the country to reexamine what "corrections" is.

Social sentiment about providing corrections in the community began to evolve quite quickly in the mid to late 1970s. The crime rate began to surge during this time. News stories about "ex-cons" committing crimes began to make headlines as more Americans watched TV. The birth of a brand new offender, the "serial killer" made people like Ted Bundy and John Wayne Gacy infamous while spreading fear. Also, the development of the "Drug War" and the criminalization and increase in punishment for a host of new crimes primed corrections for a drastic shift from community corrections to a much more punitive and incarcerative landscape. The purpose of corrections shift from correcting behavior to punishment and warehousing.

## 8.  Just Desserts Era (1980–2008)

This era is exemplified by a "Get Tough on Crime" approach where punishment (i.e. corrections) entered into the political arena on a scale not seen before. Politicians clamored for more severe punishments for a variety of different crimes. This era is a return to the theory of Rational Choice and more specifically the concept of deterrence. General deterrence is exercised in this era by the implementation and importantly the notoriety of punishment for certain crimes. News organizations and marketing campaigns sponsored by governmental agencies begin warn the public of the consequences of using and selling drugs for instance.

The incarceration rate grew over 200% from 1980 to 1996 (Blumstien, 1999). This growth has largely been attributed to four areas. First are actual offending rates increased. Secondly, arrests per offense increased as well. Thus when crime rates increased police were more successful at arresting people. Third criminal punishments began more sever and so people were going to prison for offenses that had resulted in imprisonment in the past. Lastly, people were serving longer prison sentences which resulted in an accumulation of inmates (Blumstien, 1999).

U.S. Violent Crime Rate 1980–2015

| YEAR | INCARCERATION RATE |
|------|--------------------|
| 1980 | 596.6 |
| 1985 | 558.1 |
| 1990 | 729.6 |
| 1995 | 684.5 |
| 2000 | 506.5 |
| 2005 | 469.1 |
| 2010 | 404.5 |
| 2015 | 375.7 |

Source: Bureau of Justice Statistics 2017.

In order to house this burgeoning number of inmates more prisons had to be built. Since 1970 more than 1,200 new prisons were constructed (Prison Policy Initiative, 2019). Every state and the federal government built or modified prisons in order to house everyone.

> **Class exercise**—Find out what the current population and capacity for your state's prison system. Discuss ways in which the number of inmates can be reduced.

Even with this new building binge 17 states currently operate at or beyond capacity (Wilson, 2014). The rate of states and federal prisons being built has sharply decreased. However, the number of private prisons and jails is growing. Many governmental entities are contracting with private corporations to house prisoners.

As was noted in Chapter 1 of this text the incarceration rate has slowed and is even showing signs of abating. The social appetite to send copious numbers of people to prison has considerably diminished. The cost of housing thousands of inmates has also contributed to a search for alternatives to incarceration. Programs and policies that are non-incarcerative have proven to be effective at reducing recidivism while also costing considerably less than prison. Agencies are refocusing toward evidence-based practices as a result of social and financial pressure.

## C. AMERICAN PRISONS TODAY

We are entering a new era of imprisonment and indeed how we are approaching corrections. State and federal correctional agencies are looking at and investing in alternatives of incarceration. The recently passed, **First Step Act** (December 14, 2018) is an attempt by the federal government to address prison overcrowding, public sentiment about incarceration, and use resources more wisely. The first goal is to utilize evidence-based practices in order to reduce inmate recidivism. Reentry programs are a main focus. The second focus is directed at expanding good time credits and other early release incentives. The final focus is an effort to amend federal sentencing laws whereby sentence lengths and mandatory terms of incarceration for many crimes would be reduced or eliminated (National Conference of State Legislatures, 2018).

The new Evidence-based Era currently appears to be the newest paradigm in corrections. The punitive and "just desserts" era still occupy a place in corrections just as other pieces from other eras still remained during the Just Desserts era. The purpose of punishment continues to evolve and we find ourselves entering a new era.

# D. THE PRISON LANDSCAPE

Despite recent small drops of the number of prisoners in the U.S. we still incarcerate more people than any other country in the world. There are approximately 2.3 million people in American prisons and jails today. The majority of these inmates are in state prisons (1.3 million). There are another 615,000 in county jails, the vast majority (76% or 465,000 inmates have not been convicted and are awaiting trial). Still another 225,000 inmates are in federal custody (Wagner, 2019).

The prison system is complex. Prisons are administered by a state department of corrections. The Secretary of corrections is appointed by the governor or each state. The Secretary is responsible for establishing the policy and programs within each correctional department. There are nuances in how prisons are run in each state and even within states. The prison **warden** is responsible for maintaining security and order within their prison.

The Federal Bureau of Prisons (BOP) is responsible for the care and custody of federal inmates. There are 142, BOP facilities. These are scattered throughout the nation. Each of these facilities also has a warden.

Not all facilities are the same. Each prison is designated as a certain type of facility or affixed a **custody level**. The prison will hold a certain inmate that corresponds to their custody level. The prison can also be designated to care for inmates with special needs such as medical or mental health. Some prisons have different custody levels within the institution. There are often referred to as **units**.

The custody level for state prisons often is broken into three different categories:

Minimum security—This is the least amount of security of the facility custody levels. Accordingly these places have inmates with limited criminal histories. They are often not incarcerated for a violent crime, but violent offenders can be housed due to **working their way down** or are close to releasing from prison. Inmates may have job duties that may take them off of prison grounds such road maintenance. Inmates have access to more educational or vocational programs. Visitors are often allowed physical contact with the inmate and the frequency of visits are more often allowed than in medium security.

Medium security—Inmates in these institutions are often incarcerated in these prisons for a number of different types of crime. They are usually housed in 2 person cells but they can also live in **pods.** There are less restrictions concerning access to education or other resources. Inmates here often leave their cells for limited work details within the prison such as laundry or kitchen duty. Visitors can typically have some type of limited physical contact (i.e. an embrace). The number of visits allowed are more frequent than maximum security. The prison is usually surrounded by high walls or some type of string fencing with razor wire. The inmate to staff ratio is less here than in maximum facilities.

<u>Maximum security</u>—Inmates with long criminal histories (particularly violent histories), a history of escapes, a new court commitment with a long prison sentence, a history of violence while in prison, affiliation with a security threat group (i.e. prison gang). Inmates in maximum security often do not leave their cells for much of the day. They are usually housed in 1 or person cells. Access to resources such as education, or treatment is limited. There is usually not no physical contact allowed with visitors. These prisons typically surrounded by high walls, razor wire, and other security measures. The inmate to staff ratio is particularly low here in order to maintain control.

# E. SUPERMAX

In order to address prison violence a new type of prison was built or in some prisons a prison was built within the walls. These facilities or prison units are often referred to as "supermax" facilities. They are distinctively different from other classifications. These institutions severely restrict inmate movement and contact not only with other inmates and prison staff but with people outside of the prison. The primary purpose of the prison is security and control. These places are designed to minimize inmate movement as inmates rarely get an opportunity to leave their one person cells. Inmates are typically in their cells for 23 hours a day. They eat in their cells and receive any type of treatment in their cells. An hour outside of the cell usually includes some type of recreation either indoors or outside. Even while outside of the cells inmate to inmate contact is kept at a minimum. The purpose again is to eliminate any opportunity for inmates to assault one another as well as staff.

Inmates housed in these conditions typically have a history of severe violence against other inmates or staff. Other inmates can be housed at a supermax prison because of the severity of their offense. Yet others may be housed in these places due to past escapes or attempted escapes. One of the most well-known supermax prisons is in Florence Colorado. It's known as ADX Florence. This is a Federal Bureau of Prisons (BOP) institution. The "ADX" is a designation of the BOP and signifies the institution as a

> **Class Exercise**—Find out if and where your state has a supermax facility. Talk about the potential positives and negatives that an institution like a supermax represents.

supermax prison. This prison houses some of the country's most notorious inmates such as Ted Kaczynski otherwise known as the "Uni Bomber", Robert Hanssen who spied for Russia when he was employed with the FBI, and Barry Mills and Robert Bingham who as senior members of the Aryan Brotherhood prison gang were responsible for a number of prison homicides.

## F.  INMATE CLASSIFICATION

Much like the classifications of prisons inmates are designated or classified with a risk level. These levels can change though an inmate's period of incarceration. Inmate classification occurs after the inmate has been taken into custody by the correctional entity (i.e. state department of corrections) after sentencing. Inmates are transported from county jails to a prison that's primary purpose is to assess and classify the inmate whereby they are transferred to a prison that corresponds to their classification. These reception and diagnostic prisons perform a number of different evaluations for each inmate. Medical and mental health screenings are done in order to identify any special needs the inmate may have. A review of court records like a pre-sentence investigation helps prison staff determine if there are past histories of violence, gang affiliations, social, and educational backgrounds. All of the factor into classifying the inmate as a minimum, medium, or maximum risk inmate (North Carolina Department of Public Safety, 2019). One of these three classifications to an inmate is designated, however each state and the federal prison system have nuances in classifying inmates in their custody.

### 1.  Minimum

Inmates at this level have the least amount of restrictions. They have access to more programs both educational and vocational than other levels. This is because they are deemed to be at such a low risk to harm others and a low risk to escape they are granted more access to these programs. Inmates personal area are dormitory or barrack's like. Inmates typically are assigned some type of job and if the institution is equipped may have a job with a private company housed on the prison grounds.

### 2.  Medium

Inmates classified in medium custody have more restrictions than the minimum level inmates. They may spend more time in their cells. Two or more inmates typically occupy a cell. Jobs are earned in order to leave the cell or **cellblock**. A job is seen as a privilege. Inmates have some access to programs like education but this access is less prevalent than minimum custody. An inmate's time is moderately controlled and structured.

## 3. Maximum

Inmates classified at the maximum level typically spend the majority of the day in their cell or cell block. Cells are limited to single or double occupancy. Inmate movements are closely monitored and the structure is stricter than lower levels. Inmates may have jobs within the cellblock but do not usually leave the cell block unless accompanied by correctional staff or otherwise closely monitored.

## 4. Security Threat Groups

Gang activity in prison is not a new problem. Street gangs have migrated into the prison system however, some were established within the prison system. Some gangs operate in both environments while others involved in prison gangs stop gang involvement after they leave confinement. Every state and federal correctional institution houses inmates affiliated with a gang. Inmates often self-segregate into these groups. There are areas of the prison which inmates with certain gang affiliations do not go out of fear or through an understanding that doing so would cause violence.

The establishment of prison gangs and the dramatic increase in these gangs can be traced back to the 1980s when prison population began to dramatically increase. Prior to the 1980s gangs or loose affiliations amongst inmates existed but not in the fashion they do today. Prior to the massive increase in inmate populations a social order largely existed in the form of an "inmate code". However, the social structure transitioned as more inmates and many first time offenders became incarcerated. Some brought with them affiliations and grudges experienced as members of street gangs and still others recognized that a break in the "inmate code" of the past was largely disregarded by these new more plentiful numbers in of inmates and thus the culture of person changed (Wood, 2014).

Prison gangs are responsible for a great number of violent acts and other types of crime like drug trafficking in prison. Many prison gangs have evolved and become more sophisticated over the years. Several gangs that started out in one prison have grown throughout the country and almost franchised their organization. Many resemble national organized syndicates responsible for violence outside of prison walls. Breaking these gangs up has become problematic as transferring members to new prisons provides opportunities to spread an organizations influence. Often correctional officials tolerate gangs because just as they can create havoc and violence they too can serve to keep the peace and order in prisons just like the inmate code of earlier inmates and eras (Lessing, 2016).

## G. PRIVATE PRISONS

The U.S. not only has the largest inmate population in the world we also have the largest number in inmates incarcerated in private prisons. There were 128,063 inmates held in private prisons in 2016 (Gotsch, 2018). That means that almost 1 in every 10 inmates was being held in a private prison. About 75% of people detained for immigration reasons are held in a private facility (Gotsch, 2018).

What is a private prison? These are prisons built by privately held companies such as Core Civic (formerly Corrections Corporation of America) and GEO Group. These two companies alone have about 80% of the prison market. Private companies build, maintain, and staff facilities across the country. Governmental entities such as states and the federal government in turn pay or contract with these companies to house inmates. The private prison industry is a $5 billion dollar industry (The Week, 2018).

Visit this weblink—https://www.sentencingproject.org/publications/capitalizing-on-mass-incarceration-u-s-growth-in-private-prisons/

The federal government utilizes private prisons more often than states in that last from the year 2000 to 2016 the number of inmates in federal custody housed in private prisons grew 120% from 15,524 to 34,159. The number of people in federal custody for immigration detention grew during that same period by 442%, from 4841 to 26,249 people (Gotsch, 2018). Immigration and Customs Enforcement pay private prisons $159 per day per inmate.

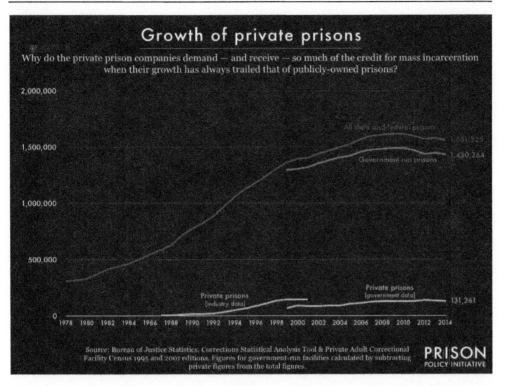

One of the biggest reasons for housing inmates in private facilities is cost. The amount of money a state spends on average per prisoner varies widely across states. For example the state of Alabama spends $14,780 per inmate per year and the state of New York spends $69,355 per inmate per year. The bulk of the money it costs to incarcerate a person is primarily due to paying the salaries of correctional professional salaries. 68% of the cost to for confinement is associated with staff salaries (Hendrichson, 2012). The private prison industry were supposed to be more cost efficient than those run by states and the federal government.

When we look at what the research concludes about cost savings and private prisons a different picture emerges. The General Accounting Office (GAO) is a federal governmental entity that studies four states and concluded that no substantial cost savings occurred. The states of Utah, Ohio, and Arizona also conducted studies and concluded that there were no cost savings and in the case of the Arizona study the state spent more on medium security beds for a private facility than it would have had the inmates been housed in a similar state run facility (Gotsch, 2018).

The real cost of private prisons are becoming increasingly more of a concerns as have conditions of the facilities and treatment of inmates. The Justice Department's Office of the Inspector General is tasked with a number of responsibilities, one of which is oversight of federal prisons (both private and

Bureau of Prisons (BOP). Their 2016, report concluded that private prisons had more security violations per inmate than BOP prisons and that inmate-on-inmate assaults were 28% percent higher in private prions than BOP facilities. Inmate-on-staff assaults were twice as high in private prisons than BOP prisons.

---

### Corrections in Action

The Management and Training Corporation (MTC) is a private prison company that runs two federal facilities and over 20 other state facilities across the country. The American Civil Liberties Union (ACLU) and the Southern Poverty Law Center (SPLC) filed a federal civil right lawsuit on behalf of the inmates in 2017, and during the trial many serious issues were revealed. The then Warden of Eastern Mississippi Correctional Facility testified that correctional officers, "did their best" to keep inmates in cells but could not guarantee the prison was capable of performing this basic duty. In another instance a mentally ill inmate that was on suicide watch hung himself. Gang members were allowed to beat other inmates, while cries for medical attention were ignored by staff. After listening to numerous inmates recount stories of neglect and abuse the trial judge complained of exhaustion.

The purpose of the private facility is to save the state money. Mississippi required (MTC) to operate 10% lower than similar state facilities. In order to meet this requirement the number of staff on duty is lower than similar prisons. The access to and resources for medical and mental health is also scarce. Security staff earn less than $12 per hour. This staff also receive 3 weeks of training instead of the 6 weeks state correctional officers receive in the state.

The facility is designated to hold inmates with mental health issues. Four out of five inmate receive medication but the facility was without a psychiatrist for almost a year. Mississippi's prison mental health director is not a medical doctor but rather a family and marriage therapist. The Chief Medical Officer had never even been to the prison despite being in her position for approximately 10 years.

The ACLU and SPLC are seeking changes ordered by the court. The outcome of this case has not been determined prior to this texts publication.

---

## H. RESEARCH AND POLICY/PRACTICE

One of the most frequently asked questions about prisons seems to be do they deter people from crime? In essence do prisons specifically deter people from committing crime? That is a rather simplistic question which often results in a complicated answer. If however we do look at it in the simplest of terms we know that a very large number of former inmates are rearrested within ten years of their release from prison. One recent Bureau of Justice Statistics report (2018) conducted a follow-up study of 401,288 inmates from 30 different states across the country and found that within 9 years of their release from prison 83% of inmates had at least 1 arrest. 68% of those released were arrested within 3 years of their release (Alper, Durose, & Markham, 2018). These numbers are stark indeed but we need to remember that arrests often do not result in convictions and that many of those arrests involve technical violations of release (i.e. parole violations).

There are many different programs and treatment inmates can have access to. However, this access and the resources state and federal agencies have differ from jurisdiction to jurisdiction. Some correctional departments have very little resources to devote to education and other programming or even health and mental health services. Agencies strive to find **programming** that is effective. One of the most important programs is education for inmates. The Rand Corporation conducted a **meta-analysis** of other research and concluded that inmates who participate in some type of educational program have 43% lower odds of returning to prison than those that do not participate in education while in prison. Inmates that received some type of educational programming while in prison had 13% higher employment rates than those that did not (Davis, Bozick, Steele, Saunders, & Miles, 2013).

Access to education while in prison can be difficult. Paying for education in the case of earning college credit can be almost impossible. However, that was not always the case. Inmates had access to Pell Grants until 1994. These grants allowed inmates to pay for college credit but he Crime Control Act passed by Congress in 1994, disallowed inmates from receiving federal monies to obtain higher education credit. This despite empirical data that showed that for every $1 that was spent on inmates for college credit $4–5 was saved. The Second Chance Act of 2015, allowed for a pilot program of $30 million in Pell grant monies to be set aside for inmates seeking higher education credit. This investment in inmates represented only 1% of total Pell Grant monies for 2016. 12,000 inmates in 67 schools participated in the program.

# I. CONCLUSION

The U.S. has the highest number of people in prison in the world. Prison is a big part of many people's lives whether they know it or not. The impact can be direct such as who are incarcerated or who have a loved one incarcerated, it they work in prison or provide technology or support work for a prison to operate. Many Americans own stock in private prisons. Thus they may have a personal financial interest in prison.

The U.S. basically invented prison or at least how we see it today. People came from all over the world to study prisons like Eastern Prison in Pennsylvania or the Auburn Prison in New York in the middle 1800s. They replicated mass incarceration elsewhere, within and outside of the U.S. Today incarceration is a multi-billion dollar business in some regards. It's beyond private prisons as there are any number of entities that provide contact support work from food service to medical care of inmates.

The trend of increasing inmate populations appears to be slowing. There are a number of different pieces of legislation such as the Second Chance Act, the Fair Sentencing Act, and most recently the First Step Act that seek to reduce prison populations and use evidence-based practices to inform policy.

## Discussion Questions

1.  Discuss the evolutionary nature of U.S. prisons.

2.  What are some factors that led to changes in U.S. prison eras?

3.  Explain the medical model of imprisonment.

4.  Why did the incarceration rate grow exponentially during the "Just Desserts" era?

5.  Discuss the impact of recent legislation on prisons/inmates.

6.  Explain the different security levels of prison.

7.  Why do prisons have different security levels?

8.  What role do private prisons have in the U.S. today?

9.  How do the custody levels impact inmate management?

10. What are the benefits and negatives of private prisons?

## Student Exercises

1.  Research what if any private prisons are in your state. What sort of inmates do they house? Discuss with other students if private prisons are beneficial or not.

2. Research 8th Amendment issues that "Supermax" prisons represent. Discuss with the class the purpose of these types of prisons and if they represent cruel and unusual punishment.

## Key Terms

**Cellblock**—a group of cells that represent a distinctive part of the prison.

**Custody level**—prisons are affixed a level of custody that determine which level of inmate can be housed there The custody level of the prison dictates inmate behavior and also the physical makeup of the prison.

**First Step Act**—act of Congress passed in December 2018. The act mandates a number of requirements. An important piece of this act relates to the Federal Bureau of Prisons uses policies and programs based on evidence-based practices.

**Halfway house**—a facility which houses inmates. The facility is typically not secure but has rules which inmates have to follow.

**Medical model**—the method of treating inmates as patients in need of diagnosis and some type of prescribed care.

**Meta-analysis**—a statistical analysis of other scientific studies.

**Penitentiary**—large prisons initially to house inmates in single cells.

**Pods**—a living area within a prison which house a small group of inmates.

**Programming**—educational, vocational, substance abuse, and mental health therapy or any number of different programs or therapies meant to assist inmates in rehabilitation.

**Supermax prison**—a newer type of prison where inmates movements are severely restricted. Inmates in these institutions are generally regarded as more dangerous than other inmates.

**Unit or prison unit**—a segment within a prison with a specific custody level.

**Warden**—official charged with the responsibility of managing a prison.

**Working their way down**—inmates can move from a higher custody level to a lower level through good behavior and completing programs.

## CHAPTER 7

# Prison Subculture

**Chapter Objectives**

- Students should be able to understand the nuances of inmate subcultures in men's prisons.

- Students will be able to understand staff subculture of prisons.

- Students will analyze how staff and inmate subcultures operate in prison. Specifically how they harmonize and create discord.

- Understand staff roles.

- Understand the importance of inmate characterizes when considering prison management.

## A. INMATE SUBCULTURE

As we know millions of people are currently being held in prison and millions more will serve a prison sentence at some point in their lives. Prisons are referenced to as **total institutions**. These of course are places that control or attempt to control every aspect of life. They are not simply places where people sit and completely lose **human agency**. In fact this unique environment allows for subcultures to emerge. The establishment of these subcultures dictates the norms of behavior. For instance an often accepted norm is to settle disputes among inmates, often through violence. Where outside of prison the culturally accepted norm would have been to call police and have them settle disputes, in prison such a move would often result in further violence toward the person responsible to altering correctional officers. Values and beliefs are often distorted from the mainstream in an effort to conform to unwritten rules amongst inmates.

These subcultural "rules" determine a great many things. What we take for granted or don't even think about such as sitting at a certain table or standing in a certain area can be taken as major offences in prison. The consequences of such a "violation" can result in a physical assault or worse. These rules also allow the prison to function without violence, if these "rules" are adhered to. Trying to learn these norms of behavior can be difficult. One way to attempt to appreciate being removed from one culture and thrust into another is by remembering your first couple weeks, semester, or even first year at a university. Learning the norms, values, beliefs (i.e. student subculture) can be daunting. For many this may be the first time away from home for an extended period of time and being immersed in this new subculture can be overwhelming. Fortunately students have the ability to reconnect or leave the situation and return to wherever they came. Inmates of course cannot.

The development of culture, or in this case a subculture allows inmates to know how to act and react in situations. These behaviors don't only appear as simple behaviors but can permeate and change thinking or cognition within inmates. The need for self-preservation and control or manipulation of others can take precedent. People can and do change as inmates. We often refer to this as **institutionalization**. Here the inmate because so accustomed to the cultural "norms" of prison becomes difficult to function outside of prison. Imagine someone that has been removed from society for 10 or 20 years and then suddenly put right back into it. Think of how many things have changed, not only from a technological standpoint but overall with society.

> **Class exercise**—Imagine you have been incarcerated for the past 20 years. As a class think of how many things have changed in culture over the last 20 years. Come up with a list. Secondly, discuss the problems you might encounter as a person removed from mainstream culture reentering society.

## B.  INMATE SUBCULTURE FORMATION

Subculture formation is a process. Just as one learns new norms of behavior in a new environment so do inmates. The immersion is a complete one, not only does an inmate learn the official staff rules that are written and enforced through formal means inmates must quickly learn the unwritten rules of the inmate world. The following is an example students in the author's class discovered upon a visit to a local private prison often used by the U.S. Marshall's Service as an inmate transfer hub. An inmate was discussing inmate protocol as this facility:

*"We can sit where we want in the chow hall here. There are no rules about that since this is a temporary place. When I get designated then that will change real quick."*

—unidentified inmate

Many places within prison are segregated by race. Black, white, Asian, and Hispanic inmates often self-segregate in prison. Native American and other ethnic groups often form smaller groups. These groups are not all gangs or gang members. That is to say prison is not an amalgamation of separate gangs. That is important to understand. However, prison gangs do play a major role in inmate life.

Studying subculture formation is critical to understanding inmate behavior and how to effect change in not only individuals but the entire management of the prison. At least 95% of inmates will be released back into the community (Bureau of Justice Statistics, 2018). Understanding how to impact these individuals' behaviors while they are incarcerated is essential when considering reducing recidivism rates and ultimately public safety.

## C. THEORIES OF SUBCULTURE FORMATION

There are a couple of theories relating to prison subculture formation. We will discuss two here: Deprivation Theory and Importation Theory. These theories are both credible but also have limitations too.

## D. DEPRIVATION THEORY

Deprivation theory relies on the idea that a socialization process occurs once the inmate enters prison. This theory is largely based on the work of criminologist, Gresham Sykes (1958). Sykes conducted an **ethnographic study** of inmates in a New Jersey prison. He posited that as a result of the unique environment prison offers that inmates adapted or were resocialized as a result of the following **pains of imprisonment:**

1. Loss of liberty—The fundamental purpose of prison is to remove a person from society. The inmate's movement is severely restricted often time to a single room (i.e. cell). The purpose of this loss of liberty and confining inmates are supposed to protect the general public, which it seems to accomplish that goal quite effectively (Shammas, 2017). While this goal is achieved another latent effect takes place. Inmates through all their differences share the common bond of being an inmate. This commonality ties them together and becomes a shared affliction. No matter their race, type o crime, or other affiliation they all have lost an enormous amount of freedoms.

2. Loss of goods and services readily available to society—The deprivation here is relative. In many cases inmates were homeless and went without basic necessities such as food for extended

periods of time (Shammas, 2017). Thus for some prison may offer more goods, services, and access to healthcare than when they were not incarcerated. However, even those with very little while outside of prison can and do experience deprivations such as access to certain types of food, substances like tobacco and services such as mental health in some cases or illicit services. These deprivations can be a catalyst for making positive life choices or can provide avenues for illegal measures and **contraband** inside prison. Deprivation conditions are ripe for an underworld in illicit trade to emerge.

Just as the purpose of prison is to deny liberty the purpose of prison is largely seen by many to provide a deterrent effect. Prison is supposed to be an uncomfortable place where the amenities of home are removed. The "pains" of imprisonment are meant to remind us of the "pain" involved in the pain versus pleasure principle of deterrence. A balance between too much deprivation and too much access is difficult to achieve.

3.  The loss of heterosexual relationships, both sexual and nonsexual—Sykes believed that the loss of heterosexual sexual and non-sexual relationships for inmates was profound (Shammas, 2017). Today we recognize both heterosexual and homosexual voluntary relationships as deprivation. The key for deprivation here is the voluntariness of relationships or the lack of access to preferred relationships. This loss of access to loved ones or potential relationship development is a further indication of the removal from mainstream society and fosters the development and reinforcement of the subculture shared by inmates.

4.  The deprivation of autonomy—The loss of autonomy concerns the removal of the ability for the inmate to make even the smallest decisions for themselves (Shammas, 2017). Inmates are told when they can eat, when they should go to sleep, who they can associate with, what sorts of items they can and cannot have in their cells, amongst other directives. This represents not only a loss of liberty as was discussed in #1 above, but control beyond simple restriction of movement. This complete control is exercised on all inmates further alienating them from mainstream culture and shaping a subculture where this group of inmates again shares that common bond.

5.   Deprivation of security—This deprivation represents division amongst inmates. The difference between this deprivation and the afore mentioned deprivations concerns inmate divisions amongst each other (Shammas, 2017). The other deprivations were experienced by all inmates as a result of sharing the social position of an inmate. Deprivation of security represents concerns of security that other inmates cause their peers to experience. Inmates are not concerned about assaults from staff but from each other. Thus the deprivation of security results in inmates forming groups or gangs inside prison to protect themselves from other inmates.

Deprivation Theory focus is on the unique environment of the prison. Prisons are naturally meant to deprive people of a great many things that seems to be the retributive purpose of prisons. This line of thinking adheres to the concept of deterrence. One must consider the depth of these deprivations and how they impact an inmate's socialization. These deprivations seem to remove an inmate from mainstream culture and reinforce negative behavior. Considering well over 95% of inmates will be released back into the community with these developed norms of behaviors we can begin to see difficulties inmates experience upon release, not to mention how these institutionalized norms of behaviors can permeate norms, values, and beliefs outside of prison and into communities.

# E. IMPORTATION THEORY

Importation theory relies on the idea that inmates bring their norms, values, and beliefs with them to prison. Contrary to Deprivation Theory which posits that inmate behavior is shaped while in prison. Thus behaviors are imported into prison and just displayed while incarcerated. Behavior is a reflection of the outside community. This theory seems to make sense as inmates do not lose their set of values and beliefs once they reach prison doors.

Perhaps the best example of importation theory affecting prison life is represented by the rise of gangs in prison. The numbers of street gangs and overall gang membership skyrocketed in the late 1980s and early 1990s (Howell, 2010). As gang members began to become incarcerated the number of prison gangs and the impact they have on the inmate subculture became apparent (Wood, 2019). It's well documented that as gang membership increases the chances of being involved in serious crimes such as assault, weapons violations, and homicide increase (Huff, 1998). Prison violence as a result of gangs increased dramatically during this time (Lessing, 2014). Street gangs also began to become established as prison gangs too. Thus street gangs such as the Mexican Mafia, Blood and Crips, etc. began to establish themselves within prisons. Some posit the establishment of these prison gangs allowed gangs to expand their reach not only in prison but beyond it into the community as well (Lessing, 2014). Further evidence concerning the importation of street gangs to prison gangs lies in gang hierarchy. Often gang leaders (i.e. **shot callers**) will continue to lead the street gang while in prison.

Gang influence is just one example of importation theory. Importation theory goes beyond gang involvement and the nuances of gang activity. Criminal thinking such as predatory behavior and anti-social manifestations are prevalent as well. This "criminal thinking" was honed prior to entering prison. The responsibility of prison is not to refine these socially and personally destructive behavior but to address them in a way to effect change. This as anyone can imagine is extremely difficult when the social environment calls for the opposite.

## F. INTEGRATION MODEL

The integration model combines Deprivation and Importation theories. **Socialization** is a lifelong process. Many of the same values and beliefs learned as children or young adults are carried with us through the life course while other values, beliefs, and morals evolve. The development of culture or in this case subculture changes too. Just as some accepted practices within conventional culture change so does subculture eve deviant subcultures such as those in prison. Many inmates that eventually end up in adult prison spent some amount of time incarcerated as a juvenile. These experiences as a juvenile in a correctional setting help cement criminal thinking. It establishes early in life the mindset of an inmate.

## G. INMATE CODES OF CONDUCT—NORMS, VALUES, AND BELIEFS

The subculture or the environment helps determines individual behavior. Think for a moment about the accepted rules of the classroom. University students learned have learned proper classroom etiquette over a number of years and copious amounts of time spent in a classroom. University professors typically do not deal with classroom behavior issues because the students occupying seats in a university classroom have learned and adhere to acceptable behavior. Behavior that is disruptive in university classrooms is not only unacceptable to the teacher but also to the students taking the class. The norm of behavior in this case is frequently observed. People tend to want to assimilate to accepted standards or norms of behavior and prison is no different. However, the consequences of violating norms of behavior or what is typically known as the **convict code** in prison can have serious consequences.

Prisons have very strict codes of conduct. There are standard codes of conduct throughout a prison system and individual prisons may have additional rules. These rules are formal in nature and if there is an infraction they are dealt with by the prison staff. The convict code on the other hand are the unwritten rules inmates enforce upon each other. If these rules are violated inmates enforce them. Chief among these rules concerns not involving the prion staff in any inmate matters. The label of a **snitch** can have deadly consequences.

---

### Corrections in Action

James "Whitey" Bulger was a notorious Boston, MA area organized crime figure in the 1980s and early 1990s. Bulger led a life of crime, at one point serving prison time in Alcatraz Federal Prison. He continued to commit numerous crimes including serval armed robberies and murders. During his time as a mob boss he secretly worked as an FBI informant for almost 20 years. During his time as an informant FBI agents handling Bulger looked the other way and did not pursue any charges against him while he and his gang continued to murder others and commit various serious crimes. In 1994, Bulger fled Boston and became a fugitive from justice after FBI agent John Connolly tipped him off that he was about to be indicted on federal charges.

Bulger spent the next 16 years as a fugitive. At one point he became one of American's 10 most wanted fugitives along with Osama Bin Laden. He was arrested on June 22nd 2011, after a neighbor recognized a photo of him from a TV program. He was eventually indicted for several crimes including 19 murders as head of the South Boston Winter Hill Gang. He was sentenced to 2 consecutive life sentences in Federal Prison on Nov. 14 2013.

After sentencing his custody was transferred to the U.S. Bureau of Prisons. Bulger was eventually transferred to a high security prison (USP Hazelton) in Bruceton Mills, West Virginia. Bulger had not been in the prison for more than 24 hours when on Oct. 31st it is alleged that Bulger, now wheelchair bound, was approached by two inmates. One of the inmates Fotios "Freddy" Geas a convicted Boston area hitman serving a life sentence and one other inmate approached Bulger in his cell and beat him to death as he sat in his wheel chair.

Brian Kelly, a former federal prosecutor who was part of Bulgers prosecution team advised that he was not surprised Bulger would meet a violent end given the life he led and that, "Prison is a violent place and informants are not too popular, so these things can obviously happen if proper precautions are not taken" (DeCosta, 2018).

The convict code is much more involved than "snitching". It's an aspect of informal social control that permeates throughout prison life. Just like anybody would adhere more or less to norms, values, and beliefs shared in a neighborhood inmates are no different. Their neighborhood or environment is simply the prison. Therefore what to wear and how to wear clothes, even prison jump suits, becomes part of the norm. Where to sit in the **chow hall** or physically be in a prison commons area such as the **yard** is important also.

Often inmates will develop language specific to prison life. This may seem somewhat inconsequential however it is one of the most outward indications of a subculture. By developing a **prison argot** or unique language only those familiar with the terms are privy to the meanings. Sharing a language or idiosyncrasies of a language help define and distinguish the "us" from "them".

The norms and values of male and female inmates share similarities such as not "ratting" on fellow inmates about virtually anything. Telling prison official's mundane information like who inmates associate with to keeping quiet about much more serious matters like which inmate assaulted another inmate can often be met with serious consequences. However, female and male inmate subcultures within prison can be strikingly different.

## H. MALE INMATE SUBCULTURE

Culture and subcultures are all about identifiable norms of behavior and shared values and beliefs that exist within groups of people. Prisons are unique places which allow subcultures to develop. Inmates come from a variety of different backgrounds and experiences but when they enter prison they share one commonality that pervades their life behind prison walls and often even when they are back in the community. The role of the inmate is shared by violent and property offender, by gang member and those not affiliated with a gang, and by inmates from every socio-economic status and race. Their shared status as an inmate dictates the role they'll abide by and thus how a person behaves in prison.

The social position or status a person can occupy changes many times throughout life. In prison inmates gain these status by achievement or through ascription. The status and then role and subsequently behavior can be achieved through any number of methods. For instance one can become known as an enforcer or someone known to be violent through of course being violent toward other inmates as well as staff. Others still can be known as inmates that can obtain items not readily available to others. The point is some inmates obtain their status or social position within the institution by "earning" that status. Others earn their status through ascription. In this case social status is ascribed upon an inmate by others. One of the most obvious is the status of a sex offender in prison, especially an inmate who has victimized children. In the male inmate world this status is often viewed as the lowest status inmate. Often inmates that do not have this type of conviction do not want any association with these inmates. Even in an atmosphere where the "convict", "inmate", or "felon" is met with considerable stigma from mainstream culture the prison subculture seems to want to distance itself from those offenders. Inmates with this type of offense often attempt to hide it from others as best they can.

The inmate world is an ultra-masculine environment. Physical and mental toughness is a top priority. A Criminologist Walter B. Miller (1962) (Greene, 2017) theorized about the elements of subculture that he viewed has valued attributes by members of the lower socio economic strata. These elements are shared by inmates also:

| Concern | Explanation |
| --- | --- |
| Excitement | Defining what is "exciting" is often a matter developed along cultural/subcultural lines. Inmates can find excitement through fighting, manipulation of others (i.e. officers and inmates), and using or dealing in contraband. |
| Toughness | Being physically tough is prized in a prison environment. Inmates with this characteristic are often revered by other inmates and even staff. |
| Smartness | Obtaining and using being "street smarts" to outwit others. Knowing and manipulating other inmates as well as staff. |
| Trouble | Being in trouble or having to be disciplined by prison staff is not met with stigma or being chastised by other inmates but instead is prized and seen as a badge of courage/honor. |
| Autonomy | The idea that inmates even though they are in prison, one of the most controlled places in the world still have autonomy to control their behavior and others behavior too. |
| Fate | Inmates see their future as determined. They have been labeled as a "felon" or "offender" and will not be able to |

> shed this label. Accordingly rather than fight to shed the label it's embraced and becomes a self-fulfilling prophecy.

Violence in male institutions is a very real threat. Prison gangs, also known as security threat groups are responsible for a large portion of that violence. Sexual violence is also a real concern for male inmates as well as female inmates. Sexual violence for both male and female inmates have very serious consequences. However, when we examine sexual assault amongst male inmates versus female inmates this type of behavior is contextually different in many respects. In male institutions sexual assault occurs in many cases with respect to one inmate wanting to show power and control over another inmate. Inmates that are preyed upon sexually are often referred to as a **"punk"**. The label is meant to degrade the person it's affixed to and often times the inmate identified as a "punk" will be a target for continued victimization.

---

### Corrections in Action

The Prison Rape Elimination Act (PREA) was passed with unanimous support by Congress in 2003. The purpose of the act was to provide local, state, and federal correctional institutions with accurate data concerning sexual assault that occurs in prisons and jails. By understanding the scope, extent, and nature of sexual violence in prisons resources could be targeted more effectively in hope of decreasing or even eliminating this type of crime in prisons. Thus funding that supports research in this area was made available through the Bureau of Justice Statistics and the National Institute of Justice.

This act also created the National Prison Rape Elimination Commission. This commission is charged with developing standards for prisons and jails to follow in the hope that these standards will eliminate or severely decrease the number of sexual assaults of inmates while in custody. Today many state local institutions strive to meet these standards. The U.S. Department of Justice adopted the standards set by this commission in 2012. Today these standards apply to all federal institutions and their contract institutions.

> **Class exercise—**Contact staff at a jail or prison near you and inquire about what that institution does to comply with PREA standards. Discuss in class.

Today the National PREA Resources Center provides federally funded training and technical assistance to state and local institutions to address this issue. The resource center also serves to assist those conducting research in this

> area as well as helping those interested agencies reach compliance with standards.

The U.S. Department of Justice releases PREA data each year. In the most recent report prior to the publication of this textbook (2018) there were 24,661 reports of sexual victimization in American prisons and jails. However, only 1,473 of those reported could actually be **substantiated**. The sharp disparity between reported sexual victimization and those cases that were actually reported is an indication of how difficult it is to calculate and fully understand the problem. This is not surprising considering the subculture that exists within the inmate community and coupled with the multitude of other factors that hinder reporting such as fear of retaliation and shame of victimization. However if we look at the substantiated cases we see that:

- Substantiated cases in private and local jails doubled from 2011 to 2015, from 284 in 2015 to 576 in 2015.

- Substantiated cases rose from 605 to 873 cases of sexual assault in federal prisons (up 44%).

- 58% of the substantiated cases involved inmates assault other inmates while 42% were perpetrated by staff members.

- Prisoners have higher rates of sexual victimization than jail inmates (Bureau of Justice Statistics, 2018).

Sexual violence in prison is a substantial issue for corrections and correctional administrators in particular. The reasons behind this type sexual violence perpetrated is mirrored in the general public. The environment of the prison is certainly unique but the motivations for such crime are similar. Sex crimes are vastly underreported in the general public but most definitely are underreported in prisons due to the subculture that exists. Reporting any type of victimization in prison is fraught with danger let alone reporting sexual victimization as a male inmate.

Institutionalization can take place after being immersed in an environment for a period of time. Erving Goffman considered prison a "total institution". The longer a person is subjected to this environment the more stable the patterns of behavior becomes. The more "normal" the behavior is considered. This behavior is an adaptation to the environment one finds themselves in. In this case the prison, where violence to staff and other inmates and silence concerning involving authorities are valued. These norms of behavior and values can be difficult to shed. We know that 95% of inmates will eventually be released from prison at some point (Hughes, 2019). Those that have adopted and adhered to institutionalized behavior do not simply leave these norms and values at the prison door. They carry these into the communities they inhabit. Sometimes the continuation of institutionalized behavior is reinforced or at the least not challenged upon release and thereafter. This can create a cycle or feedback loop where the focal concerns we reviewed previously aren't challenged in the community or in prison and are in fact adopted in both environments.

## I.   STAFF SUBCULTURE

Prison not only offers a unique environment which fosters inmate subcultures to develop them also cultivate staff subcultures. Prison staff, specifically custodial staff (i.e. corrections officers of all ranks) deal with inmates on a daily basis. They keep order in the facility and are required to do any number of tasks. Many inmates refer to them as the "police" as such because they can operate much like police do outside of prison. Even though correctional officers (CO's) do not have to stay at work thus within prison walls all day every day they are not immersed in a "total institution". However, the nature of the job is unique. It's as unique as any job within corrections. Whereas a police officer may be involved with a subject and arrest the person their contact with that subject is limited. Parole and probation officers are similar in that the duration of the contact can be measured in minutes the frequency of the contact is much more than a police officer. Correctional officer contacts with inmates is substantially different. The nature of the job is dangerous but they typically do not carry any weapons, even non-lethal weapons. They spend a substantial amount of time with the same group of inmates thus the frequency and duration of the contact is extensive. The 40–60+ hours a week CO's spend with inmates is a unique situation within the criminal justice system. Officers and inmates can get to know each other quite well.

The inherent danger of the prison environment for all staff is present at all times. Correctional officers act as first responders within the prison. It is their job to respond to incidents of every nature (i.e. fights, medical emergencies, etc.). This inherent danger creates a bond amongst the custodial staff.

## J.   CUSTODIAL STAFF ROLES

Culture and thus subculture consist of norms of behavior. Norms of behavior are expected behaviors or roles that are dictated by social position. For instance as a college student the norm of behavior during class is to sit and listen to the instructor while taking notes as well asking pertinent questions. This is the behavior classmates expect as well as instructors. This is the role of the student just as if someone were playing a role in a play. Social status dictates the role and role informs behavior.

The role of the correctional officer (CO) can be conflicted. An important role of the CO is to enforce the rules of the prison. This can be rather impersonal. Displaying regard of any kind can be seen as a weakness by other CO's as well as a point to take advantage of when observed by other inmates. Yet a purpose of prison is to support rehabilitation. This can result in a certain amount of conflict about what role a CO is supposed to play. If the CO doesn't put up an austere unfeeling front they could expect ridicule or other forms of sanctions from coworkers and inmates.

A balance between the role of enforcer/disciplinarian and rehabilitation/advocate is difficult to achieve. CO's manage inmate behavior in a number of different ways. Certainly CO's maintain control through administering disciplinary measures and issuance of rewards but how they achieve management was identified by a researcher John Hepburn (Hepburn, 1985):

Reward Power—CO's dispense formal and informal reward. Formal rewards can be the awarding of good time credit or lowering of custody level (i.e. from medium custody to minimum custody). Informal rewards can be job duty assignments or more time outside of the cell.

Referent Power—the ability of officers to gain or earn respect from inmates as someone who is fair with both discipline and in meting out rewards.

Expert Power—inmates perception of an officer as being experienced in and with prison operations both written and unwritten. Also inmates being able to identify officers with special skills and knowledge in areas such as counseling, treatment, or legal issues.

Coercive Power—officer perceived to be punishment oriented. They get inmates to do things simply out of threat or fear of punishment.

Legitimate Power—power officers have by the virtue of their position but that officers are seen as possessing legitimate authority from the perspective of the inmates. The officer may have power but the inmates must recognize that power.

# K. CATEGORIES OF JOB DUTIES

There are a multitude of tasks performed by different a varied assortment of professionals in prison. They are typically categorized into three different areas:

Administrative staff: The warden and their staff make up the administration of a prison. The warden is ultimately responsible for everything that happens in prison but that person has many people helping determine policy and practice. The main responsibility concerns ensuring the proper functioning of the prison.

Program staff: Program staff are those responsible for providing a number of different services to inmates such as medical and mental health care, acting as therapists or counselors for substance abuse treatment or sex offender therapy. Professionals in the program staff also provide vocational and education to inmates as well as food service. Their main responsibility are to provide services to inmates in order to foster rehabilitation.

Custodial staff: Custodial staff are tasked with maintaining order in the prison and to provide safety for inmates and all of the staff no matter what their role is. Correctional officers that work on a regular basis with inmates are often referred to as line officers. These are the people that we may often think of as the prototypical "guard". Their role is changing just like police in the communities role is changing from strictly enforcing the law to more problem solving so are correctional officer duties changing. Their first priority is to ensure the safety of everyone in prison but increasingly they act in many different capacities.

## L.  CORRECTIONAL OFFICER DUTIES

Correctional officers have many different job assignments. These assignments differ depending where they occur in prison and the nature of the specific type of work required. They are all similar the primary duty concerns ensuring the safety of inmates and staff.

Block or pod officers: These officers supervise inmates in or near their living quarters. They ensure inmates are behaving according to prison rules. They oversee inmates coming and going from and to the cell block. They provide small items to inmates such as toiletries. They inspect and search inmates and cells. They also are the first to report and deal with issues between inmates and seek to prevent small problems from becoming big problems. They suggest and are responsible for moving inmates within the cell block and removing them as well. These officers spend much of their time with inmates in as close to a place that inmates can call home.

Transport officers: These officers are responsible for transporting inmates to a variety of different endearments outside or prison. They take inmates to court appointments, to different prisons, to medical or other appointments as necessary.

These officers are typically armed as they are outside of prison walls and these situations can represent the best chance for an inmate(s) to escape.

Work detail: Inmates perform a variety of different tasks involving menial labor inside and outside of prison. Outside of prison they can work as road clean-up crews, work as forest fire-fighters, or a host of other jobs. Inside of prison they work in the laundry and kitchen etc. All the inmates no matter what job they are performing require some type of supervision from correctional officers.

Yard and perimeter officers: Yard officers supervise inmates who are outside of their cell blocks usually in some type of recreational activity. They ensure inmates are observing prison rules and ensuring the safety of all when inmates gather in large groups in common areas referred to as the "yard". Here inmates have a chance to socialize with other housed in other areas of the prison. These times offer inmates a chance to exercise and socialize but also traffic contraband or commit assaults.

Perimeter officers patrol the perimeter of the prison. They often carry firearms in an effort to deter or stop inmates from completing an escape.

Intelligence, investigation, and S.O.R.T.: All correctional officers provide a measure of safety and security to prisons but the main duty of these officers are to provide prison staff with proper security measures, investigate all crimes in prison, and when necessary to use force to extract an inmate(s) from their cells or end a disturbance or riot as quickly as possible. Intelligence officers become familiar with the different prison gangs, gang members, and potential issues or disturbances in order to prevent these from happening. Those involved in investigations investigate criminal activity within the prison such as assaults, drug trafficking, or other behaviors that would be viewed as a crime in the general public. These officers investigate inmates as well as other staff. The Special Operations Response Team (S.O.R.T.) is responsible for responding to prison disturbances inside the prison they work at or they can be sent to other prisons to help out at disturbances. These are teams of officers that receive special training in defensive tactics and special non-lethal weapons use.

## 1. Special Issues for Correctional Officers

Correctional officers are faced with daunting tasks every day. They work in hostile conditions, their pay is seen as low considering what their responsibilities are, and they often work in shifts thus they may have to work at odd hours or weekends and holidays. Considering these and other factors correctional officers have stressors unique to the position.

The threat of physical assault on officers is a constant threat. Correctional officers (CO's) have one of the highest rates of nonfatal work-related injuries in the U.S. (Konda, Tiesman, Reichard, & Hartley, 2013). CO's experienced four times as many injuries sustained on the job which resulted in at least one day of missed work as compared to all other occupations. There are on average 11 work related fatalities for CO's every year (Konda, Tiesman, Reichard, & Hartley, 2013). Besides the threat of physical assault many officers receive copious amounts of verbal and emotional harm. Many assume this is a part of the job but the toll of such mental stress has consequences. Schaufeli and Peeters (2000) conducted a metanalysis of several studies concerning correctional officer stress. They found four different stress reactions from these studies:

1. Withdrawal behaviors—Withdrawal in this context concerns withdrawing from the profession. Careers in entry level corrections such as correctional officers experience very high **turnover** levels. Turnover rates for some prisons and entire correctional systems are higher than 30% (Fiflied, 2016). Absenteeism is also associated with withdrawal. CO's in New York state corrections have 300% higher absenteeism rates than all other occupations in the state (Konda, Tiesman, Reichard, & Hartley, 2013).

2. Psychosomatic disease—mental stress can result in physical ailments. CO's have higher rates of hypertension (i.e. high blood pressure) than police. CO's have higher rates of heart disease than police officers 3.5% compared to 1.4% for police as well.

3. Negative attitude—CO's also have high rates of job dissatisfaction when compared to other occupations with respect to similar level of pay an education. CO's experience high levels of alienation, occupational tedium, powerlessness, and pessimism (Schaufeli, 2000).

4. Job burnout—Approximately one third of CO's experience emotional exhaustion on the job. Still others evaluative their careers negatively (Schaufeli, 2000).

> **Class exercise**—Locate correctional officer compensation for an entry level officer in your state. Compare that compensation with at least 1 other adjacent state. Does Your state pay less? More? The same?
>
> Why would an hourly wage be more beneficial for officers than a yearly salary?

The compensation CO's receive affects recruiting and retaining people. Correctional officers are typically paid an hourly wage as opposed to a yearly salary. The average annual national compensation for CO's is $43,550. The range however from the highest to lowest is quite varied. For example the hourly mean wage in Mississippi is $12.88 per hour. At the other end of the pay spectrum New Jersey CO's make $33.32 per hour. Federal correctional officers earn an average of $41,868 per year.

# M. CHARACTERISTICS OF CORRECTIONAL OFFICERS

As we see from the chart below correctional officers are overwhelming white and male. Approximately 70% of officers are white. African Americans make up most of the rest. Fully 72% of officers are males. Consider that minorities are over represented as inmates in jails and prisons the racial divide between officers and inmates presents a real issue for corrections as a system and prisons in particular. Students may ask why this racial disparity would matter. It really involves the ability for people to relate to one another. One who has never experienced racism or bigotry may easily say it does not exist because it has not happened to them. Also, the ability to form some type of personal yet professional connection between an inmate and an officer(s) is helpful in many different ways.

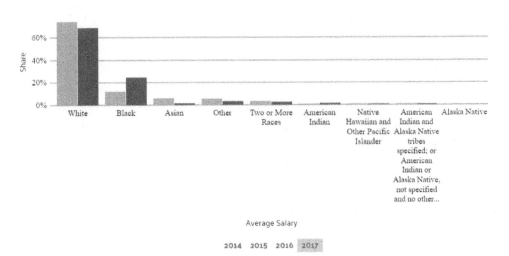

Average Salary

2014  2015  2016  2017

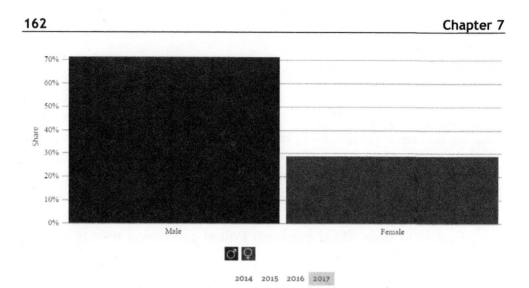

(DataUSA, 2019).

Corrections officers help define what correction in the U.S. Their job is often thankless and dangerous. Yet, many men and increasingly women work in this area. The responsibilities and duties are changing in order to fit inmate needs. As the number of inmates with mental health issues grows, the number of inmates with substance abuse issues remains, and the challenges that technology present the challenges correctional officer's face evolve. This field is at the forefront of implementing evidence-based practices.

# N. RESEARCH AND POLICY/PRACTICE

One of the keys to retaining corrections officers is to recognize that this type of job has unique risks both immediate physical risks and long term psychological risks. Correctional administrators are beginning to take notice that in order to keep officers who they have made a substantial investment in training and the that the knowledge seasoned officers have are important to the functioning of the prison and in the best interest in rehabilitative efforts. Some institutions have implemented employee assistance programs and peer support groups. There are attempts to change the "machismo" culture of corrections officers. Receiving assistance is not a sign of weakness. The National Institute of Justice (NIJ) released findings relating to correctional officer well-being. They recommended the following policies:

- Improve inmate intake procedures to identify problematic inmates.

- Improve communication channels between correctional staff at all levels.

- Separation of gang members.

- Ensure officers have backup when dealing with troublesome offenders.

- Training to de-escalate volatile situations.

- Provision of therapeutic services, where possible, for offenders with mental disorders.

The NIJ has pledged resources to institutions across the country in order to combat officer stress and address safety issues.

# O. CONCLUSION

Prison is one of the most unique places in the world. Culture and therefore subculture are human creations whereby we adapt to the social and physical environment. Inmates and prison staff adhere to the written and unwritten rules of these subcultures. They are meant to be places where inmates correct their illegal behavior, but as we have seen they can have a counter-productive effect. To be sure not all people who enter prison leave it only to commit future crimes. For some inmates a single stint in prison will be the first and last time they set foot in prison. On the other hand for many others prison and returning to prison can become a way of life. It can be a place where inmates leave worse off than when they arrived. It's our duty as corrections officers, program staff, prison administration, and very importantly the general public to ensure that fewer people return to prison. Use of evidence-based practice and policy help us reach that goal.

## Discussion Questions

1. What is a subculture?

2. Explain what deprivation theory is.

3. Explain what importation theory is.

4. What is a role?

5. How do subcultures impact roles and thus behavior?

6. How can we change a violent prison subculture?

7. What are some stressors for correctional officers?

8. How can we decrease the stress of correctional officers feel?

9. Why is it important to have a diverse correctional workforce?

10. Explain two ways to recruit more correctional officers besides an increase in pay.

## Student Exercises

1. View the Stanford Prison Experiment and discuss the establishment of inmate and staff roles.

2. Research the demographic characteristics of correctional officers in your state and report on it. How do you propose to recruit and retain women and minorities as officers?

## Key Terms

**Chow hall**—cafeteria or lunchroom in a prison.

**Contraband**—disallowed items identified by prison staff.

**Convict code**—informal social control exerted in prison; the unwritten rules of inmate behavior.

**Ethnographic study**—scientific study of people and culture through qualitative means.

**Human agency**—the capacity for people to make choices through free will.

**Institutionalization**—the process in which an inmate adopts the norms, values, and beliefs of the inmate prison environment.

**Pains of imprisonment**—5 different deprivations inmates suffer identified by criminologist Gresham Sykes.

**Prison argot**—language and euphemisms developed by inmates and that are unique to inmates.

**Punk**—inmate who is used as a sexual object and subjected to numerous degradations.

**Shot callers**—gang leaders in prison.

**Snitch**—an inmate who cooperates with prison staff.

**Socialization**—the process by which individual norms, values, and beliefs are formed through the life course.

**Substantiated**—proven with evidence.

**Total institutions**—closed system which strict norms, rules, and schedules are enforced either through formal or informal social control.

**Yard**—the outside commons area of a prison where inmates can exercise and communicate freely.

## CHAPTER 8

# Women Offenders

**Chapter Objectives**

- Understand the differences between female and male inmates.

- Explain what gender responsiveness is and how it informs correctional policy and practice.

- Compare the different social structures of men's and women's prison.

- Explain how children of incarcerated womens are impacted by their absence.

- Describe how treatment programs and policies should be implemented in a gender responsive way.

- Describe how treatment programs and policies should be implemented in a gender responsive way.

- Summarize how community corrections can be more gender responsive.

## A. WOMEN INMATES

Today in the U.S. male inmates outnumber women approximately 11:1. Womens make up only about 7% of the entire prison population (Bronson, 2019). As we have seen inmate populations in the state and federal prison systems have decreased slightly in last couple of years. However, women inmate populations have decreased more slowly than males.

2016 7 Percent change, 2016–2017

**Prisoners under jurisdiction of state or federal correctional authorities, by jurisdiction and sex, 2016 and 2017**

| Jurisdiction | 2016 | | | 2017 | | | Percent change, 2016–2017 | | |
|---|---|---|---|---|---|---|---|---|---|
| | Total | Male | Female | Total | Male | Female | Total | Male | Female |
| U.S. total | 1,508,129 | 1,396,296 | 111,833 | 1,489,363 | 1,378,003 | 111,360 | -1.2% | -1.3% | -0.4% |
| Federal[a] | 189,192 | 176,495 | 12,697 | 183,058 | 170,525 | 12,533 | -3.2% | -3.4% | -1.3% |
| State[b] | 1,318,937 | 1,219,801 | 99,136 | 1,306,305 | 1,207,478 | 98,827 | -1.0% | -1.0% | -0.3% |

Source: Bronson and Carson BJS 2019.

As we can we from the chart above women incarceration rates have fallen just as the male incarceration rate has fallen just at a slower rate? There are differences in the type of crime or **new court commitment** a person is incarcerated when we consider gender. Only 37% of women inmates in 2016, were incarcerate for a violent offense while approximately 57% of males were in state prisons because of a violent offense. However, about 26% of women inmates were in prison for a property crime as compared to males (16.9%). There were greater rates of womens in prison for drug offenses too.

**Sentenced prisoners under jurisdiction of state correctional authorities, percentages by most serious offense, sex, race, and Hispanic origin, December 31, 2016**

| Most serious offense | All prisoners[a] | Male | Female | White[b] | Black[b] | Hispanic |
|---|---|---|---|---|---|---|
| Total | 100% | 100% | 100% | 100% | 100% | 100% |
| Violent | 55.2% | 56.5% | 37.5% | 47.6% | 60.1% | 60.4% |
| Murder[c] | 14.2 | 14.3 | 12.0 | 10.5 | 16.3 | 15.5 |
| Negligent manslaughter | 1.3 | 1.3 | 2.5 | 1.3 | 0.8 | 1.0 |
| Rape/sexual assault | 12.8 | 13.6 | 2.4 | 16.4 | 8.3 | 14.0 |
| Robbery | 13.1 | 13.5 | 8.0 | 7.2 | 19.3 | 12.7 |
| Aggravated/simple assault | 10.5 | 10.6 | 8.8 | 9.1 | 11.8 | 13.3 |
| Other | 3.3 | 3.2 | 3.8 | 3.1 | 3.7 | 3.8 |
| Property | 17.5% | 16.9% | 26.4% | 23.8% | 14.5% | 12.3% |
| Burglary | 9.4 | 9.6 | 7.1 | 11.5 | 8.7 | 7.1 |
| Larceny-theft | 3.4 | 3.0 | 8.4 | 5.4 | 3.0 | 2.1 |
| Motor vehicle theft | 0.7 | 0.7 | 0.8 | 1.0 | 0.6 | 0.9 |
| Fraud | 2.0 | 1.6 | 7.1 | 2.9 | 1.2 | 1.0 |
| Other | 2.0 | 1.9 | 2.9 | 2.9 | 1.0 | 1.1 |
| Drug | 14.8% | 14.0% | 24.8% | 15.4% | 13.8% | 13.9% |
| Drug possession | 3.5 | 3.2 | 7.3 | 4.1 | 3.2 | 3.2 |
| Other[d] | 11.2 | 10.7 | 17.6 | 11.3 | 10.6 | 10.7 |
| Public order | 11.9% | 12.0% | 10.2% | 12.4% | 11.2% | 13.1% |
| Weapons | 4.2 | 4.4 | 1.7 | 2.6 | 5.4 | 5.3 |
| DUI | 1.9 | 1.9 | 2.6 | 2.7 | 0.7 | 2.6 |
| Other[e] | 5.8 | 5.7 | 5.8 | 7.1 | 5.0 | 5.1 |
| Other/unspecified[f] | 0.6% | 0.6% | 1.1% | 0.8% | 0.4% | 0.4% |
| Total number of sentenced prisoners[g] | 1,288,500 | 1,194,000 | 94,400 | 401,100 | 419,700 | 278,400 |

Source: Bronson and Carson BJS 2019.

---

**Class exercise**—Locate the women's prison(s) in your state. Where are they? Why do you think they are located where they are? What are the demographics of the inmates in a particular prison? What types of crimes are they in prison for?

---

The number of women's correctional institutions usually reflects the typically smaller total women inmate populations as well. The same is true on a national level as well. The Federal Bureau of Prisons (BOP) reports that women make up 7% of the total federal inmate population and that there are 29 facilities of varying security levels across the country. This compared to 93 BOP facilities across the country (Federal Bureau of Prisons, 2019).

Since there are fewer facilities and numbers of women inmates resources devoted to this population of offenders sometimes are not sufficient. For instance simply due to the few places a women inmate can be housed may cause a hardship for the inmate as their family or other means of support may live several hundred miles away thus making visiting difficult. Some may say this is a small hardship but this lack of support can hinder reintegration and rehabilitation efforts. These efforts not only reduce the chances the person would end up back in prisons but also impact community safety. Many women's prisons offer similar educational and treatment programs that males have but women's inmates differ from their male counterparts in significant ways. Women are more likely than men to suffer economic hardship, employment instability, lack vocational skills when compared to male inmates. Women inmates also suffer higher rates trauma and abuse than men. The type of court commitment, different levels of abuse and trauma, and women inmates as parents or as a new mother mean prison officials from correctional officers to wardens have to recognize the differences in custody and care women inmates represent.

The need for correctional institutions was made clear in a 2002, report from the National Institute of Corrections. In it **gender responsiveness** was a focal point. Even acknowledging there is a difference between male and women needs of inmates was an important step. However, the report is a great illustration of evidence-based practice at work. There were several findings that have impacted women inmates since its release.

The report drew three different conclusions. First, that there were differences between male and women pathways into criminality. Secondly, that men and women react differently to custody/imprisonment. Lastly, that realizing the differences between men and women as inmates are real thus treating and handling inmates based on varied needs increases the chances for inmates to be successful when released. Lastly, the report surmised the following concerning gender responsive strategies:

- Management of women offenders would be more effective.
- Correctional facilities would be more suitably staffed and funded, which would decrease staff turnover and improve services to inmates.
- Decrease the likelihood of litigation from staff and inmates.
- Increase gender appropriate services.

(Bloom, Owen, & Covington, 2002).

# B. CHARACTERISTICS OF WOMEN INMATES

Racial disparities for women inmates exists just as they do for males. African Americans represent about 13% of the general population in the U.S. yet about 50% of the women prison population are minorities Black women are also eight times more likely to be incarcerated than are white women (Covington, 2000). The imprisonment rates for black womens is almost twice that of white inmates. Tackling this disparity has become a major focus of correctional officials, courts, and politicians.

The vast majority of women in corrections are under some form of community supervision (85%) (Bloom, Owen, & Covington, 2002). Interestingly about two thirds of probationers are white womens as compared to two-thirds of those in jail or prison are African American or Hispanic (Carson, 2017).

Since womens often have a different pathway toward criminality than males the correctional efforts should recognize this differing pathway. Thus correcting women offending is not the same for womens as it is for males. Pathways toward criminality for womens often involves the following gender-based experiences and thus different consequences:

Family background—women in the criminal justice system are more likely to come from single parent homes than the general population. These women are more likely than men to have at least one incarcerated family member as well.

Substance abuse—Over 80% of women in prison have a substance abuse problem at the time of their arrest. Fully half of those women arrested for the offense for which they were currently serving prison time for were under the influence of alcohol of drugs at the time of their arrest. Even when compared to male inmates women inmates reported using a mind altering substance just before committing their **instant offense**.

Physical Health—women enter jail and subsequently prison with more health concerns than their male counterparts. Poor health is often due to poverty, poor nutrition, inadequate healthcare, and substance abuse (Reviere, 2002).

Abuse—women inmates suffer higher rates of abuse (physical, mental, and sexual) than their male counterparts. Tis abuse can be current or past trauma from childhood. Abuse in the women inmate population is higher than the general women population. Thus these past and current traumatic events can play a role in physical and emotional health of inmates. Since there are higher rates of several types of abuses in women inmate's correctional official must be aware of these needs.

Employment and education—About half of women in prison and jail had completed their high school degree upon entering the institution. The rate for federal women inmates was much higher than state women inmates (56% state women inmates compared to 75% of federal women inmates). Only about 40% of women reported being employed at the time of arrest. Most of those employed were working in low skill and low wage jobs. Women were also much less likely to be engaged with some type of vocational training prior to incarceration as well (Bloom, Owen, & Covington, 2002).

Children—Unlike their male counterpart's women that end up in prison were far more likely to be caretakers of children than males. Males were almost as likely to have children as womens but the role of caretaker was largely women versus males. Almost 70% of women under some type of correctional supervision had at least one child under 18 years of age. Approximately 1.3 million children have a mother under some type of correctional supervision. Almost a quarter of a million children have a mother that is incarcerated (Cecil, McHale, Stozier, & Pietsch, 2008).

That national profile of women inmates can be summarized as follows:

- Women inmates are disproportionately women of color.
- They tend to be in their early to mid 30s.
- They are most likely to be incarcerated for a non-violent offense.
- A fragmented family who in turn have family members in the criminal justice system.
- Are survivors of mental and/or physical trauma.
- They are likely to have physical and/or mental health issues.
- Be unmarried and have children.
- Likely to possess a high school degree or GED but have limited work experience.

(Bloom, Owen, & Covington, 2002).

## C.  GENDER RESPONSIVENESS AND CORRECTIONS

Understanding the characteristics of women offenders and how they become involved in crime is key to understanding rehabilitative efforts with all offenders regardless of gender. The effects of gender in criminality and therefore in how we deal with offenders is well documented. Understanding this difference allows corrections officials to offer more client direct services and meaningful rehabilitative efforts. Correctional polices and management are typically gender neutral yet we know that corrections is not a one-size-fits all effort. Gender differences have been found at all stages of criminal justice processing from defining what is criminal, types of crime committed, to sentencing (Bloom, Owen, & Covington, 2002). Since we are focused on corrections we will look at how classification, services and programs offered in prison and through community corrections, staffing and training or prisons and community corrections, and finally staff sexual misconduct impact women offenders and thus corrections.

Classification is the process of identifying inmate's risks and needs. If you recall classification is done upon entering the prison. There are numerous evaluations done in order to identify what risks the inmate may present to staff and other inmates as well as what sorts of needs the inmate may have such as mental health treatment or substance abuse issues. These measure are typically done with the male inmate in mind but utilized for womens as well. The same tools used to identify risk and needs of the male inmate may not offer as accurate results for womens. There has been a call for more research in this area (Bronson, 2019).

Women's services and programs also often mirror what is provided to males in prison. Yet in order to address women criminality services and programs that are focused and gender responsive offer better results. The factors that often facilitate women toward crime are: violence, substance abuse, and struggling to provide for themselves and/or their families (Pollack, 2002). Thus all services rendered should consider gender differences not only in substance but in delivery and teaching methods. Planning and funding considerations should be considered at the executive level. Some have pushed for the creation of a "Women's Services" branch in corrections to delineate it from male corrections (Bloom, Owen, & Covington, 2002).

As we have discussed previously staffing any prison is a challenge today. Recruiting and training staff is one of the most pressing issues for prison administrators today. Specialized training concerning women inmates is lacking in corrections. Few state correctional organizations offer specialized training for dealing with women inmates (Corely, 2019). Considering women inmates make up a small portion of the total inmate population it can be easy to overlook the importance of differentiating training. Training for corrections officers is male oriented and women offenders are often lumped into the training mix without appreciating the differences. Yet we know that demographically and criminogenic risks and needs can be substantially different between males and womens.

Lastly sexual misconduct is higher in women's facilities than at men's institution. Rates of inmate-on-inmate sexual violence was 4 times higher for womens than males (212 per 1000 for womens and 43 per 1000 for males). Misconduct does not always involve rape of sexual assault. Inappropriate language, verbal degradation, intrusive searches, and unwarranted visual inspection are all considered sexual misconduct. This type of misconduct by staff can be easy to disguise. Also procedures to address this type of behavior sometimes put the inmate in difficult or impossible situations where they fear retaliation by staff that can come in various ways. Considering many women inmates have backgrounds involving their own abuse these types of searches or the use of isolation techniques can exacerbate a situation.

Women and male inmates share one commonality: they have been convicted of a crime that sent them to prison. However, this is where the similarities diverge in many instances. Recognizing the pathway toward criminality is often times different for men than it is for women is an important distinction to make. Recognizing this allows corrections officials to implement policy and procedures that are tailored to the women inmate. Thus rehabilitative efforts are easier to instill. Litigation can also be avoided to a great degree as a result as well. Additionally, the functioning of the prison overall is affected by understanding the nuances between male and women inmates.

# D. PSEUDO FAMILIES

Just as there are differences concerning the makeup of men's and women's facilities so to are there differences in the social structure of men's and women's prisons. Perhaps one of the most striking differences concerns the development of **pseudo families**. Instead of prison gangs being the dominant social structure feature as in men's prisons women's prisons tend to have a predominant social structure that revolves around family like structures. These pseudo families mirror a family structure in free society. Just like prison gangs in men's institutions pseudo families provide kinship and support. Granted pseudo families tend to provide more emotional support than gangs do. The development of these are seen as a coping mechanism considering the unique environment that prison provides. Just as gangs develop due to prison deprivations or importing behavior from the outside world so pseudo families develop out of the same deprivations and importations.

The family structure is much like that of a family outside of prison. An inmate assumes the role of patriarch and another matriarch. Also other inmates assume roles of siblings and so on. As opposed to their male counterparts who gravitate toward power womens relate on a more emotive and expressive level. The women inmates who are more likely to be in need of emotional support, advice, and assistance to making an adjustment to prison life are more likely to become a member of a pseudo family (Kolb, 2018). Unlike men's prison gang's women pseudo-families are a virtual melting pot. Family members from a variety of racial backgrounds exist. There are associated behaviors one must conform to considering these roles. In other words inmate's behavior and behavioral expectations are dictated by the role one assumes. This that assume a fatherly role "protect" the family. Those that do not assume a parental role can be told what to do and receive punishment for not adhering to the rules.

Sexual relationships within women's prison take place for the same reasons they do in men's prisons. Sometimes intimate relationships are a need to relieve loneliness. They can be consensual in nature. Alternatively, sexual relationships can and are sexual assaults just as elsewhere. The reasons for which these tale place occur because of a multitude of reasons.

## E.  CHILDREN AND WOMEN INMATES

Approximately 70 percent of women in prison and jail have at least one minor child. Over two thirds of women in state prisons lived with their child before entering prison. Approximately 2.3 million children are separated from their mothers each year (Sawyer, 2018). The number of women inmates with children doubled since 1991 (+131%) (Glaze, 2008). Almost 2.3 % of children in the U.S. has an incarcerated parent. Considering many of these children are dependent on their mothers this can represent a hardship for children and the families. One also has to balance that some of these women can be abusive or neglectful of their children also. Separating a child or children from their mother can be difficult but sometimes is necessary for the safety of the child. It is one of many challenges the entire criminal justice system must deal with concerning women offenders and inmates.

Some women are pregnant before being incarcerated and some become pregnant during incarceration. Approximately 5.2% of white womens, 6.7% black womens, 5.9% of Hispanic womens are pregnant upon entering prison. Almost 4,000 women inmates give birth each year (Snell, 1994).

Percent of State and Federal Inmates Who Were
Parents of Minor Children, by Age and Gender

| Age of inmates who were parents of minor children | Percent of parents in state prison | | | Percent of parents in federal prison | | |
|---|---|---|---|---|---|---|
| | Total | Male | Female | Total | Male | Female |
| **All inmates** | 51.9% | 51.2% | 61.7% | 62.9% | 63.4% | 55.9% |
| 24 or younger | 44.1% | 43.5% | 55.4% | 45.8% | 45.7% | 47.5% |
| 25-34 | 64.4 | 63.3 | 80.7 | 74.1 | 74.1 | 74.5 |
| 35-44 | 58.9 | 58.3 | 65.7 | 71.9 | 72.1 | 68.2 |
| 45-54 | 31.0 | 31.4 | 25.8 | 47.0 | 48.3 | 31.2 |
| 55 or older | 12.6 | 12.9 | ^ | 23.8 | 25.3 | ^ |

Note: See appendix table 16 for estimated total counts.
^Estimate not reported. Sample size too small (10 or fewer) to provide reliable data.

Source: (Glaze, 2008).

As we can see from the chart above the majority of inmates of both sexes have at least one minor child. However, women especially those 25–34 are very likely to have at least one minor child of which they very often lived with just prior to being incarcerated creates not only a burden for the inmate and her children but also the families of the inmate/children.

Percent of Minor Children of Parents Aged 25–34
in State and Federal Prison by Gender

| Age of minor child | Percent of minor children among parents in state prison | | | Percent of minor children among parents in federal prison | | |
|---|---|---|---|---|---|---|
| | Total | Male | Female | Total | Male | Female |
| **Total** | 100.0% | 100.0% | 100.0% | 100.0% | 100.0% | 100.0% |
| Less than 1 year | 2.4% | 2.5% | 1.6% | 0.7% | 0.7% | 1.1% |
| 1-4 years | 20.0 | 20.3 | 16.7 | 15.1 | 15.3 | 12.6 |
| 5-9 years | 30.2 | 30.3 | 29.1 | 33.8 | 34.0 | 30.1 |
| 10-14 years | 31.6 | 31.4 | 33.8 | 35.1 | 35.0 | 35.8 |
| 15-17 years | 15.8 | 15.5 | 18.8 | 15.3 | 15.0 | 20.4 |

Source: (Glaze 2008).

Women inmates that do have minor children as tend to have young children. About half of womens in prison have a child 9 years of age or less. Considering womens are more apt to be the caregivers of young children the absence of the mother can be quite distressing to the child. Due to the young age of these children the absence of the mother at such a young age can result in a cascade of issues for the youth of these women.

## F. THE IMPACT OF INCARCERATION ON CHILDREN

The impact of incarceration is dynamic and the effects on inmates and children differ considering the type and nature of the relationship the parent and child had prior to incarceration. The types of and nature of relationships vary with each family unit. We know that incarcerated fathers tend to have the child's mother care for the child (90% of the time mothers assume caregiving responsibility after the father goes to jail). Compare that when a mother goes to jail only 28% of the time does the father assume caregiving responsibility (Parke, 2001). It is important to note that women tend to spend far less time in prison than males do (80 months for males and 49 months for womens). However, as we discovered previously a large portion of children of incarcerated womens are young and therefore missing on child development in the formative years has negative consequences for the child, mother, and ultimately society.

The effects of incarceration have short term effects and long lasting effects for both parents and children. Again, the effects are not confined to the family but usually have community ramifications. Having a child witness the arrest of a parent can be traumatic in itself. Usually there are not resources for children that have this experience. Often children do not understand what is occurring. The event can present a host of problems beyond witnessing the immediate arrest. School days may be lost, living situations can change, loss of resources can also occur. The arrest of a caregiver has many collateral consequences that often are not addressed. There are also long-term effects for incarcerated mothers. Those that do give birth in prison often get only a few days before the baby is removed from the mother. The chance to bond at the very early stages of development is critical for both mother and child at this stage (Myers, Smarsh, Amlund-Hagen, & Suzanne, 1999). When mothers are released and assumes caregiving responsibility to a child or children where the emotional bond is weak children have a higher likelihood of more emotional and behavioral problems (Travis, Solomon, & Waul, 2001).

The effects of an incarcerated mother for school aged children are also evident. Children with incarcerated mothers had higher rates of aggressive behavior in school, poor academic performance, and increased school absence. Students with incarcerated at least one incarcerated parent were also more likely to dropout of school than children who didn't not have a parent incarcerated (Parke & Clarke-Stewart, 2002).

There are also notable differences concerning the impact of incarceration of a parent for boys and girls. Boys are effected more adversely to stressful situations than girls are (Lansford, 2009). That said, the impacts of incarceration for both boys and girls can be negative. There is not much research concerning the removal of a parent as being a positive experience, but for some the absence may not have near as many negative consequences especially if the parent was abusive or neglectful. We do see that boys react differently than girls do when a parent is incarcerated. Boys are more likely to externalize issues through behavioral problems while girls are more likely to internalize problems (Brock, 2016).

# G. BUFFERING CHILDREN'S REACTION TO PARENTAL INCARCERATION

That nature of the relationship prior to incarceration is important to understanding the impact of incarceration has on a child. If we assume the nature of the relationship was positive then the absence of the parent may be devastating and not only have acute short term consequences but also long term outcomes that plague a child for years. If however that relationship between the parent and child was already negative or the parent was not a factor in development the consequences of parental incarceration can be positive or moot. Assuming either or does not allow us as students, practitioners or academics to fully appreciate the situation.

If we assume the relationship was positive than the importance of extended family relationships is important for these children. Also, non-family informal social networks are important for emotional support as well as finding material resources such as financial help. The community responding to children and understanding that dealing with all people impacted by crimes and subsequent arrests and ultimately incarceration is important. Courts and the community at large understanding all of the fallout from crime becomes important to limiting the damage crime causes not only for the direct victim but the family of the perpetrator.

One of the main factors in limiting harmful consequences of incarceration for children of inmates is to maintain positive contact between the child and the inmate (Parke & Clarke-Stewart, 2002). The ability to visit the inmate can be quite difficult. Sometimes the prison is far away from where the child or children reside. Thus visiting can be quite a hardship. If the child is placed in foster care then visiting may not be an option or even a consideration. Institutions can also be an impediment to maintaining contact. Visiting hours and regulation regarding juvenile visitors can make visiting difficult. The physical makeup of the visiting area within the prison can be intimidating and scare children. Sometimes contact between the inmate and visitor is restricted to talking on a phone and seeing the other party through thick glass while other rules curtail physical touching. These rules are not meant to be punitive but rather help the prison maintain security as contraband can be moved through other less restrictive measures. The key is to find a balance and not sacrifice security while being humane to the inmates and their families.

The incarceration of a parent regardless of gender can have negative consequences for both the inmate and the children of those inmates. These children are also harmed by the actions of their parents, though the harm is typically less direct. These are often forgotten victims of crime as well. Direct victims no doubt need attention but to deny children of inmate's resources because of the actions of their parent's only serves to help perpetuate a myriad of social problems.

# H. TREATMENT

The largest percentage of women inmates are incarcerated for drug offenses. Thirty-four percent of womens inmates in state prisons are serving time for drug offenses while an overwhelming majority of womens in federal prisons (72%) are incarcerated for drug crimes (Bloom, Owen, & Covington, 2002). Not all persons in prison for drug crimes have substance abuse issues. However, approximately 80% of women in state prisons have substance abuse problems (Acoca, 1998). Thus long term substance abuse is a significant problem for women inmates. Also the impact of substance abuse on criminality is well documented ((Bloom, Owen, & Covington, 2002). Almost half of all women inmates used either alcohol or another type of substance at the time of their offense. Another third of those inmates reported committing their Instant offense (es) in order to obtain money to support a drug habit. The second largest percentage of women inmates incarcerated in state prisons are serving sentences related to property crime. (27%) (Center for Substance Abuse Treatment, 1997). Women reported higher substance abuse usage than their male inmate counterparts. Treatment for this segment of the offending population is a critical factor concerning community safety (i.e. recidivism) and the health of the offender which can also become a community responsibility.

A vast body of research outlines the differences between male and women substance use and abuse. Gender differences plays a role concerning early opportunities to use substances and the social inhibitors and reinforces of abuse. The differences include **etiological, physiological, psychological, sociological**, and familial factors. The pathway to use and subsequent abuse is more complex for womens than males. It often involves familial and social factors. Bloom, Owens, and Covington(2002) reported a few major points of women inmate substance abuse:

> **Class exercise**—Have a class discussion about how society differentially encourages or reinforces the use of some substances while discourages the use of others.
>
> How can culture promote or inhibit the acceptance of drug use as a potential way to reduce recidivism?

- The onset of substance use is gradual and begins as the result of depression or a family problem.

- Women users have a greater number of life problems besides criminality than do male abusers.

- Race, culture, and ethnicity greatly impact the development of women substance abuse. When low income, and low level of education are also present there is a degree of alienation and powerlessness.

- Treatment programs for women recognize need for not only dealing with the substance abuse issue but also that this specific issue can be addressed through dealing with a number of different issues (i.e. prior physical and/or mental abuse).

There is now a recognition that just as there are different pathways toward criminality for males and womens so too is there a different pathway to male and women substance abuse. Substance abuse treatment providers are recognizing that arbitrarily lumping women offenders in with male offenders for treatment purposes may but be the best use of resources. Also that using a substance abuse as a one-size or one-gender fits all approach may not be the most efficient way to deal with this problem.

# I.  MENTAL HEALTH

Many women who end up in the criminal justice system had prior contact with the mental health system as well. Just like the male inmate population the women prison population has a higher rate of mental health disorders when compared to the general U.S. population. Approximately 73% of women inmates in state prisons had a mental health problem. In federal prisons the rate was lower (61%) (James & Glaze, 2006). 23% of women inmates reported they had been diagnosed with a mental health disorder prior to being incarcerated. When only 8% of males reported the same. Keep in mind that womens are more apt to seek out mental health services than are males. Young inmates, those 24 years old or younger, were also more likely than older inmates to have some type of diagnosed mental health issue.

The major types of mental health issues differ from male inmates. Women inmates suffer from high rates of depression, post-traumatic stress disorder (PTSD), and substance abuse than do males. Women offenders also experience high rates of past physical, sexual, and emotional abuse thus impacting the numbers of PTSD cases. Almost a quarter of women inmates receive some type of medication for a psychological disorder.

Treating women's mental health issues again is different than it is more men's issues. Men and women suffer with many of the same afflictions but how best to treat mental health issues diverges when we consider gender. Again the divergence is due to the differing underlying issues. Recognizing these differences and devoting resources based on gender responsiveness is an effective method to reduce mental health issues and thus reduce recidivism. Recognizing that depression affects women inmates twice as often as it affects male inmates allows more and varied programs that deal with depression, especially causes of women depression to be implemented. Again, dealing with depression in a generic one-gender fits all modality does not effectively address the issue.

Women inmates are more likely than males to have children and be the head of household. This represents a significant amount of potential stress and thus obvious mental health issues. As the women head of the house and considering womens are significantly more likely to experience low levels of education and thus job opportunities the access to resources are very limited. Women offenders are often underserved when it comes to mental services even though they report mental health issues to practitioners more freely than do men. Only one quarter of the women inmates needing treatment for mental health issues receive any service (Belle, 1994).

Recognizing the different reasons that men and women abuse substances as well as the differing pathways affecting mental health represents a start toward more effect services in those areas. Attitudes about devoting resources to and dealing with women offenders should also evolve. Rasche (2000) refers to correctional officer difference in attitudes and thus service as "male inmate preference". According to this attitude women inmates are seen as "harder to work with". During a discussion with a Kansas Correctional Sergeant he stated, male inmates just do what they're told but womens always ask why and want to argue". There appears to be a pervasive attitude than since women inmates present such a small portion of the total prison population and that their crimes are viewed as less serious or violent than males they are "not worth the time" (Bloom, Owen, & Covington, 2002).

## J. COMMUNITY CORRECTIONS

The number of womens under probation supervision increased almost 100% between 1997 and 2007 (Statistics, 2008). Managing and supervising women under any type of community corrections supervision in a gender responsive way is also necessary. In this environment it's actually much easier to place women into men's treatment groups because they are not physically separated by prison walls. It can be seen as cost effective to include womens into male oriented treatment, especially in rural areas where access to treatment groups of any kind can be limited at best. Bloom, Owen and Covington (2002) found that womens under community corrections supervision tend to have the following differences:

- Women tend to take more of an officers time during office contacts.

- Women have an expectation that officers will provide help such as navigating community resources and providing direct assistance.

- Officer tend to "burn out" at higher rates because women offenders are more demanding of services.

- Women offender tend to make or want to make stronger personal connections with parole and probation officers.

- Since womens are often the heads of households there can be difficulty meeting all the needs of community supervision such as treatment or employment. Upon release it can be difficult for women parolees to reunite or gain partial or full custody of children thus creating issues beyond reunification.

- Family members that took care of children upon a mother's incarceration expect her to take responsibilities of childcare immediately upon release creating difficulties with reintegration.

- Officers tend not to recognize gender responsive needs of offenders.

Understanding gender differences in women versus male offenders in the community is important. As the head of household women inmates can experience different stressors than do male offenders. Allowing for these differences can reduce revocations and thus incarceration rates for womens. Probation and parole officers knowing that these differences can affect success of offenders under supervision is critical to community corrections effectiveness. Officer may need to coordinate with several community agencies in order to increase chances of success. **Case management** practices may need adjusting to accommodate these needs and risks.

## K.  RESEARCH AND POLICY/PRACTICE

Women offenders present different challenges to reducing recidivism than do males. We have discussed the importance of gender responsiveness in a number of different areas. Thus recognizing these differences is necessary but not sufficient when thinking about change in the correctional system. Gender responsive strategies, policies, programs, and practices need to be developed to recognize these differences. As evidenced throughout the course of this chapter significant differences exist between male and women pathways toward or away from criminality. Understanding why people commit crime informs us how to correct that behavior. Effective probation measures that target women vulnerability toward crime can be implemented. The *Moving On Program* uses three different approaches:

Relational Theory—type of theory based on the idea that mutually satisfying relationships with others are necessary for one's well-being. (Psychology Today, 2019).

Motivational Interviewing—technique of interviewing which the person interviewing the subject encourages change and help the subject to solve problems (Rollnick, 2019).

Cognitive-Behavioral Intervention—intervening on behalf of a person involved in destructive behavior by reformatting thought processes by instilling coping mechanisms (wisegeek, 2019).

The primary goal of this gender responsive program concerns using existing strengths each participant has while developing less honed ones. Using community resources to help develop and polish strengths are important. Participants are treated with respect and dignity, provided an environment that is supportive and collaborative both with other participants as well as facilitators, and challenges women to improve (Bauman, Gerhing, & P, 2007). The program is based on 26 sessions where participants address different modules:

- Setting context for change.

- Women in Society.

- Taking Care of yourself.

- Family messages.

- Relationships.

- Coping with emotions and harmful self-talk.

- Problem-solving.

- Becoming assertive.

- Moving on.

The effect of the program has sown to reduce recidivism. Specifically that this program is gender responsive is significant since the risk factors of the sample were unique to women. It also show that the particular type of program, in this case a cognitive program was effective for women offenders. Programs such as this have impacted correctional treatment in as much that it is an evidence-based practice that when implemented for women can effectively reduce recidivism.

Understanding gender responsiveness as a correctional strategy or corrections philosophy is essential to promoting effective evidence-based programs. Strategy informs community level programs that can be tailored to meet the needs of specific communities.

# L. CONCLUSION

Women inmates and offenders have outpaced the growth of males. The needs and risks they present differ from males. Using the exact same policies and practices to effect women offenders does not address the differences each present when we consider pathways toward criminality. As we know understanding why a person commits a criminal act helps corrections professionals prevent future crime from occurring. Corrections is not a one-size fits all venture. Using evidence-based practices and recognizing that gender responsiveness are important variables to understand strengths our ability to promote rehabilitation and affect the families of offenders and the community as a whole.

## Discussion Questions

1. Explain what gender responsiveness is and how it impacts women corrections.

2. Why are more womens entering the criminal justice system today?

3. What are some hardships that women inmates face that many males do not?

4. Describe 2 characteristics of women inmates.

5. Why is it important to understand the characteristics of women inmates?

6. Should prison staff receive specialized training for dealing with women inmates? Explain your answer.

7. What are pseudo families and why are they prevalent in women prisons?

8. What sort of issues do children of inmates have?

9. Explain the potential impact of having a mother incarcerated has on a child.

10. How should corrections programs be different for womens than males?

## Student Exercises

1. Visit the website crimesolutions.gov and do the following:

   A. Find a program which is focused on women offenders and summarize it.

B.  Is it effective and producing results? Explain.

C.  Can this program be implemented in your community? Explain.

2.  The separation of women inmates from their children can have a negative impact for the child and the mother. What are some ways these negative consequences can be alleviated?

## Key Terms

**Case management**—a management plan specific for each offender that address their unique needs and risks.

**Etiology**—science of causation.

**Gender responsiveness**—recognizing that females and males respond differently to correctional measures. Understanding that pathways towards female criminality can differ from males and that correctional policy and programs should be geared with this understanding.

**Instant offense**—the crime(s) for which the offender is currently incarcerated for.

**New court commitment**—the placement of an offender in prison due to a new court conviction.

**Physiology**—the physical and chemical makeup of people. The bodies physical reaction to substances.

**Pseudo families**—a family group formed by female inmates that simulate a traditional family. These groups are formed to facilitate emotional needs.

**Psychological**—the mental aspect of a person.

**Sociological**—the social factors that influence use and potential abuse of substances. Society may encourage or discourage the use of a substance.

## CHAPTER 9

# Specialized Populations

**Chapter Objectives**

- Describe what a special needs inmate is and how these inmates present management challenges.

- Explain what Crisis Intervention Teams (CIT) are.

- Understanding what communicable diseases present a danger to staff and inmates.

- Explain how important of least eligibility is and how it impacts the administration inmate healthcare.

- Discuss the issues that inmates with mental health problems present to correctional officials.

- Understand the legal issues special needs inmates present to correctional administrators.

## A. INTRODUCTION

Inmates in jails and prisons today are as varied as people outside of prison. They too have many of the same issues that plague the general public. Issues like providing health care and mental health care are a growing challenge for prisons and jails. Inmates with mental health issues, intellectual disabilities, and health issues are considered **special needs** inmates. Since they have this distinction a great number of needs must be satisfied in order to protect this population from harm, prevent spread of disease, and treat those with varied afflictions.

An estimated 40% of state and federal inmates reported having a current chronic medical condition. The rates of inmates having HIV/AIDS, hepatitis B or C, and tuberculosis is much higher than the general population. Since many of these diseases are communicable prisons and jails are not only dangerous because an assault may occur they are also places where disease can be spread much more easily not only to inmates but also staff. It's also important to remember that well over 90% of inmates will be released some day and the diseases they acquired while incarcerated are carried outside of prison walls. Wildeman (2016) (Wildeman, 2016) reported that due to mass incarceration the overall life expectancy in the U.S. remained stable at 78.8 years instead of growing like other comparable nations such as Spain, Sweden, and Japan due to health issues from mass incarceration. The mental health issues inmates present has been a growing concern for many years since states began to defund community non-incarcerative mental health services. Inmate with mental health issues grew tremendously in the past 30 years. Special needs inmates present unique challenges both financial and legally to corrections staff at every level. Corrections administrators must be cognizant of legal and financial concerns while those that deal directly with special needs inmates often require specialized training and must take precautions to avoid harming the inmate of being harmed themselves.

## B. CLASSIFYING OR IDENTIFYING SPECIAL NEEDS INMATES

> **Class exercise**—Research how many inmates or what percent of inmates in the local jail have a chronic mental health issue. Discuss with your classmates how jails and the community at large can reduce the number of people entering jail or remaining in jail for long periods of time.

All correctional facilities (i.e. jails and prisons) classify inmates. Probation and parole agencies also classify inmates and offenders. Classification not only designates an inmate as a certain level of security risk but also identifies any physical or mental health needs an inmate may have. Identification of these issues typically occurs at intake or booking in jail or when an inmate is sent to prison for long term incarceration they usually spend several weeks at a facility designated to perform diagnostic evaluations (in this case physical and mental health evaluations). Reception and diagnostic units (RDU's) then classify a risk level such as minimum, medium, or maximum custody as well as any special needs the inmate may have such as medical disability or mental health concern. After classification inmates can then be sent to facility that address risk factors while also meeting the needs of the inmate.

Some facilities main purpose are to house inmates with special needs. Access to programs and treatment both mental and physical are necessary for inmates. The **Americans with Disabilities Act** requires many institutions to accommodate inmates with physical impediments. This legal act creates a **legal liability** for jails and prisons to make either physical structural accommodations to facilities or change policy to accommodate and adhere to the requirements of this act.

The pre-sentence investigation (PSI) is also an essential tool for identifying an inmate with a special need. If you recall from Chapter 5 in this textbook we discussed the pre-sentence investigation (some jurisdictions refer to this as a pre-sentence report which is the same as a PSI). Prison officials review the PSI for not only risk concerns but any special needs that the facility should be aware of.

Identifying special needs inmates does not end once an inmate leaves RDU. Inmates are of course under constant supervision to ensure they are following prison rules but they are also being monitored by all prison staff for changes in physical and mental health. Probation and parole officers also continually monitor offenders in order to address any concerns for those under community corrections supervision as well. Corrections staff, especially these that work with offenders and inmates on a daily basis receive training to identify changes in mental or physical health. Thus they are not only law enforcers or disciplinarian but trained to spot the nuances of mental and physical health symptoms people can present.

---

### Corrections in Action

Approximately 44% of jail inmates in America and 61% of inmates in prison were found to have a mental health problem according to the Bureau of Justice Statistics (2016). While jails perform a number of different functions one of their more frequent functions are to hold inmates awaiting some type of transfer for mental health evaluations. Prisons of course are house inmates for a longer period of time so the commitment and effort to house inmates with mental health issues requires a more long term solution. Regardless of how long an inmate is incarcerated corrections officers in jails and prisons are required to handle more inmates with mental health problems than ever before. One of the more recent responses to deal with these inmates are for corrections officers to receive crisis intervention training (CIT).

The National Institute of Corrections (NIC) in associate with the National Alliance on Mental Health (NAMI) have created training for correctional officials to identify the scope and impact of mental health illness in corrections, identify core elements of what a Crisis Intervention Team (CIT) should include, the benefits of CITs, and how to establish CIT's and partnerships. It's beyond the scope of this text to discuss all of these segments, so here we will focus on what a CIT is and its core elements (National Institute of Corrections, 2019).

A crisis intervention team (CIT) are a group of people specifically trained to identify a person undergoing a significant mental health crisis and de-escalate the situation in a peaceful manner. The team should be able to respond to situations 24 hours a day and they consist of people from a number of different fields (correctional line officers, administration, mental health, and other collaborative personnel). Corrections officer are often first responders in the facility therefore these people are critical when identifying the possible mental health issue(s) and using non-forceful techniques to calm a tense or violent situation down. CIT, has been empirically validated as a way to reduce the number of use of force incidents thus preventing harm to inmates and staff while additional reducing the number of legal actions that result from use of force incidents (National Alliance on Mental Illness, 2019).

CIT's are now used in many different jails and prisons. They address the need to identify inmates that are currently experiencing a substantial mental health issue and rather than using force to control the situation less violent means are utilized. These teams represent a significant evolution in managing an inmate population that increasingly has varied and serious mental health issues. Utilizing an evidence-based approach like CITs to address acute mental health issues will reduce harm to inmates and staff alike.

Classification and placement of inmates with mental health issues is important to the management of any facility. We know that just as people in the general population needs change so do prisoners. An inmate may be perfectly healthy upon entering prison but for any number of reasons their health both physical and mental change as people age and environments change.

## C. SPECIAL NEEDS POPULATIONS IN PRISON

There are many different categories of special populations in prison, jail, and in community corrections. The few we have mentioned here and we will elaborate on further here. However, we can break down special needs into many different categories such as those convicted of sex crimes as a special needs population or those in need of substance abuse treatment. About 74% of state prison inmates who had a mental health issue also met the criteria for substance dependence/abuse (Glaze, 2006). So we can see that there is significant correlation between substance abuse/dependence and mental health. However causation of one upon the other is not typically the case.

Here we will split up special populations into two broad categories. The first category we will focus on are those with health problems. A great number of inmates are serving a great number of years in prison. As they grow older health problems naturally occur and it's the prisons and ultimately all our responsibility to ensure those inmates receive medical care. In this category we will look at communicable diseases in spread. We will look at the prevalence and incidence of it and the serious concerns about the spread of such **communicable diseases** to other inmates, prison staff, and even into the general population outside prison. We will specifically focus on HIV/AIDS, hepatitis B and C, and finally tuberculosis. They are certainly other diseases we could include such as sexually transmitted diseases other than HIV/AIDS but that's outside of the scope of this textbook. These diseases and their spread is of particular concern to correctional professionals and those interested in entering the field as exposure to these diseases are as dangerous as any sort of violent act perpetrated by an inmate.

The second large category we will concern ourselves with here is a focus on mental illness. Prisons and jails have seen a massive increase in the number of inmates with mental health issues. Its accurate to say that we have gotten better at identifying mental illness so numbers of inmates increase but also due to inadequate funding and other resources we have seen those not treated for mental illness be arrested and subsequently end up in jail awaiting trial or serving a sentence or ending up in prison. We will discuss the reasons for this rise and the correctional response.

# D. ELDERLY INMATES

The number of older prisoners grew by 280% from 1999–2016, from 43,300 inmates that were 55 and older to now more than 164,400. The number of older inmates continues to climb even though we have started to see our prison populations shrink for the first time in several decades. The increase in the number of elderly inmates are largely due to the harsher or longer prison sentences meted out by courts. Older inmates now represent approximately 11 percent of the total prison population (McKillop, 2018). Compare this to 1999, when the population of prisoners 55 and older were only about 3%.

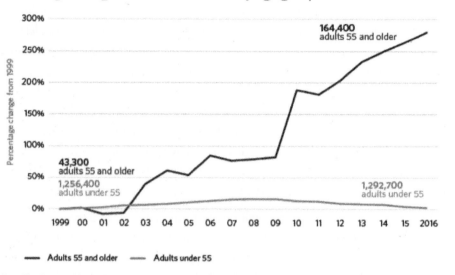

## The Number of Older Prisoners Grew by 280%, 1999-2016
Percentage change in sentenced adults by age group

Note: The Bureau of Justice Statistics estimates the age distribution of prisoners using data from the Federal Justice Statistics Program and statistics that states voluntarily submit to the National Corrections Reporting Program. State participation in this program has varied, which may have caused year-to-year fluctuations in the Bureau's national estimates, but this does not affect long-term trend comparisons. From 2009 to 2010, the number of states submitting data increased substantially, which might have contributed to the year-over-year increase in the national estimate between those years.

Source: Bureau of Justice Statistics

© 2018 The Pew Charitable Trusts

Source: Pew Charitable Trusts 2018.

Just like older people outside of prison require more medical care so do inmates. However, unlike elderly people in the non-incarcerated world inmates suffer higher rates of dementia, hearing loss, and, impaired mobility. Older inmates experience the effects of age sooner than the non-incarcerated population. This results a high rate of elderly inmates with chronic or long term medical conditions. Elderly inmates also present a host of difficulty for staff. Staff certainly need special training in dealing with inmates who have dementia, supervising this group of inmates more closely to prevent them being taken advantage of is also necessary (Maruschak, 2015). Their mobility and access to areas of prison is not only important to the management of the prison but can present legal liabilities. Some states and the federal government devote entire facilities or large segments of the prison to the caring for elderly inmates.

The impact on the management of these inmates presents special challenges to staff that deal with these inmates on a daily basis but also to administrators when it concerns paying for the cost of these inmates. Elderly inmates typically cost 2 or 3 times as much to treat in prison as those who are not incarcerated

(McKillop, 2018). A report from the Federal Bureau of Prisons found their institutions with the heist percentage of aged inmates (55+ years old) spent 5 times more on medical acre per inmate and 14 times more per inmate for those in need of medication. A report from the National Institute of Corrections identified the following management issues that elderly inmates present:

- Vulnerability to physical or mental abuse.

- Being taken advantage of concerning money issues.

- Not being able to establish social relationships with younger inmates.

- Increased need for physical accommodations.

- Needs for special programs and privileges.

- Transportation costs (staff and financial resources).

(Anno, Grahman, Lawrence, & Shansky, 2005).

The "**greying of America's prisons**" has been a focus of corrections for many years. The increase of the elderly inmate population has been impacted by the demographics of the U.S. population. **Baby-boomers** are one important reason for the increase in elderly inmates. Again, a reflection of society's influence on prison demographics. A large number of new admissions to prison of people 55 years and older has been occurring. From 2003–2013 the number of 55+ new court commitments to prison increased by 82% (McKillop, 2018). However, there is much more to this increase. The largest contributing factor to the greying of our prion system concerns the longer prison sentence being given in court. A large number of inmates are severing more time in prison than they have previously. Long prison sentences mean that young inmates will of course grow old in prison. Today about 1 in 7 inmates is serving a life sentence.

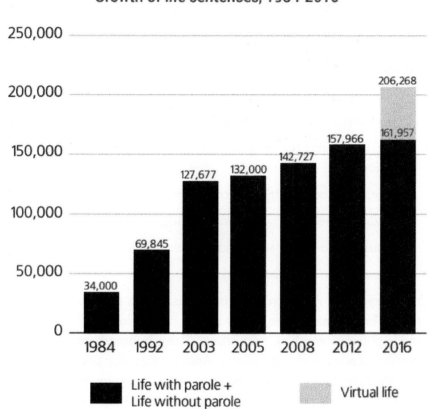

## Growth of life sentences, 1984-2016

(The Sentencing Project, 2018).

The number of elderly inmates will surely grow as those convicted at a young age grow old in prison while those that already are considered elderly remain. Prison officials are legally obligated to adhere to not only Americans with Disabilities (ADA) requirements but also a host of legal and humanitarian obligations. There is a considerable amount of anxiety amongst correctional administrators and legislators about the rising cost of healthcare for this population.

## E. DEALING WITH ELDERLY INMATES IN THE FUTURE

Inmates have a legal right to a standard of care. The level is care is referred to as the **principle of least eligibility.** Which means they are entitled to care for serious medical needs. They are entitled to care that is medically ordered and medical issues are addressed unimpeded by correctional professionals and are made according to medical standards.

One of the impediments toward gaining effective healthcare is the lack of centralized administration of services (Anno, Grahman, Lawrence, & Shansky, 2005). Institutions operate separately from other institutions in the same jurisdiction. Healthcare for the general public operates more efficiently when the costs of healthcare are spread out. They typically are not for prison healthcare systems. A complete sophisticated range of services is called for inmate healthcare. A multi-disciplinary approach which includes not only medical care for immediate concerns but also preventative care that can address issues before they become more serious and costly. Incorporating psychological, social, and dietary, as well as spiritual disciplines can be helpful. A holistic approach addresses not only physical but mental health problems and even serves as a preventive measure. Often we see services that address acute or immediate issues like a heart attack, when services that deal with hypertension and proper diet can prevent such major medical events and are far less costly from a financial consideration.

# F. CHRONIC AND COMMUNICABLE DISEASES

There are three forms of hepatitis. We will concern ourselves with hepatitis B and C, since these are communicable diseases. Hepatitis B and C are especially a concern to inmates and staff because how easily its spread. Considering the nature of prison and the potential to come into contact with blood and other fluids that carry the virus staff and inmates should take extra precautions to prevent its spread.

About 1% of the general public have hepatitis C in contrast 17.3% of inmates in the U.S. have this disease (He, Li, Roberts, & Spaulding, 2016). Since hepatitis B and C can ultimately destroy the liver it's not surprising to see that deaths from liver disease for inmates has increased even past inmate deaths attributed to HIV/AIDS. Hepatitis C also follows inmates after release from prison as a full 30% of all Americans with hepatitis C had at least spent part of a year in a correctional facility (He, Li, Roberts, & Spaulding, 2016).

Hepatitis B and C are highly communicable diseases. They are spread through sexual contact, sharing toothbrushes (blood on the toothbrush), needles from drug paraphernalia and/or tattooing equipment, or during childbirth. Both inmates and prison or jail staff need to be highly aware of contracting this disease. Both hepatitis B and C can lead to serious health complications or even death through cancer or cirrhosis of the liver. However, there are new medicines available that can now help cure this once incurable disease. Costs for the drug and screening are significant. One study estimated the cost per week at about $8,500 (He, Li, Roberts, & Spaulding, 2016). One of the best and most cost efficient ways to curtail the spread of the diseases concerns identifying inmates entering the prison with either strain of hepatitis. Empirical data tells us that by detecting and treating these with hepatitis by $260–$680 million (He, Li, Roberts, & Spaulding, 2016). The saving would be significant but the initial costs would be cumbersome. Budgeting money for this creates a significant burden on correctional budgets and ultimately taxpayers.

## G. HIV/AIDS

Human immunodeficiency virus (HIV) is spread through certain bodily fluids (namely blood and semen). The virus attacks the body's immune system. Overtime, if left untreated, infections that might otherwise be healed by the body take hold and the Acquired Immune Deficiency Syndrome or AIDS (the most severe phase of the HIV virus) overcomes the body's immune defenses (HIV.gov, 2019).

About 1.1 million people in the U.S. have HIV today. About 15% of those people do not know they have the virus. Every year approximately 38,000 people get infected with the HIV virus (HIV.gov, 2019). There are 17,150 state and federal inmates reported to have HIV. This number was actually down from the 1991, HIV number of 17,740 which was the first year HIV numbers of inmates were recorded. It's a significant departure from the peak HIV number of 25,980 inmates reported to have the HIV virus.

**Number of prisoners who had HIV and rate of HIV per 100,000 in the custody of state and federal correctional authorities, 1991–2015**

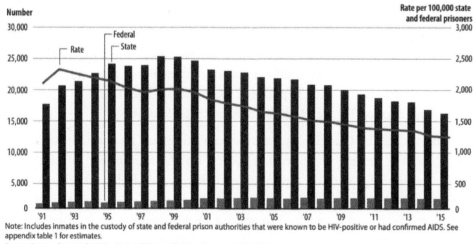

Note: Includes inmates in the custody of state and federal prison authorities that were known to be HIV-positive or had confirmed AIDS. See appendix table 1 for estimates.
Source: Bureau of Justice Statistics, National Prisoner Statistics Program, 1991–2015.

As we can see from the figure above the number of HIV cases have been falling since their peak in 1998. This of course is promising but what is even better news concerns the **mortality rate** for this population. The figure below illustrates a dramatic reduction in the number of inmates dying from the disease. This reduction is due to several factors which relate to the overall reduction in HIV cases in the general public as well as detection of inmates with the HIV virus and medications associated with reducing the diseases progression into the AIDS phase. While this is good news U.S. prison inmates are 3 times more likely to have the HIV virus than the general population. Inmates in state prisons in Florida, Maryland, and New York have an inmate **prevalence rate** of 3% higher than the national rate which is which is on par with sub-Saharan Africa, which is known to have the highest HIV rates in the world (Westergaard, Spaulding, & Flanigan, 2013).

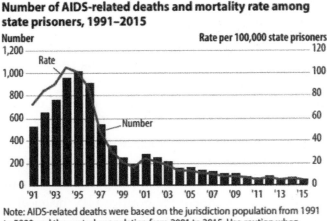

**Number of AIDS-related deaths and mortality rate among state prisoners, 1991–2015**

Note: AIDS-related deaths were based on the jurisdiction population from 1991 to 2000 and the custody population from 2001 to 2015. Use caution when comparing data prior to 2001 to data from 2001 and beyond. Jurisdiction refers to the legal authority of state and federal correctional officials over a prisoner, regardless of where the prisoner is held. See appendix table 2 for estimates.

Source: Bureau of Justice Statistics, National Prisoner Statistics Program, 1991–2000; and Deaths in Custody Reporting Program, 2001–2015.

Reception and diagnostic units for state correctional agencies now test for the HIV/AIDS virus in 15 states. 17 other states reported that inmates can opt-out of testing for the virus. In eight states an inmate could request a HIV/AIDS test (Maruschak L. a., 2017). The Federal Bureau of Prisons (BOP) provided testing to all incoming prisoners. Inmates here could opt-out of the testing.

Of course inmates can acquire the virus while in prison so testing upon entry into the correctional system tells us some of the issue. However, limiting the spread of the disease for inmates while they are incarcerated is vitally important as prisons don't want to be a place where any virus, especially not one as deadly as HIV/AIDS can spread among inmates and subsequently into the community.

Staff too can come into contact with fluids that contain the virus and they too can contract the disease, so their protection is paramount as well.

Inmates in the U.S. have a disproportionately high risk of HIV infection. The nature of prison certainly impacts these rates as wells as inmates having risk factors such as substance abuse (i.e. using needles to administer drugs), unprotected sex, poor access to healthcare, and a general mistrust of prison staff. Testing and identifying inmates for the early stages of HIV infection is very important in order to prevent its spread. Inmates who are detected with this virus can obtain the proper medical treatment and staff can take precautions to protect themselves. Collaboration between clinicians, correctional personnel, and public health practitioners is an important strategy for preventing the spread of the virus (Westergaard, Spaulding, & Flanigan, 2013). Success depends on increased efforts to test inmates and then apply the proper medical treatment. Although testing is important for jail inmates as it is for prison inmates the length a jail inmate is incarcerated for is about 2–5 days, which makes testing and receiving the results of such a test then counseling the inmate about the medical care needed difficult. However when we examine empirical data concerning quick testing and turnaround we see that it is feasible from both a time perspectives as well as a financial one (Beckwith, Bazerman, AH, & E., 2011). The option to be tested for jail inmates or a mandatory test allows inmates who don't have access to routine healthcare or may not have even considered the possibility that they might be infected a chance to receive treatment for positive HIV diagnosis. This can be critical to preventing the spread of the disease not only inside jail but since jail inmates are released into the community rather quickly the chance to prevent its spread to community members.

# H. TUBERCULOSIS

Tuberculosis (TB) is a potentially serious infectious disease that mainly affects a person's lungs. If TB is not treated properly it can become fatal (American lung Association, 2019). The virus is spread through saliva droplets released into the air via sneezing or coughing. TB was not uncommon in the late 1800s in the U.S. However, people infected with this virus began to decrease significantly in the 1920s and '30s. TB cases remained relatively low until the HIV/AIDS epidemic in 1985. The HIV virus weakened people's immune system and allowed prevalence of this disease to surge.

Approximately 4–6% of all TB cases in the U.S. are inmates. This is a small percentage of cases but inmates contain a high proportion of people at greater risk than the general population to become infected with TB. Since this group is at greater risk of contracting this disease it makes sense to alert people of the possible issues.

The **Centers for Disease Control** (CDC) have identified the following prevention and control efforts to reduce or prevent the spread of TB:

- Early identification of persons with TB through entry and follow-up testing.

- Successful treatment of TB and latent infection TB.

- Use of appropriate airborne precautions.

- Comprehensive discharge planning.

- Thorough and efficient contact investigations when TB has been identified in order to alert other who may be infected due to living in close proximity to the infected person.

(Centers for Disease Control, 2019).

The number of TB cases is small but the consequences are considerable. In 2016, 5579 inmates were diagnosed with TB and 299 correctional employees had the virus. The median incidence rates for TB were 29 per 100,000 jail inmates and 8 per 100,000 prison inmates. The federal system saw higher rates at 25 per 100,000. Some of the results for federal inmates were the result of those under Immigration and Customs Enforcement (ICE) holds (Lambert, Armstrong, & Lobato, 2016). Detection and treatment remains a major focus for preventing the spread of TB.

# I. MENTAL HEALTH INMATES

More than 37% of prisoners in the U.S. have been informed by mental health professionals that they have a mental health disorder. Many inmates (Bureau of Justice Statistics, 2017) are diagnosed with depressive disorder (24%), bipolar (18%), post-traumatic stress disorder (13%), and schizophrenia or another psychotic disorder (9%). The same rate of mental health disorder hold true for jail inmates as well where 44% of jail inmates have some form of mental health disorder. Female inmates were more likely than males to meet the criteria for serious psychological distress (SPD). 66% of female inmates and 35% of males were told by a mental health professional that he had a PSD. Jail inmates reported about the

> **Class exercise**—Locate the state correctional departments website in your state. What is the prevalence of inmates with mental health issues for those inmates? What sort or programs or other initiatives are being implemented to address mental health inmates in your state?

same rates of mental health illness (females 68% and males 41%) (Bureau of Justice Statistics, 2017). In 44 states jails or prisons hold more mentally ill individuals than the largest remaining state psychiatric hospitals. There are approximately 3 times more seriously mentally ill persons in jail or prisons than in hospitals (Treatment Center Advocacy, 2019).

## J.  THE RISING NUMBER OF INMATES WITH MENTAL HEALTH PROBLEMS

Psychiatric hospitals have been part of the state health system for well over a century. They were established to address mental health in the communities and were seen as providing a social function much like education or any welfare safety net. The primary purpose of state mental health institutions were to decrease the numbers of mentally ill in prisons, on the street, or in poor houses. In the 1950s states began closing asylums in exchange for more community based services (Vera Institute of Justice, 2019). The movement was known as **deinstitutionalization**.

The intentions of those seeking deinstitutionalization were humanistic. Practitioners and the public were becoming disenfranchised by the use of public funds for the purposes of housing large number of mentally ill. There were also advances in **psychotropic medication,** stricter due process for **civil commitment,** and the growing influence of non-residential mental healthcare (Vera Institute of Justice, 2019). The financial resources to successfully deal with the number of mentally ill after deinstitutionalization never matched the need. Therefore the commitment to implement mental health services adequately in the community failed. There were dramatic cuts to various social services in the 1980s and into the 1990s. This meant that those with mental illness went untreated. The War on Drugs also resulted in more punitive incarceration for possession offenses. Today nearly 68% of jail inmates and over 50% of prison inmates have a diagnosable substance abuse disorder. Many inmates have a co-occurring substance abuse and mental health disorder. 72% of jail inmates have a substance abuse issue and a co-occurring mental health issue (Vera Institute of Justice, 2019). We must note that just because someone has a mental health problem that does not mean will commit a crime. Also, substance abuse often times does not result in causing a mental health disorder. Rather people with mental health disorders may **self-medicate** in order to sooth the symptoms of their disorder. By not treating and addressing mental health disorders people are more at risk to be incarcerated because they are buying **illicit drugs,** obtaining prescription drugs illegally, or committing some type of property or violent offense.

## Corrections in Action

The use of solitary confinement is now regularly referred to as administrative segregation. The use of solitary confinement was largely discontinued in 1890 (see *In re Medley*, 134 U.S. 160, 168) when the U.S. Supreme Court expressed concerns about the impact on an inmates mental health. In 1958 the U.S. Supreme Court again noted that solitary confinement may not leave physical scars to be cruel and unusual punishment. The 8th Amendment of the U.S. Constitution prohibits cruel and unusual punishment.

Yet today about 4.4% of federal and state inmates are held in administrative segregation. Almost 20% of prison and 18% of jail inmates had spent some amount of time in administrative segregation (Beck, 2015). Entire prisons are devoted to housing only inmates for solitary confinement (see ADX Florence and Pelican Bay State prison in California as examples.) Inmates stay in solitary confinement in some cases for years.

**Class exercise**—Discuss the effects of solitary confinement on an inmate's mental health. What are the consequences for the inmate? Prison? Society?

How can we manage inmates who are violent toward inmates or staff?

Time in solitary confinement can exacerbate a pre-existing mental health issue or a mental health issue can manifest as a result of being in solitary confinement. Many inmates end up in solitary confinement for creating disorder or assaulting inmates or prison staff. Almost a third (29%) of inmates that exhibited symptoms of mental health or psychological distress ended up spending time in solitary confinement. Data shows that inmates that did not spend any time in administrative segregation had lower levels of psychological distress. In fact rates of inmates with no symptoms of psychological distress prior to entering administrative segregation were found to be significantly higher after they left administrative segregation (Beck, 2015).

Solitary confinement or administrative segregation is largely recognized as a punishment within prison walls when very little else can be taken away from an inmate only the circumstances of how the inmate serves that time can be used as punishment. It becomes difficult to draw the line between punishment and what can be considered cruel and/or unusual punishment. Isolation is a psychological stressor (Metzner, 2010) (Weir, 2019). For some it can and does result in a significant mental health problem. For others it can exacerbate an existing issue. Yet some can cope with periods of solitary confinement.

The courts will continue to decide the efficacy of administrative segregation. There is no doubt about the negative impact that type of confinement has on

> people's psychological health. There's only the question of how much harm is being done not if any occurs.

Correctional staff from wardens and jail directors to correctional officers deal with inmates that have mental illness. They represent significant challenges across the correctional spectrum. A bigger issue to consider is placement of people with mental illness in a correctional facility. Are prisons and jails the proper places to house and treat those with mental illness? Addressing this issue will require a societal response. Corrections will need to be a part of the conversation on this topic and correctional officials input should be respected. Decision makers need to be informed about topics they make decisions on. It's correctional professional's responsibility to inform those decision makers.

## K.  LEGAL ISSUES WITH SPECIALIZED POPULATIONS

Even though inmates are deprived of many rights they are not exempt from still enjoying some basic legal rights. When it comes to healthcare, both physical and mental, care are protected. The U.S. Constitution, federal statutes, state constitutions, and state statutes are the legal foundations which inmates can seek remedies to issues concerning healthcare. The courts have generally recognized four legitimate institutional needs that justify some restrictions on the constitutional rights of prisoners:

1.  Promotion of the rehabilitative rights of inmates.

2.  Safety and security of inmates and staff.

3.  Maintenance of institutional security.

4.  Maintenance of institutional order.

When it comes to health care we noted earlier in this chapter that principle of least eligibility is applied to administering healthcare in prisons and jails. This means that the entity housing the inmates (local jail or state/federal corrections) must provide healthcare services. In 1976, the U.S. Supreme Court affirmed that failure to provide basic medical care is a violation of the 8th Amendment of the U.S. Constitution (*Estelle v. Gamble*, 429 U.S. 97 (1976)). Since then a number of court cases have been decided on the issue of healthcare of inmates.

In order to ensure inmate healthcare needs are being met organization like the American Correctional Association and the National Commission on Correctional Health Care have set standards for facilities to follow. However, these standards are voluntary. It may be difficult from correctional agencies to adhere to guidelines because of financial constraints. As a result litigation is the mainstay of enforcing correctional healthcare standards. Correctional healthcare improvements are piecemeal and typically involve struggling just to reach the minimum standard of care.

There are currently about 2 million people in the U.S. under correctional custody and almost 10 million people every year cycle through custodial care (AC, Seals, & MJ, 2009). The sheer numbers of inmates cycling through the system make it difficult to say the least to ensure reasonable and adequate care is given to inmates. We discussed earlier in this chapter that inmates are growing older in prison and as such the need to provide healthcare is only going to grow as well. Correctional administrators are in a precarious spot because if they fail to give adequate healthcare they can be held legally liable. Yet in order to gain or adhere to standards they need more money. However, one of the first items to be cut in a budget are programs like medical services and treatment. If correctional agencies demonstrate a **deliberate indifference** to the medical needs of an inmate they are held legally liable. The U.S. Supreme Court ruled in *Rufo v. Inmates of Suffolk County Jail*, 502 U.S. 367 (1992) that the infliction of pain by not providing medical services violated the 8th Amendment protection of inmates. Court cases dealing with mental health and inmates protections also impact prison and jail management. *Washington v. Harper*, 494 U.S. 210 (1990) allow prison staff to forcefully administer psychotropic medication to an inmate who is a danger to themselves or other. While *Knecht v. Gillman*, 488 F.2d 1136 (Iowa 1973) prohibit medications being forced on inmates for aversion therapy if the substance was applied without the inmate knowing the consequences of injecting the drug.

The legal consequences of administering or withholding healthcare weather its mental health or physical health is a complex landscape to navigate in the correctional world. It's important to understand that inmates do have rights, however diminished. Correctional staff are tasked with understanding the general nature and purpose of these rights.

# L.  RESEARCH AND POLICY/PRACTICE

If we look at the median amount of money we spend on prison and jail inmates every year is $5,720. This national median number varies greatly from state to state. California spends the most at $19,796 per inmate per year in 2016, while Louisiana spent the least per inmate at $2,173 (McKillop, 2017).

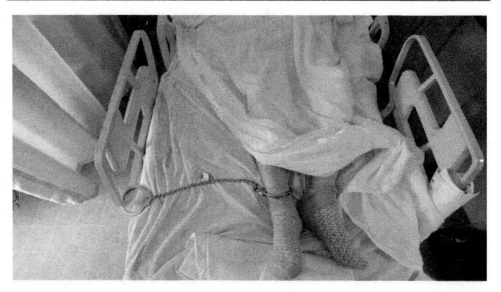

Noah Berger/The Associated Press

Source: (Pew Charitable Trusts, 2018).

Most healthcare for incarcerated inmates takes place inside prison walls. It's well known that healthcare is expensive but it's even more so when it's provided for in prison due to the obvious precautions taken with inmates. The Pew Charitable Trust and the Vera Institute of Justice conducted a research program in 2015, which surveyed state prison officials about healthcare concerns for inmates. The empirical data gathered allowed corrections officials, legislators, and the public insight about how to curb costs while also providing reasonably adequate care for inmates. The study concluded that:

- Off-sight healthcare costs are a significant part of healthcare budgets. Some states spend as much as a quarter of their healthcare budgets on off-sight medical care.

- The model used by most state correctional agencies when considering off-sight services is contingent upon the on-sight medical officials making arrangements for hospitalizations and determines which entity pays the bills.

- The Affordable Care Act (ACA) offers state policy makers to elect to expand their Medicaid programs' eligibility as a way to reduce costs.

- Inmates will continue to have to be transported outside of prison for healthcare, but some states are trying to reduce this number by innovating and saving money.

The research also revealed that's states tend to use one of the four models below.

1. Direct model—clinicians are employed by the state and provide most if not all on-sight care.

2. Contracted model—clinicians are employed by private entities and deliver most of the care on-sight.

3. State university model—the state's public medical school or affiliated organization is responsible for all or most the care on-sight.

4. Hybrid model—on-site care is delivered by some combination of the other models.

**Delivery System Organization Structures, Fiscal 2015**

| Delivery system | States | Number of states |
|---|---|---|
| Direct | Alaska, California, Hawaii, Iowa, Nebraska, Nevada, New York, North Carolina, North Dakota, Ohio, Oklahoma, Oregon, South Carolina, South Dakota, Utah, Washington, and Wisconsin | 17 |
| Contracted | Alabama, Arizona, Arkansas, Delaware, Florida, Idaho, Illinois, Indiana, Kansas, Kentucky, Maine, Maryland, Massachusetts, Mississippi, Missouri, New Mexico, Tennessee, Vermont, West Virginia, and Wyoming | 20 |
| State university | Connecticut, Georgia, New Jersey, and Texas | 4 |
| Hybrid | Colorado, Louisiana, Michigan, Minnesota, Montana, Pennsylvania, Rhode Island, and Virginia | 8 |

Note: New Hampshire did not provide data.

© 2018 The Pew Charitable Trusts

Source: Pew Charitable Trusts.

No one model appears to be more cost efficient or patient response that the other models. The best way to save money while also providing adequate care is to prevent off-sight hospitalizations. The best way researchers found to prevent that from happening was to ensure preventative medical care occurs and that once a health issue arises in an inmate that issue is dealt with promptly. States like Pennsylvania review each inmate's medical history that receives off-sight care to ensure that some type of treatment in prison could have prevented the off-sight hospitalization.

Another issue of importance was re-admittance to an off-sight hospital. The Federal Bureau of Prisons found that 1 in 5 of their Medicare inmates were readmitted to an off-sight hospital 30 days after the initial admittance. California found that focusing on certain prisons with the highest hospital readmission rate is important to identify inmates at the greatest risk for readmission. They developed an **algorithm** to help identify these inmates. As a result the readmission rate fell from 9.3 to 2.4 percent (Pew Charitable Trusts, 2018).

# M. REDUCING THE COSTS

The Affordable Care Act (ACA) is commonly referred to as Obamacare after former president Barack Obama. This healthcare act is extensive and involves many different facets. One of the most important for correctional officials is the ability for states to optionally expand the eligibility for **Medicaid** coverage for people under 65 years of age. Today all but 17 states have expanded Medicaid coverage under the ACA (Henry Kaiser Family Foundation, 2019). This legislation allows more inmates to be covered for medical expenses through federal monies as opposed to state monies. The ACA also holds healthcare vendors financially at risk for off-site inpatient care. Officials in states where Medicaid has been expanded have saved millions of dollars in saving because most correctional hospitalizations have qualified for coverage. Still other states who have expanded their coverage were able to benefit by shifting the processing of hospital claims to state Medicaid agencies. This relieves state correctional officials of that function (Pew Charitable Trusts, 2018).

There are also other ways to save money on off-sight services. Telemedicine allows doctors to video-conference with healthcare personnel inside and outside of prison. This saves money through preventing transportation costs and inmate supervision from officers. Off-sight specialists can identify subtle issues that might otherwise get overlooked by general care staff, thus preventing small medical issues from becoming major issues. Yet another cost saving approach is procurement of mobile medical care. States like Montana use a mobile mammography van to provide services to female inmates where they might otherwise have to transport inmates for serval hundred miles to obtain the service (Karishma, Simon, & DeFrances, 2016).

# N. CONCLUSION

Special populations of inmates present a host of management challenges. Prisons are not unlike the outside community as there are social problems beyond criminality. Prisons and jails cannot avoid the realities and challenges of managing special needs inmates. Those entering the field of corrections must be able to enter this challenging arena with that understanding. Policy makers at the local, state, and federal level are becoming fully aware of what correctional professionals at all levels of the profession have known for many years now.

## Discussion Questions

1.  What is a special needs inmate?

2.  How do special needs inmates present a management problem?

3.  Why is classifying an inmate as "special needs" is an important designation?

4.  What is a Crisis Intervention Team (CIT)?

5.  Why is it important to address communicable diseases of inmates?

6.  What special issues do elderly inmates present to correctional administrators and line staff.

7.  What is the principle of least eligibility?

8.  How does the principle of least eligibility impact how inmate healthcare is administered?

9.  What management issues do mental health inmates present?

10. What are some legal issues that special needs inmates present?

## Student Exercises

1.  Research the number and percent of elderly inmates in your state. How much money and what percent of the state corrections budget is spent on healthcare? Discuss with classmates how healthcare costs of inmates could be reduced. Discuss early release of inmates with serious healthcare issues.

2.  Research the impact solitary confinement has on a person's mental health. Do you thinks solitary confinement is cruel and unusual punishment? What can be done with inmates that are violent or continue to be a danger to staff and other inmates?

## Key Terms

**Algorithm**—a mathematical calculation used to solve a practical or social problem.

**Americans with Disabilities Act**—federal civil rights law that prohibits discrimination against people with disabilities in all areas of public life.

**Baby-boomers**—generational cohort born in the decade after World War II (1945–1955). This cohort increased the entire American population significantly.

**Centers for Disease Control**—federal agency that supports health, prevention of diseases, creates and disseminates health reports, and promotes health care among the general populace.

**Civil Commitment**—the institutionalization or detention of a person based on a court order. Detention is based on the finding that a person is a danger to themselves or others.

**Communicable disease**—infectious disease that can spread from one person to another directly (i.e. sexual contact) or indirectly (a person sneezing on their hand and then touching a surface that another touches).

**Deinstitutionalization**—an era when many public mental health asylums were closed or defunded. As a result people once housed in the facilities were released into the community often without any support system.

**Deliberate indifference**—the conscious or reckless disregard of the consequences of one's actions.

**Greying of America's prisons**—term used to describe how a larger portion of inmates are becoming elderly in prison.

**Illicit drug**—any type of drug that is either illegal to possess without a prescription or is not prescribable.

**Legal liability**—corrections officials are legally responsible by law to adhere to law. In this case inmates can civilly sue a governmental entity or official to obtain legal relief.

**Medicaid**—is a combination of state and federal resources that helps people with limited financial means obtain medical care.

**Mortality rate**—the number of deaths in a given time period or area.

**Prevalence rate**—the number of cases of disease present at a particular time in a particular population.

**Principle of least eligibility**—legal principle which advises prisoners must be given a level of care equal to those at the poverty line.

**Psychotropic medication**—any medication capable of affecting the mind, emotions, or behavior.

**Self-medicate**—when a person uses a substance not prescribed by a licensed mental health or health professional in order to remedy an ailment.

**Special needs inmate**—prisoners who have physical, mental, or programmatic needs that distinguish them from other inmates and whom prison officials respond to in extraordinary ways.

## CHAPTER 10

# Parole and Post-Release Supervision

**Chapter Objectives**

- Define what parole is.

- Understand how and why parole was established.

- Explain the contemporary issues of parole in the U.S.

- Know the difference between discretionary and mandatory release under supervision.

- Understand the basic concepts of parole supervision.

- Explain the efforts to control parole revocations.

- Know what best practices are for parole supervision.

## A. COMMUNITY CORRECTIONS

Community corrections is one of the most frequently used types of correctional measures used in the U.S. today. It often takes one of two forms. The first is probation which we discussed earlier in this text. The other is **parole.** Although probation and parole are two forms of community corrections there are many aspects of parole that are different than probation, of which we will discuss later in this chapter. For now it's important to understand that parole is conditional release from prison into the community.

There are approximately 4 million people under some form of community corrections, the vast majority of them are under probation supervision (3.7 million adults in 2016, that's over 80% of the entire community corrections population). The number of parolees is actually much smaller at 874,000 adults. The number of probationers fell to levels last seen in 1999, while parole number actually increased by .5% (Kaeble, 2018).

There are number of reasons community corrections is utilized at such rates. First, it's rather cost effective. It can cost as much as $25,000 to $47,000 a year to incarcerate one adult in prison and as much as $96,000 to incarcerate a juvenile[1]. Compared to $1,500 to $3,000[2] a year to supervise a person in the community. Secondly, there is greater access to treatment for any number of issues such as mental/physical health, substance abuse, and anger management just to name a few when compared to treatment possibilities in prison.[3] People under community supervision also have greater employment prospects and earning potential than prison offers. There are numerous positive aspects to community supervision however, there are potential negative outcomes for the community. Namely, when someone on community supervision commits a crime. Parole is increasingly acting as a release valve to reduce the number of inmates crowding prisons. This might be one reason for the slight increase in the number of parolees.

Lastly, community corrections and specifically parole is an alternative form of punishment to prison. Here the control is applied in the community and not behind prison walls. There in essence are invisible handcuffs placed on the offender. The goals of community corrections often mirror the socially acceptable goals of the wider scope of punishment. The goals of community corrections are frequently a combination of retribution, rehabilitation, restorative justice, deterrence, and even unique efforts of incapacitation. Just as the wider criminal justice system applies more focus on a particular purpose of punishment, for example focusing more toward retribution than rehabilitation, so too does community corrections change its focus. Parole unlike probation typically allows less leeway concerning technical violations or release. Thus revocation rates can be higher than probation and less intermediate sanctions applied before a parole officer seeks revocation.

## B.  HISTORY OF PAROLE

Parole like probation was established about the same time, mid 1800s. Unlike probation parole was not started in an urban environment where an increase of court cases coupled with a societal change helped facilitate its growth and social acceptance. Initially, judges started to transfer the custody of felons to private businesses. A fee would be paid to those businesses to transport inmates to the American colonies. The practice became an effective way to populate a land that few people dared to go as America at the time was not a preferred destination. This practice lasted until the Revolutionary War started in 1775. When transporting inmates to America was no longer possible a new destination was found. A prison administrator, British Captain Alexander Maconochie, was posted to a penal colony in Australia. He instituted what was known as a "tickets of leave". These tickets were promissory notes issued to inmates that allowed their conditional release from prison. These penal colonies were set up so a prisoner would progress through stages. The first of course involved incarceration. The second was the actual **"ticket of leave"** which allowed the inmate to be conditionally released into the community. These tickets were earned through good behavior. If the conditions were violated the offender would be returned to prison. The final stage involved a complete restoration of liberty. Sir Walter Crofton, a prison administrator in Ireland and employee of the British government also began to allow tickets of leave in 1854. His system was a bit more structured it involved the following:

- Report to the constable (police) upon release from prison and subsequent arrival to the place of residence.

- Abstain from any law violation.

- Refrain from habitually associating with those of notorious bad character.

- Obtain employment and/or refrain from living and idle life.

- Produce the ticket of leave when requested by police or a magistrate.

- Notify the constable prior to changing residence.

Many ideas about corrections were being shared between Britain and the U.S. during this time. The concept of parole was no exception. It did not take long for parole to become implemented in some areas of the U.S. Zebulon Brockway (1876) is largely credited for establishing parole here. Mr. Brockway was a prison administrator at the Elmira Reformatory in New York.[4] During this time correctional sentencing was undergoing a change. Flat-time prison sentences were being replaced by an indeterminate sentencing structure. If you recall from Chapter 3 of this text indeterminate sentencing allows the judge to sentence the inmate to a range (i.e. 3–7 years). Indeterminate sentences allow prisoners to be released early on parole.

## C. CONTEMPORARY PAROLE IN AMERICA

We noted earlier the entire parole population increased slightly n 2016 (.5%). However, the rate increase was the slowest since 2010 (Kaeble, 2018). The number of people under parole supervision has been growing slowly and steadily each year for the

> **Class exercise**—Find the parole population report from your states department of corrections website. What are the demographics of the people on parole on your state? What are some special issues parolees encounter upon release from prison?

better part of the last decade. Each year almost 700,00 people are released on parole (Kaeble, 2018). This is no doubt due to the large number of people incarcerated previously that are now nearing the end of their prison terms and now being released on parole. As the prison population slowly reduces the number of people on parole will grow.

Figure 10.1

Adults on Parole in the U.S., 2016

| Jurisdiction | Parole population December 31, 2015 | Parole population January 1, 2016 | Entries Reported | Entries Estimated | Exits Reported | Exits Estimated | Parole population, December 31, 2016 | Change, 2016 Number | Change, 2016 Percent | Number on parole per 100,000 U.S. adult residents, December 31, 2016 |
|---|---|---|---|---|---|---|---|---|---|---|
| U.S. total | 870,526 | 870,657 | 422,975 | 457,100 | 428,022 | 456,000 | 874,777 | 4,120 | 0.5% | 349 |
| Federal | 114,471 | 114,746 | 45,469 | 45,469 | 48,108 | 48,108 | 114,385 | -361 | -0.3% | 46 |
| State | 756,055 | 755,911 | 377,506 | 411,700 | 379,914 | 407,900 | 760,392 | 4,481 | 0.6% | 303 |
| Alabama | 8,138 | 8,150 | 2,515 | 2,515 | 2,103 | 2,103 | 8,562 | 412 | 5.1 | 227 |
| Alaska | .. | 2,100 | 717 | 700 | 1,005 | 1,000 | 1,812 | -288 | -13.7 | 326 |
| Arizona | 7,379 | 7,379 | 11,481 | 11,481 | 11,360 | 11,360 | 7,500 | 121 | 1.6 | 140 |
| Arkansas | 23,093 | 22,910 | 10,868 | 10,868 | 9,902 | 9,902 | 23,792 | 882 | 3.8 | 1,038 |
| California | 86,053 | 86,053 | 26,007 | 53,100 | 23,212 | 45,600 | 93,598 | 7,545 | 8.8 | 309 |
| Colorado | 10,269 | 9,953 | 7,657 | 7,657 | 7,424 | 7,424 | 10,186 | 233 | 2.3 | 236 |
| Connecticut | 2,939 | 2,939 | 2,591 | 2,591 | 2,151 | 2,151 | 3,379 | 440 | 15.0 | 119 |
| Delaware | 425 | 425 | 129 | 129 | 167 | 167 | 387 | -38 | -8.9 | 52 |
| District of Columbia | 4,594 | 4,548 | 1,330 | 1,330 | 1,853 | 1,853 | 4,025 | -523 | -11.5 | 713 |
| Florida | 4,611 | 4,611 | 6,110 | 6,110 | 6,155 | 6,155 | 4,566 | -45 | -1.0 | 27 |
| Georgia | 24,130 | 24,413 | 9,434 | 9,434 | 11,461 | 11,461 | 22,386 | -2,027 | -8.3 | 285 |
| Hawaii | 1,540 | 1,479 | 629 | 629 | 822 | 822 | 1,367 | -112 | -7.6 | 122 |
| Idaho | 4,875 | 4,875 | 3,055 | 3,055 | 2,876 | 2,876 | 5,054 | 179 | 3.7 | 402 |
| Illinois | 29,146 | 29,629 | 23,889 | 23,889 | 25,083 | 25,083 | 29,428 | -201 | -0.7 | 298 |
| Indiana | 9,434 | 9,420 | 7,056 | 7,056 | 8,091 | 8,091 | 8,385 | -1,035 | -11.0 | 165 |
| Iowa | 5,918 | 5,901 | 3,810 | 3,810 | 3,660 | 3,660 | 6,051 | 150 | 2.5 | 251 |
| Kansas | 4,331 | 4,331 | 4,465 | 4,465 | 3,966 | 3,966 | 4,830 | 499 | 11.5 | 220 |
| Kentucky | 16,563 | 16,536 | 10,757 | 10,757 | 11,910 | 11,910 | 15,383 | -1,153 | -7.0 | 448 |
| Louisiana | 31,187 | 31,187 | 15,888 | 15,888 | 16,168 | 16,168 | 30,907 | -280 | -0.9 | 864 |
| Maine | 21 | 21 | 1 | 1 | 1 | 1 | 21 | 0 | -- | 2 |
| Maryland | 10,887 | 10,887 | 4,295 | 4,295 | 4,877 | 4,877 | 10,305 | -582 | -5.3 | 220 |
| Massachusetts | 1,978 | 1,995 | 2,111 | 2,111 | 2,255 | 2,255 | 1,851 | -144 | -7.2 | 34 |
| Michigan | 17,909 | .. | .. | .. | .. | .. | .. | .. | .. | 216 |
| Minnesota | 6,808 | 6,810 | 7,129 | 7,129 | 6,864 | 6,864 | 7,075 | 265 | 3.9 | 167 |
| Mississippi | 8,424 | 8,424 | 6,597 | 6,597 | 6,376 | 6,376 | 8,645 | 221 | 2.6 | 381 |
| Missouri | 17,694 | 17,657 | 13,255 | 13,255 | 13,120 | 13,120 | 17,792 | 135 | 0.8 | 377 |
| Montana | 1,092 | 1,092 | 533 | 533 | 551 | 551 | 1,074 | -18 | -1.6 | 131 |
| Nebraska | 1,043 | 1,050 | 1,537 | 1,537 | 1,499 | 1,499 | 1,088 | 38 | 3.6 | 76 |
| Nevada | 5,507 | 5,507 | 3,635 | 3,635 | 3,881 | 3,881 | 5,261 | -246 | -4.5 | 230 |
| New Hampshire | 2,451 | 2,451 | 1,461 | 1,461 | 1,476 | 1,476 | 2,436 | -15 | -0.6 | 226 |
| New Jersey | 15,180 | 15,180 | 5,539 | 5,539 | 5,591 | 5,591 | 15,128 | -52 | -0.3 | 217 |
| New Mexico | 2,888 | 2,763 | 2,384 | 2,384 | 2,367 | 2,367 | 2,780 | 17 | 0.6 | 175 |
| New York | 44,562 | 44,562 | 20,443 | 20,443 | 20,579 | 20,579 | 44,426 | -136 | -0.3 | 285 |
| North Carolina | 11,744 | 11,744 | 13,647 | 13,647 | 12,388 | 12,388 | 12,726 | 982 | 8.4 | 161 |
| North Dakota | 644 | 634 | 1,545 | 1,545 | 1,375 | 1,375 | 804 | 170 | 26.8 | 138 |
| Ohio | 18,284 | 18,284 | 8,085 | 8,085 | 6,735 | 6,735 | 19,634 | 1,350 | 7.4 | 218 |
| Oklahoma | 2,116 | 2,116 | 383 | 383 | 604 | 604 | 1,895 | -221 | -10.4 | 64 |
| Oregon | .. | 24,077 | 9,561 | 9,600 | 8,927 | 8,900 | 24,711 | 634 | 2.6 | 760 |
| Pennsylvania | 112,351 | 112,351 | 61,179 | 61,179 | 62,443 | 62,443 | 111,087 | -1,264 | -1.1 | 1,097 |
| Rhode Island | 433 | 441 | 239 | 239 | 220 | 220 | 460 | 19 | 4.3 | 54 |
| South Carolina | 5,021 | 4,963 | 2,460 | 2,460 | 3,076 | 3,076 | 4,347 | -616 | -12.4 | 112 |
| South Dakota | 2,652 | 2,673 | 1,788 | 1,788 | 1,774 | 1,774 | 2,687 | 14 | 0.5 | 410 |
| Tennessee | 13,093 | 13,063 | 3,353 | 3,353 | 4,324 | 4,324 | 12,092 | -971 | -7.4 | 234 |
| Texas | 111,892 | 111,892 | 35,398 | 35,398 | 36,003 | 36,003 | 111,287 | -605 | -0.5 | 537 |
| Utah | 3,506 | 3,502 | 2,640 | 2,640 | 2,435 | 2,435 | 3,707 | 205 | 5.9 | 172 |
| Vermont | 1,090 | 1,083 | .. | 600 | .. | 700 | 935 | -148 | -13.7 | 185 |
| Virginia | 1,576 | 1,576 | 711 | 711 | 601 | 601 | 1,650 | 74 | 4.7 | 25 |
| Washington | 11,198 | 11,131 | 5,782 | 5,782 | 5,591 | 5,591 | 11,322 | 191 | 1.7 | 198 |
| West Virginia | 3,123 | 3,123 | 2,113 | 2,113 | 1,686 | 1,686 | 3,550 | 427 | 13.7 | 244 |
| Wisconsin | 19,453 | 20,241 | .. | 6,500 | 1,450 | 6,400 | 20,401 | 160 | 0.8 | 453 |
| Wyoming | 812 | 783 | 691 | 691 | 632 | 632 | 842 | 59 | 7.5 | 189 |

Source: BJS Kaeble 2018.

As we see in Figure 10.1 the largest number of people on Parole in the U.S. are from the federal prison system. We need to be aware the term "parole" is a bit of a misnomer since parole in the federal system was abolished in the late 1980s. If we are going to be precise they have the largest overall number of people under post-release supervision. This is due to the federal prison system (Bureau of

Prisons) holding the highest number of inmates. In response to the slowly rising numbers of people on parole the resources in funding and personnel will need to grow. Technology and addressing parolee's risks and needs will be one of the responses to a growing population. As we noted in Chapter 9, there are a number of inmates with physical and mental health issues, substance abuse problems, amongst other impediments. Upon release those issues do not go away. Those issues may become exacerbated by incarceration. When the person is released on parole they not only deal with those issues but now have to find a place to live, employment, meet parole requirements, all while encountering many of the same social influences that facilitated their criminal behavior to begin with. Succeeding on parole can be a difficult prospect for many. The job of a parole officer can certainly be challenging.

The major issues parolees and those that administer parole are:

Parolees:

1.  Receiving health care (physical and mental)—Care upon release and maintaining support throughout the term of supervision and beyond has become a major issue. Well over 95% of inmates will be released we know from Chapter 9 in this text that a large number of prison inmates have mental health issues. Finding services in the community for inmates can be challenging. Heading off issues that may result in revocation or new criminal charges is a pressing concern.

2.  Employment—Over a quarter of those released are unemployed. Far more are **underemployed**. A job, especially a job that pays well and has good benefits (i.e. insurance and pension) not only benefits the parolee but also means the person is paying taxes, keeping occupied in a prosocial manner, and recidivism rates are vastly reduced. Unemployed offenders under supervision had a renovation rate 500% higher than those who were employed (Rakis, 2013).

3.  Housing—Almost 10% of those leaving a correctional facility are homeless in the months prior to and upon leaving prison (McKernan, 2019). Those with parolees with mental illness have even higher rates of homelessness than other parolees (Aidala, 2014).

4.  **Revocation**—Of course is a concern for both parolees and corrections officials. Almost a quarter of people on parole will be

reincarcerated for a parole violation (Laskorunsky, 2019). The first six months after release is the most likely time during a person's release where they are likely to have their parole revoked (Petersilia, 2003).

5.  Education and **vocational training**—41% of prison inmates do not have a high school diploma or a **GED**. Education and vocational training are directly related to employment and employability.

6.  Reintegration—Reintegration involves what was addressed above (i.e. education, employment, and housing). However, there are some nuances outside of those areas that all parolees or people convicted of certain offenses have that make it difficult from them to transition back into the mainstream of society. For instance in many jurisdictions people convicted of felonies are not allowed to vote. This can create a level of **disenfranchisement.** Unless otherwise sealed by a court of law and adults criminal record is a public record. People can access these records quite easily through many different methods, but this access has been made very easy though internet services. Sex offenders and others convicted of certain other crimes must register their whereabouts with authorities and in many cases their whereabouts are made public. These can create problems for parolees trying to find housing or jobs.

## D. DEMOGRAPHICS OF PAROLEES

**Weblink**—Visit the following website to view your state's parole statistics information:

https://nicic.gov/state-statistics-information

The characteristics or demographics of a state's parolee population is fairly diverse. It typically mirrors the characteristics of the prison population. That said as we know from Chapter 6, in this text there are a disproportionate number of minorities in prison and thus we see a disproportionate number of minorities on parole as well. Please visit the web link on this page for more information about the demographic makeup of your state. Figure 10.2 below is a look at the aggregate numbers of parolees in the U.S.

Figure 10.2

Adult Parole Demographics in the US

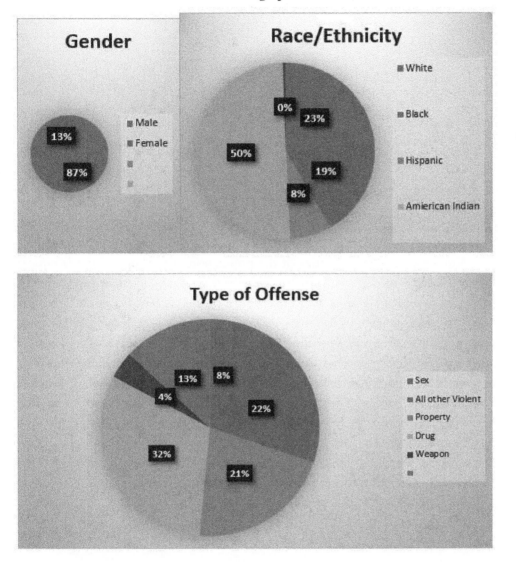

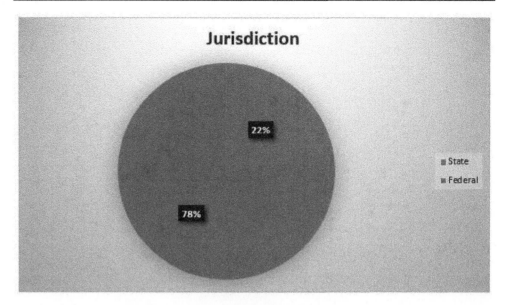

Knowing the characteristics of the population under supervision is critical. Figure 10.2 tells us some information but there are many more nuances that are particular to each state or even to areas with a state. Parolees from rural areas can offer challenges to supervision that is not a factor to parole officers in urban areas. For instance parolees must usually be seen at home. **Home contacts** are a regular part of parole supervision but some if these people may live in rural areas far from parole offices, thus parole officers spend several hours each week making required home contacts. Services such as drug and alcohol treatment, mental and physical healthcare, and sex offender therapy may take hours to get to in rural areas. As a result some urban or cities large enough to support such services can become cities where parolees must live to obtain parole required services. The "Corrections in Action" segment below details this problem.

## Corrections in Action

Wichita, KS has a population of almost 400,000 people. It lies in Sedgwick County which has a population of 513, 607 people. It is located in the south central part of the state and is the most populous city and county in the state. In fiscal year 2018 1,041 people were sent to state prison from Kansas courts. Yet in that same year 1,243 people were released on post-release supervision (i.e. parole) (Kansas Department of Corrections, 2018). Johnson County, which is in the greater Kansas City metropolitan area, received the second most releases at 356 parolees. Sedgwick county and the city of Wichita receive almost 31% of the entire state of Kansas parole releases.

On any given day one out of three suspects in crime is a parolee or registered offender (Potter, 2019). "Many are serious crimes from theft to murder" notes Wichita Police Chief Jose Salcido (Potter, 2019). In one recent case citizens called police about a "suspicious vehicle" upon further investigation by police they discovered a registered sex offender from north-central Kansas was attempting to solicit children for sex. What is drawing parolees and registered offenders are the promise of jobs. Employment opportunities are much more abundant in urban areas like Wichita than in rural Kansas. Also there are a number of resources like mental health clinics who can provide services not available in rural areas or small towns.

The large number of parolees coming to Wichita has put a strain on resources. About a quarter of homeless resources go to homeless parolees. It's not only resources that are strained by the influx of parolees. In 2015, a parolee named Robert Greeson was sent to live at the only men's state correctional work release facility which is in Wichita. This is a 250 bed facility. His convictions were from counties in the southeast part of the state. After spending a few months at the work release facility he went on a crime spree which ended in a shootout with police. He was killed in the shootout but not after fatally wounding Sedgwick County Sheriff's Deputy Robert Kunze.

Wichita is unique in Kansas because it has resources that draw parolees to it for employment, therapy and mental health resources amongst other features that make it attractive. Yet it's not unique when we consider other states that have seen rural and small town employment opportunities vanish. Closing mental and physical care facilities has hit nonurban areas especially hard as many clinics and treatment facilities have contracted back to cities.

## E. PAROLE AND POST-RELEASE

Every state has some type of supervised release for inmates leaving prison. However, not all inmates will be under some form of community supervision as some inmates **max out** their time while in prison. Those that do not max out their time in prison will undergo some type of supervision. The mechanism of release for these people differs with each jurisdiction. The mechanism of release is either discretionary or mandatory. Parole in the true sense of the word is discretionary. An inmate is seen by a **parole board** and they have the discretion to release the person on parole or continue to incarcerate them. The mechanism of release in jurisdictions that require inmates to be mandatorily discharged from prison is referred to as post-release. The mechanism of release for inmate under post-release supervision is simply time. The inmate will serve a determined amount of time in prison and once that time has expired they are mandatorily released under post-release supervision. Jurisdictions that use post-release still refer to this practice as "parole" as it is a more common term and more easily understood than post-release.

Figure 10.3

Parole and Post-Release

| PAROLE | POST-RELEASE |
|---|---|
| • Mechanism of release is discretionary. A parole board meets and decides release or continued incarceration<br><br>• Utilized in an indeterminate sentencing model<br><br>• Revocation for technical violations can result in the parolee serving years of incarceration | • Mechanism of release is mandatory. An inmate must be released by law when they have served the time allotted at sentencing<br><br>• Utilized in determinate sentencing models<br><br>• Revocation for technical parole violations result in a specific and determined period of incarceration, typically a few months |

Historically states and the Federal prison system used parole and an indeterminate sentencing model. However, in the late 1970s and into the early 1990s prison systems began to shift to a determinate sentencing model. This shift was due to several factors. One of those factors was based on what was at the time accepted empirical data whereby a researcher, Robert Martinson, claimed that "nothing worked" in reference to prison rehabilitation programs and by proxy rehabilitation anywhere in corrections (Liptin, 1975). This position was supported by people wanting to become tougher on crime and at the other end of the spectrum from those that saw prison as no place to "force" treatment upon people who were not truly seeking treatment modalities (Cullen & Cullen, 1988). The

Weblink—Even though there is no longer "parole" in the federal criminal system there is still a U.S. Parole Commission. Visit the following website to see that this agency does:

https://www.justice.gov/uspc

combination of research that advised, "nothing works", growing public sentiment for more harsh correctional measures, and an increase in correctional funding that fueled a prison building boom contributed toward a shift to determinate sentencing and thus 19 states currently have either completely abolished parole or severely limited it use choosing instead to replace it with post-release supervision. The Sentencing Reform Act of 1984, does not allow people convicted of federal crimes after November 1st 1987. This act effectively eliminated parole for federal crimes.

> **Class exercise**—Find out if your state has mandatory (i.e. post release) or discretionary release (i.e. parole). Which type of release do you think is more effective at rehabilitation and thus community safety?

There are advantages and disadvantages of parole and post-release. Some states offer a mix of mandatory and discretionary release in an attempt to maximize the benefits of both types of release. States like Missouri and Tennessee have discretionary release for some types of crime while keeping mandatory release for other types of crime.

Figure 10.4

| Parole Advantages | Post-Release Advantages |
|---|---|
| • Incentivizes good behavior in prison which fosters a safer prison environment<br>• It can influence inmates to take and complete a variety of programs (i.e. education, substance treatment, anger management, life skills, etc.)<br>• It allows officials to release those deemed as a reduced risk to reoffend and lessen the prison population | • The inmate knows exactly when they are going to be released from prison so they can plan their release<br>• There is no discriminatory release thus there is no opportunity for discrimination impacting release<br>• Victims and the community know when the inmate will be released thus a sense of justice is established |
| Parole Disadvantages | Post-Release Disadvantages |
| • Parole Boards can release inmates that appear to be at a reduced risk to reoffend only to have them continue to commit crime once released<br>• Since the release is discretionary this allows an opportunity for discriminatory releases (i.e. white | • The inmate is released regardless of poor behavior (if exhibited) while in prison<br>• There is no "release valve" for overcrowded prison systems<br>• Revocation for technical violations of parole are not lengthy thus violating parole |

| | |
|---|---|
| inmates being released at higher rates than minority inmates<br>• The community and victims view of parole can be that it allows inmates to release early and "escape justice" | does not carry much of a consequence |

The benefits and cost of each type of release is debatable. The evolutionary nature of corrections and specifically parole or post-release will change as more research is collected. The decision to use mandatory or discretionary release may be one of the most influx aspects in corrections as some states that switched to a determinate sentencing model and mandatory sentences are now starting to implement more discretionary types of release (Ireland, 2005).

## F. PAROLE HEARING

34 states currently use discretionary release or parole (Rhine, Watts, Alexis, & Reitz, 2018). In order for an inmate to be granted parole an inmate must convince a panel of parole board members to release them from prison early. Parole boards consist of 3 to as many as 19 members. Many states allow an inmate parole based on a majority vote. Each state has their own parole process. Below is the state of Michigan's parole process:

# Parole - The Parole Process

PAROLE BOARD DECISIONS

Normally, the prisoner first comes to the attention of the Parole Board as he/she nears the end of the minimum term imposed by the court. The date of parole eligibility is often called the Earliest Release Date (ERD). Approximately 8 months prior to the parole eligibility date, a Parole Eligibility Report is prepared and the prisoner will be scheduled for consideration by the Board. The Board considers many factors to determine whether parole should be granted. State law holds that "A prisoner shall not be given liberty on parole until the board has reasonable assurance, after consideration of all of the facts and circumstances, including the prisoner's mental and social attitude, that the prisoner will not become a menace to society or to the public safety." Most prisoners are interviewed by one member of the Parole Board. The scope of the interview includes the prisoner's criminal, social and substance abuse history, previous adjustment on parole or probation, conduct in prison, programming, parole plans, and other factors. The prisoner may have a representative at the interview, although the representative cannot be another prisoner or an attorney. The parole decision is made by majority vote of a three member panel of the Board. If granted a parole, the prisoner is allowed to return to the community under the supervision of a Parole Agent for a specified term. The release is conditioned upon the parolee's compliance with terms set by the Parole Board.

Below is the public telephone number and address for the Michigan Department of Corrections Parole Board. Please feel free to contact them with any concerns or problems related to prisoner parole issues. Public correspondence regarding a possible parole remains in an offender's file and is read prior to a parole board hearing. If you want to write a letter of support for a prisoner, you should do so and send it to the prisoner directly. That way the prisoner can bring it to the Parole Board interview.

Source: Michigan Department of Corrections.

As you note from the Michigan Process 8 months prior to the earliest release date (ERD) the inmate eligibility report is prepared. The inmate will be interviewed by a board member. In other jurisdictions the eligibility even to be seen by a parole board depends on different factors not just the earliest release date. Below is the eligibility for an inmate in Kentucky:

**Eligibility for Parole**

Parole eligibility is established by statute and regulation. Those convicted as violent offenders, must serve 85 percent of their sentence before becoming eligible for parole. Many convicted of being a persistent felony offender are not eligible for parole until they have serve at least ten years of their sentence. Convicted sex offenders do not become eligible for parole until they have completed a sex offender treatment program administered by the Department of Corrections. All other incarcerated felons become eligible for parole after serving 20 percent of their sentence.

Eligibility for parole in no way guarantees that an inmate will be granted parole.

Source: Kentucky Department of Corrections.

**Board Decision-Making Process**

The Board has three decision options:

**Serve Out -**
The inmate must spend the balance of his/her sentence incarcerated.

**Deferment -**
The Board sets a period of months or years before the inmate will again become eligible to meet the Board;

**Parole**
In all decisions, the Board considers the seriousness of the current offense, prior criminal record, institutional adjustment, attitude toward authority, history of alcohol or drug involvement, history of prior probation, shock probation or parole violation, education and job skills, employment history, emotional stability, mental capacities, health or illness, history of deviant behavior, official and community attitudes toward accepting the inmate back into the community, oral and written statements of victims, and parole plan, which includes home placement, job placement, and need for community treatment and follow up.

Source: Kentucky Department of Corrections.

As we can see there are three possible outcomes for an inmate seeking parole in Kentucky. The first is an outright denial of parole whereby the inmate must serve out their sentence with no future hope at parole. The second is "deferment" which means the inmate does not meet the standards for release at the time but may petition for parole in the future. The last outcome is of course release on parole.

How and who staffs a parole board is jurisdictionally dependent often times the state governor will appoint members. Members can be correctional professionals, business people, clerics, etc. There typically are no qualifications for members which can lead to some trepidation amongst correctional professionals (Burns, Kinkade, & Scott, 1999). The decision to grant parole is often based on many factors some decisions can seem arbitrary and based on hunches, suppositions, and feelings. The possibility for wrong decisions is of course a possibility. Also, there is concern that discrimination plays a factor in the decision to release or not. To help aid parole boards there are now different risk and needs instruments to help boards make informed decisions about release. The use of **Structured Decision Making Frameworks** helps boards make decisions without bias and instinct. The National Institute of Corrections (NIC) helped sponsor research on this topic. This tool emphasize seven different areas of concentration:

1.  Does the inmate have reasonable post-release plans for housing, employment, community resources, intervention steps in case of crisis, familial support.

2.  The extent to which the delivery of programs while incarcerated are or can be incorporated upon release.

3. The inmates behavior while incarcerated or if previously released on parole.

4. Any unique factors such as health issues.

5. Evidence of benefits from participation in prison programming.

6. Factors that influence inmate behavior such as substance abuse history, peer influence, impulsivity etc.

7. The inmates past criminal history if any or severity of past criminal history.

Parole board decision making will continue to be scrutinized. The process of decision making will continue to evolve as more states use different tools to aid in decision making. Predicting future criminal behavior is very difficult. We look at aggregate data in order to assess some generalities and rates of offending while also looking at individual factors that change throughout the life course. The decision to grant parole or not is certainly a difficult one. A parolee committing crime in the community when they otherwise would have been incarcerated is not a pleasant thought. On the other hand how do we incentivize time spent in prison? How do we encourage change?

## G. PAROLE SUPERVISION

Regardless the type of release the main function of parole is to provide supervision to those released. What is supervision? What do parole officers do? The common thread no matter the jurisdiction is that parole officers (post-release as well) ensure that the parolee is abiding by the conditions of their release. The conditions of release vary by jurisdiction but some common conditions of release are:

- To no commit any new crimes while on supervision.

- Not to use drugs or alcohol.

- Reporting to parole officer as directed.

- Not possessing any guns or other weapons.

- Agreeing to search upon parole officer request.

- Not changing address unless parolee informs officer prior to address change.

- Enter and successfully complete any programing (i.e. drug and alcohol treatment, mental health therapy as requested by the parole officer, sex offender treatment).

Parolees typically have **general conditions of parole** which apply to everyone while on supervision. Below are the standard conditions of parole for the state of Connecticut.

Figure 10.5

State of Connecticut Conditions of Parole

Date: _____

Name of Child/Youth _____ DOB: _____

Date of Home Placement _____ End of Commitment Date: _____

The Commissioner of Children and Families, or his/her designee, having reviewed and considered your case, has decided to place you on Parole Status at:

Address of Home Placement: _____

City: _____ State: _____ Zip: _____

Parole Status is granted to you subject to the conditions set forth in Connecticut General Statutes §17a-7 and §17a-8, with the clear understanding that should you violate any condition of your Parole, the Commissioner or his/her designee may revoke your Parole Status and place you at any institution, resource, or facility administered by or available to the Department of Children and Families, including, for boys, Connecticut Juvenile Training School in Middletown, Connecticut.. Whenever problems arise or you do not understand what is expected of you on Parole Status, it is your responsibility to consult your: _____ at _____

Parole Officer Name                    Phone Number

He or she will assist you and explain your Conditions of Parole.

If at any time you believe your placement is not meeting your treatment needs, you may request a Treatment Plan Hearing, by writing to the Commissioner of DCF., specifically stating the elements of your treatment plan with which you are not in agreement. You may ask your lawyer or parent to help you do this, or you may write the letter yourself. You are encouraged to speak with your Parole Officer and to request a Treatment Plan Hearing rather than leave your placement without permission. If you do leave your placement without permission, you will be in violation of your Parole and face the possibility of admission to a secure or non-secure facility.

REMEMBER, at any time you may contact your Parole Officer to discuss problems with your placement or treatment plan, especially issues that may influence you to leave your placement without permission.

**NOTE:** *Connecticut law permits the Department to revoke your Parole status whenever revocation is determined to be in your best interests. Therefore, it is possible, although unlikely, that your Parole status will be revoked even if you have not violated a specific Condition of Parole.*

**CONDITIONS OF YOUR PAROLE ARE AS FOLLOWS:**

1. You must obey the rules and requirements of the above-named placement.
2. You must not leave the above-named placement without first obtaining permission from your Parole Officer. When you are eligible for passes, arrangements, including visit address and phone number, must be verified and approved by your Parole Officer before each pass is issued. Out-of-state visits require that one week prior notice be given to your Parole Officer. The Department reserves the right to restrict passes on certain holidays or during specific events.
3. You must not own, possess, use, sell, or have under your control any dangerous weapon or firearm.
4. You must not use, or have in your possession or control, any illegal drug or narcotic (marijuana, crack, cocaine, heroin, acid, barbiturates, etc.)
5. You must not possess or consume alcoholic beverages, or any form of intoxicant, or abuse legal or illegal substances.
6. You **must comply with random drug screening** by Parole Services or its designee.
7. You must attend school regularly and attend all classes. If you are not in school due to suspension or other educational issues, your Parole Officer must be notified. If you are not in school because of age, you must seek full-time employment.
8. You must obey all state and local laws. If you are arrested for **ANY** reason, you are required to immediately report the nature of the incident and offense(s) by contacting your Parole Officer or Connecticut Juvenile Training School at **860-638-2400** or after 4:45 p.m. at **1-860-638-2897.** If placed in detention or jail, you must inform detention or correctional officials that you are a DCF committed delinquent on Parole.

---

> **Web exercise**—Find and review the general conditions of parole in your state. Are there any you would delete or add as general conditions? Discuss why you would make those changes.

The general conditions vary by state. As we can see from the example above the person prior to release will review the conditions of parole. They sign it and a prison official such as an **institutional parole officer** also signs it. They are given a copy to take with them. Once they meet the officer assigned to them they will review the document again to address any concerns or questions. While everyone on parole must abide by general conditions some parolees may have special conditions of parole that are unique to the person being supervised. For example a common special condition or parole for those convicted of a sex offense is to not have any unsupervised contact with people under 18 years of age. The purpose of course is an attempt to reduce potential access to new victims. This condition can present a challenge to the parolee and parole officer as the only possible residence for the parolee may house children. Also, parolees with this conditions that also have children may have a difficult time residing with them. Ultimately though the condition or the purpose of the condition is to protect vulnerable potential victims. Other special conditions may revolve around the circumstances of the crime that resulted in a prison sentence such as computer crime. Therefore parolees with this type of conviction may be prevented from owning or accessing a computer. If they are allowed access to a computer software can be installed to monitor what they are accessing online. The type and number of special conditions are tailored to prevent future crimes from occurring and also as a measure of rehabilitation.

Once released the parolee is assigned to a parole officer. Every parole officer has a caseload of parolees. By assigning a specific officer to a specific parolee the parolee has a dedicated point of contact and a person that is uniquely familiar with the parolees. Some officers handle only parolees with a certain type of conviction or a certain type of parolee. This can be a past conviction for which they are no longer on parole for or their **instant offense(s).** These officers handle a **specialized caseload**. Different jurisdictions have different categories to specialize in. A few of these specialized caseloads include:

1. Specialized caseload of sex offenders—officers supervising this category of parolee "sex offender" have to be familiar with sex offender treatment which can be complex. Understanding the treatment process is essential. Sex offenders have to register as such and this too can be time consuming as well as involve specific legal information.

2. Mental health specialization—parole officers must understand different types of psychological diagnosis, treatments, and medication. It's very important that officers communicate with those providing treatment and local law enforcement in order to prevent violence.

3. High risk/violent prone parolees—parole officers receive specific training about gangs and gang violence. They work closely with law enforcement to ensure conditions of parole are met and enforced. They supervise the parolee closely often contacting the parolee at home, place of employment, or places frequented by the parolee.

The reason officers specialize is the same reason a medical doctor would specialize in a certain kind of medicine. An officer with a specialized caseload receives specific training on how to deal with a certain type of offender. Their responsibilities are often elevated when they have a specialized caseload. Specialization ensure the officer is uniquely familiar with treatment modalities, safety hazards, and evidence-based practices to be implemented in order to effectively address offense specific problems.

# H. ADMINISTRATION OF PAROLE

The administration of parole is usually done through the executive branch of government. A state governor will select a secretary of corrections. This person is responsible for parole supervision as well as institutional corrections. A deputy secretary for parole or field services, as it is sometimes referred to, is tasked with overseeing that branch of corrections. The policy or philosophy of how parole will focus is determined by those in the upper echelon of correctional administration. For instance the overall philosophy may center on rehabilitation thus the major thrust efforts with parole would gravitate toward programs dedicated to mental health or educational/vocational rehabilitation. The correctional philosophy of these administrators establishes the strategy of the agency.

> **Class exercise**—Visit your state's corrections website and learn about who your state's secretary of corrections is. Discover who the administrator for parole is. Is the agency philosophy focused on rehabilitation or strict enforcement of the conditions? Discuss with the class.

The federal government does not use parole. If you recall the Crime Control Act of 1984, removed parole for federal offenses. The federal justice system utilizes a determinate sentencing model, thus when an inmate reaches the time they were allotted to per the sentence they are released for a **term of supervision (TSR)**. Unlike most states whereby the administration of parole is done through the executive branch of government the administration of parole or the "term of supervision" is overseen through the judicial branch of government. The **Administrative Office** (AO) is part of the U.S. court system of which the U.S. Supreme Court is ultimately responsible for. The AO provides policy and guidance to each U.S. District Court. Figure 10.6 is a map of the Federal District Courts and the Court of Appeals Circuits.

Figure 10.6

U.S. District Courts and Appeals Courts

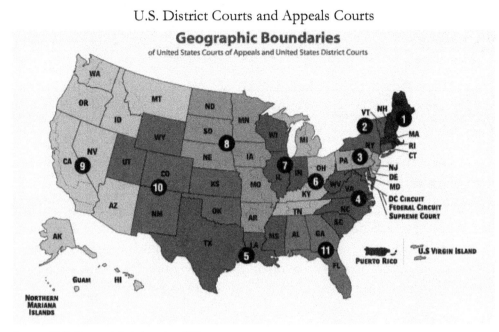

Source: U.S. Courts Administrative Office.

Some states like Idaho are a single U.S. Court District while other more populous so states like Texas have 4 separate U.S. Judicial Districts. There are 94 separate U.S. Court Districts and even though the policy for TSR (i.e. parole) is established by the Administrative Office in Washington D.C. each Federal district has some latitude about what programs they are going to administer amongst other initiatives. Every District operates under a shared national mission but management is considered local. One example concerns arming officers. For instance the Federal District of South Dakota does not currently allow federal probation/parole officers to carry firearms while on duty. It is up to the discretion of each federal district court **Chief Judge** usually in consultation with the **Chief U.S. Probation Officer** to make such decisions. Although TSR is a post-release prison function the U.S. Probation Office is responsible for probation as well as TSR. The overwhelming majority of federal offenders under community supervision are on TSR from prison.

Number of People Under Federal Community Supervision Dec. 31, 2018

| Persons Under Supervision | Parole | Probation | Term of Supervised Release (TSR) | BOP Custody | % of total on TSR |
|---|---|---|---|---|---|
| 128,412 | 908 | 15,252 | 112,148 | 104 | 87% |

Source: U.S. Courts Administrative Office (US District Courts Administrative Office, 2018).

As we can see the overwhelming majority of people under federal community corrections supervision are those that have served time in prison.

The term of supervised release is dictated by the court at sentencing and just like any other jurisdiction that uses a determinate sentencing model the offender or soon to be inmate has a good understanding of how much time they will have to spend in prison and once released how much time they will spend on community supervision if they don't have their supervision revoked.

# I.   REVOCATION

When a parolee violates the conditions of their release there are a number of intermediate sanctions that an officer can utilize. However, sometimes the violations are serious enough to warrant an immediate need to seek revocation or when intermediate sanctions fail a last resort might be to seek revocation and returning the person to prison. When parolees violate their parole by failing to follow the conditions of their parole it is referred to as a technical violation. When they violate parole it's of course a technical violation but also referred to as a new offense. As you might imagine returning to prison based on a technical violation is less serious than returning to prison after committing a new crime. In the case where a parolee commits a new crime while in the community they are subject to serving a new prison sentence based on a conviction.

When a parole officer decides to seek revocation they request a warrant or an arrest order to be issued. The parolee is taken into custody. Some states and federal districts allow the parole officer to arrest the parolee while other states or jurisdictions do not give officers the authority to make arrests. Once the person is in custody they are afforded a parole hearing. The case of ***Morrissey v. Brewer***, 408 U.S. 471 (1972) was a U.S. Supreme Court case that set legal precedent whereby parolees have the right to a hearing before a "neutral and detached" hearing body concerning the

> **Class exercise**—Discuss why or why not parole officers are or are not allowed to make arrests.

factual basis for a parole violation. The hearing body may be the parole board or a third party hearing officer. The parolee may waive this hearing or have it. The parolee is not entitled to an attorney but they may hire one if they want to. This is unlike a probation revocation as you recall the probationer is entitled to an attorney and if they cannot afford an attorney then they can have one appointed to them. This is because parole revocation hearings are an **administrative hearing** unlike a probation violation which is a court proceeding.

The amount of time a parolee will spend in prison on a revocation depends on the jurisdiction they are in. Indeterminate sentencing and those on traditional parole may spend a significant amount of time in prison for a technical violation. For instance if someone was sentenced to a term of 2–10 years in prison they could be released after serving only 2 years in prison. If their parole is revoked they could spend the next 8 years in prison as a result of the violation (It's highly unlikely they would spend the remainder of their term in prison but nonetheless possible). On the contrary a person under post-release supervision may spend as little as 90 days in prison for a technical violation. The consequences of violating release vary widely in severity.

## J.   RE-ENTRY

While all parolees are "re-entering" society the term re-entry means something a bit different to corrections professionals. Re-entry involves targeted programs to specific types of offenders such as young violent offenders. They are assigned to parole officers with a specialized caseloads that are familiar with the risks and needs of this category of offender. They are also given preference to enter certain programming like job training all in an effort to identify and help stem future criminality. If you remember we discussed Wolfgang's 6% or chronic offending. Through identifying people that present risks to the community along with understanding needs beyond punishment the hope is to prevent revocations and a revolving door in and out of prison.

There are a number of different re-entry programs in every jurisdiction. Some target employment or housing specifically. Others are more holistic and consider that one issue stems from several other problems or deficiencies.

Petersilia (2003) identified four areas which prisoner re-entry needed to be reformed.

1.   <u>Improve the prison experience</u>—provide more programming like education. Change the prison environment from a place of violence to skill building. This is done through prison administration

promoting inmate reintegration and partnering with community corrections. This can be done by implementing "tracks" or direction for inmates to follow.

2. Changing prison release and revocation practices—institute discretionary parole release. Release from prison should be based on recidivism prediction.

3. Revise post-prison services and supervision—incorporate better classification and responses to violations or observed needs in order to prevent violations.

4. Foster collaborations with the community—develop more informal social controls, develop partnerships with service providers, law enforcement, and ex-convicts, victims' advocates, and neighborhoods.

# K.  RESEARCH AND POLICY/PRACTICE

Parole supervision is an important part of not only corrections but the entire criminal justice system. Just as police, courts, and institutional corrections must improve so must parole. The Urban Institute based in New York City, NY conducted an analysis in 2008 concerning effective parole strategies. They developed 13 such strategies after reviewing a number of empirical studies concerning best practices.

We know that two-thirds of parolees will be rearrested within 3 years of their release (Langan, 2002). These arrests are for new crimes as well as technical violations of release. Technical violations have contributed to the rise in incarceration rates (Pew Charitable Trusts, 2016). In order to reduce recidivism rates and curb prison overcrowding parole administrators are looking at empirical data to inform their policy and practices.

The paper is divided into two major sections. The first covers organizational-level strategies. This level concerns establishing the philosophy of the organization. Does it lean more towards a law enforcement side or is there a need for more rehabilitative measures? The second concerns the individual level and supervision strategies at the parole officer level. These are referred to as case management strategies.

When looking at organizational level strategies the focus is on large scale policies. The first is to define what the goal is. What is success? What does success look like? Thus the first of the 13 strategies is to:

1.  Define success as recidivism reduction and measure performance. Public safety is always the first priority. Defining success though is not focused on surveillance but behavior change in parolees. Measuring success and being accountable is important to. Thus setting a goal to reduce offender recidivism by a certain percentage focuses managers and line officers to fix a goal and achieve it. As agencies begin to track their progress toward a goal they are better able to understand what is effective and ineffective at reducing recidivism.

2.  Tailor conditions of supervision. As we reviewed previously in this chapter every parolee has general conditions of release they must follow. A long and potentially unreasonable list of conditions may set a person up to fail. Surveillance oriented supervision that does not address a person's criminogenic needs does not reduce recidivism (Lowenkamp, 2004). Instead conditions of release should be:

    a.  Realistic—a parolee's ability to satisfy every requirement should be taken into consideration.

    b.  Relevant—conditions should be specific to each parolee, reflecting the risk each person presents and their unique needs.

    c.  Research-based—conditions should focus on "what works" as reflected by empirical data. A parolee's learning style should be considered. Individualized case plans can be utilized by parole officers that know the parolee.

3.  Focus on moderate and high-risk parolees. There is broad consensus by a number of different researchers concerning the focus moderate to high risk parolees should get (Andrews, 2007), (Burke, 2006). The focus is not only to identify those that present a higher risk than other but what exactly the risk is and how best to approach it is of importance. Alternatively those parolees that present a low risk need only administrative oversight. Treatment for low risk parolees tends to produce very little if any positive effect and in fact may be counter-productive (Lowenkamp, 2004).

4.  Front load supervision resources. The first days and weeks upon release are the most likely times a parolee will be rearrested (Binswinger, Nowles, & Corsi, 2011). A parolee's substance abuse, mental health, employment, and housing are especially important

during this period and contribute to the probability of rearrests. As a result waiting to release before combatting these issues is too late. Prison should focus on release. Parole staff should be involved in preplanning release. Inmates should be transported to facilities closest to the town or city they are to be released from. Frontloading parole supervision early can identify those that need the extra help and those that do not. This would reduce work load for officers. Frontloading resources means just that: providing resources to those deemed to need it more than others. It does not mean increased surveillance and enforcement.

5.  Implementing earned discharge. Parolees are often placed on supervision for a determined amount of time regardless if they are under traditional parole or post-release supervision. Implementing earned early release can be an effective means of motivating parolees to complete programs, gain or remain employed, or graduate to a less restrictive supervision. As we saw in #4 above the first year is the most likely time under supervision when a person will recidivate.

6.  Implement place-based supervision. Parolees often concentrate in relatively small areas. These are usually disadvantaged neighborhoods with high crime rates (La Vigne, Cowan, & Brazzell, 2006). This much like community policing strategies take officers out of the office and away from a 9–5 workday. Caseloads for officers are geographically based. The idea is to supervise parolees where they live as opposed to a remote office in a faraway location. Embedding within the community and seeking their help and information is key.

7.  Engaging partners to expand intervention capacities is also an important aspect. The criminal justice system is only one aspect of the community. Engaging many different governmental and non-governmental agencies is very important. Given the need for healthcare, housing, and employment are typically essential to successfully re-entry parole agencies are largely absent from implementation. Greater organization can reduce redundancy between organizations. Ensuring parolees get the services they need. Collaboration can take root at the policy level where formal agreements and informal relationships can be fostered.

The last six supervision strategies are implemented at the individual level. This level is where the case management of the parole officer takes place. The overall strategy is adopted by the agency and this is where those polices are implemented. The overarching theme here is that the parole officer and parolee have a strong interpersonal relationship that fosters accountability and change.

8.  Assessing criminogenic risks and needs. Risks and needs are not independent or mutually exclusive from each other. In fact often times they are connected. Determining risk and needs of each parolee is crucial to developing the appropriate level of supervision. There are a number of risk and needs instruments officers utilize to determine risk and needs. Using the particular instrument varies but they all should share one commonality: empirical basis. Risks and needs instruments match parolees to several different types of interventions such as substance abuse treatment. There of course are a number of different treatment modalities but selecting the proper modality to fir the parolee's learning style is very important. It may indeed be the case that there is only one of a few treatment modalities available within a geographic region so understanding the effectiveness of such treatment (regardless of substance abuse to other programming) is important. Interventions should be dynamic and focus on changeable factors like employment or education.

9.  Developing and implementation of case supervision plans that balance treatment and surveillance. Surveillance and enforcing the conditions of parole are still very important to parole, but leaning too heavily on enforcement is detrimental to the effectiveness of parole (Drake & Aos, 2009). Use of a valid risk and needs instrument as identified in #8, afore should be used to build a case plan based on strengths. Parolee input should also be utilized. Sensitivity to culture, motivation, and temperament should be considered (Clark & Walters, 2006). Case plans should be a collaborative effort between the officer and the parolee and include community resources.

10. Involve parolees to enhance their engagement in assessment, case planning, and supervision. Traditionally supervision is based on a contact-driven style of surveillance. Whereby the quantity of the contacts is more important than the quality of the contact.

Evidence-based practices suggest a behavioral management model where the parolee is an active participant be developed (Pew Charitable Trusts, 2007). Motivational interviewing has been adopted by many agencies. This engages parolees in their own supervision.

11. Engage informal social control to facilitate community reintegration. The parole officer dispensing enforcement activities and giving direction is a very small part of supervision. Utilizing a parolee's natural support (if there is) compliments the parole officer's job. Burke and Tonry (2006) argue that even fragile or limited prosocial supports improve parolee outcomes. Often times these informal social control are more effective for behavior change than any consequence a parole officer may use (National Research Council, 2007). Encouraging a parolee to use support networks is key here. Some of these include using "community guardians" to foster change.

12. Incorporate Incentives and rewards into the supervision process. Employing only punishment in parole is not effective. However, holding parolees accountable and also recognizing positive behaviors is important. The double action of reward and negative consequence serves to reinforce compliant behavior while trying to eliminate negative behavior. Drawing attention to gains or positives such as awarding certificates or small monetary rewards serves to reinforce compliant behavior. Incentivizing compliant behavior rarely takes place in parole. We might think compliant behavior is just expected behavior but as we know from classical conditioning rewards can be an effective way to change behavior.

13. Employ graduated problem-solving responses to violations of parole conditions in a swift and certain manner. Responding to technical violations of release by not using incarceration but instead community sanctions has been recognized as a way to both address violations and still maintain public safety. High risk offender can and do present a danger to the community and incarcerating a high risk parolee on a technical violation is still a good option. However, many parolees have minor condition violations and these can be more properly addressed if the actions by the parole officer are swift and certain. A gradient of sanctions can be employed that can eventually result in revocation and commitment to prison. Clearly

defined goals set by the administration and followed by line officers which specifically address the violation in a timely manner lead to improved community safety and at the same time reduce prison populations (National Research Council, 2007).

# L.  CONCLUSION

Parole is an effective community safety measure. It allows a person to gradually be released back into the community. It offers support through means of programming and a measure of structure necessary for many leaving prison but who need to assimilate into the community.

Parole just like all of corrections will continue to evolve, but it may become a tool utilized more often as the expense and overcrowding or prison seems to be untenable. These invisible handcuffs offer a measure of community safety while also a path toward proactive behavior.

Perhaps some of the most interesting data concerning parole and probationers concerns what's known as "million dollar blocks". The concept involves mapping where people are living when they are arrested and processed through to conviction. Sentences vary from probation to long prison sentences but those sentenced to the longest periods of incarceration tend to come from very small areas, in this instance certain blocks within neighborhoods. Thus the "million dollar block". The million dollars pertains to the amount of money spent on correctional involvement for people that live in a concentrated area, a city block. Location studies like this illustrate that often times where you live can impact your involvement in crime and resulting harsh punishment in the criminal justice system.

In order to reduce recidivism there's a focus on certain neighborhoods and even blocks. The purpose is to target these places and people for additional resources in order to address workforce development, addiction treatment, and mental health issues (Cooper, 2020). Community corrections officers and those that make policy and implement practice are well served when we consider they effects of place on criminal behavior.

## Discussion Questions

1.  Explain what parole is and how it differs from probation.

2.  Why do you think parole was established?

3.  Discuss some of the major issues within parole today.

4.  Why is it important to understand the demographics of the parole population?

5.  Explain the difference between parole and post-release supervision.

6.  Should parole focus more on rehabilitation or rule enforcement, explain?

7.  What are the benefits of caseload specialization?

8.  Do you think parole officers should be able to make arrests and carry firearms? Explain your answer.

9.  What is "re-entry" and summarize how Petersillia says it should be reformed?

10. Summarize one organizational and one individual level strategy to improve parole supervision today.

## Student Exercises

1.  Which do you think is more effective measure of post-incarceration community release, traditional parole or post-release? Explain your answer.

2.  Review the "strategies for parole" at the end of this chapter. Explain how 2 organizational level and 2 individual level strategies can be employed in your area to reduce recidivism.

## Key Terms

**Administrative hearing**—parole hearing in which an unaffiliated parole officer decides the outcome of a parole revocation hearing.

**Administrative Office**—the headquarters for Federal Probation and Pre-trial services, located in Washington D.C.

**Chief Judge**—the chief administrative officer for each judicial district.

**Chief Probation Officer**—the probation officer in charge of each respective judicial district.

**Disenfranchisement**—when people are deprived of certain rights or privileges based solely on having a criminal record.

**General conditions of parole**—conditions of parole which everyone on parole in that jurisdiction must abide by.

**General Equivalency Degree (GED)**—a degree equivalent to a high school diploma.

**Home contact**—parole officer typically must contact the parolee at their residence to confirm the parolee lives there and that they are abiding by the conditions of release as well as prevent any violations based on their observations.

**Instant offense**—the crime for which a person is currently under supervision for.

**Institutional parole officer**—parole officer who works inside the prison and arrangements for the release of inmates ideally help them have a home and employment upon release.

**Max out**—when an inmate has served their entire prison term.

**Morrissey v. Brewer**—court case that set legal precedent concerning parole revocation procedures, specifically giving the parolee a notice of the charges and right to an administrative hearing.

**Parole**—the conditional release of an inmate from prison.

**Parole board**—small group of people tasked with deciding to release an inmate on parole.

**Registered offender**—some offender must register their whereabouts and place of employment with authorities for a certain period of time regardless if they are under community supervision or not.

**Revocation**—when a parolee have their released revoked and they are taken into custody.

**Specialized caseload**—a parole officer who supervises a certain category of parolee (i.e. sex offender).

**Structured decision making**—a carefully organized analysis of problems in order to make decisions that are focused on achieving a particular goal.

**Term of supervision (TSR)**—a period of release for federal offenders much like post-release supervision.

**Ticket of leave**—a mechanism of release for early parole.

**Underemployment**—being employed but not full time or under their career capacity.

**Vocational training**—training to learn a specific trade or task.

---

[1]  Henrichson, Christian and Delany, Ruth (2012). The Price of Prisons What Incarceration costs taxpayers. Vera Institute.

[2]  Kaeble, Daniell; Maruschak, Laura M.; Bonczar, Thomas (2015). Probation and Parole in the United States, 2014. Bureau of Justice Statistics. U.S. Dept. of Justice.

[3]  James, Doris and Glaze, Lauren (2006). Mental Health Problems of Prison and Jail Inmates. Bureau of Justice Statistics Special Report. U.S. Dept. of Justice.

[4]   Alarid, Leanne F. and Del Carmen R. (2011). Community Based-Corrections 8th Ed. Wadsworth Cengage.

# Death Penalty

**Chapter Objectives**

- Understand the use and application of capital punishment in American history as well as its place in contemporary American punishment.

- Recognize societies role in the application of the death penalty.

- Explain how methods of execution change due to social influence.

- Compare how death row inmates differ from other inmates.

- Understand the special issues death row inmates present prison staff.

- Analyze the demographics of death row inmates and draw conclusions about it application in the U.S.

## A. INTRODUCTION

The death penalty is obviously the most severe punishment in the U.S. The purpose of execution has and for the foreseeable future remain a topic of much debate. Many individuals contend that the death penalty is purely retributive. Others contend that it serves as a deterrent to future criminality. It's obviously a very efficient method of specific deterrence but much more arguable concerning the value of general deterrence.

The death penalty is administered by the department of corrections or in the case of the federal government the Federal Bureau of Prisons. This is a unique subject within corrections. The debate about the morality and effective or ineffectiveness of execution is certainly a public debate. It's an explicit example concerning how punishment, in this sense execution, impacts corrections. Correctional professionals most certainly have an opinion for or against the death penalty. However their job duties and responsibilities of prisons and correctional staff in jurisdictions that allow the death penalty as a possible punishment are to carry out that sentence.

In this chapter we will review the history of the death penalty in the U.S. in order to provide a historical context of its use here. This examination will also allow us to make connections between the past and its current use and in many cases we will see its utility questioned and discontinued. We will also look at some general statistical information. It's important to understand who's administering and receiving this punishment, what jurisdictions allow and disallow its use, and how often are we actually using it. Also, we will examine the sociology of law concerning this punishment. This type of examination allows us to look at viewpoints that may challenge notions of what we think about this punishment as well as possibly support already held beliefs. The death penalty presents many special issues within corrections such as housing inmates with these sentences. Many are familiar with the term "**death row**". We will examine this part of the prison and how it differs from other parts of those facilities. Examining the methods of execution is also important. The way in which we execute people has changed over the course of the history of its use here. Although some methods such as hanging are still a legally recognized method many jurisdictions only allow lethal injection. No matter the method the principal of the Eighth Amendment against cruel and unusual punishment applies here in many instances. Finally we will look at the empirical data concerning the costs and benefits of the death penalty.

## B. HISTORY OF CAPITAL PUNISHMENT IN THE U.S.

Just as we have seen evolutionary developments in all aspects of corrections so too has the death penalty undergone changes from the methods of execution, to the public-to-private nature of executing people, as well as the justification of its existence. Examining the history of the death penalty in the U.S. allows us to asses justifications for its use and compare the relevance of its use throughout history and contemporaneously. The death penalty has been a part of sentencing in the U.S. even before there was a sovereign nation. Colonial America adopted much of its tradition and law from England. Crimes and punishments and their codification were carried over from England. The accepted methods of punishment were part of accept common practice and largely adopted by colonial governments.

The first recorded execution in the colonies was of Captain George Kendall. In 1608, Captain Kendall was executed for spying for the rival Spanish. Four years after Captain Kendall's execution the colony of Virginia's Governor, enacted laws that provided the legal means to execute people convicted of number of crimes from murder to trading with native peoples, killing chickens, or even stealing grapes (Death Penalty Information Center, 2019).

The justification for executing people quickly fell under scrutiny soon after the signing of the Declaration of Independence. A few of the signers of that famous document such as Benjamin Franklin and Dr. Benjamin Rush advocated for limiting the use of execution and claimed executions has a brutalization effect that made people more callous to the taking of life (Maestro, 1975). Rush and Franklin were not alone in their in criticism. Many at the time started to question all forms and purposes of punishment from corporal punishment to the use of the death penalty for any crime especially crimes not involving murder.

In 1794, Pennsylvania limited the death penalty to only crimes involving people convicted of murder (Costanzo & L.T., 1994). Many states began to develop laws that limited the use of the death penalty. Instead of executing people for less serious crimes, prisons and jails were built. These facilities, prisons, were meant to hold people for long periods of time. The idea of justice and punishment moved away from punishing the body to punishing the "soul". This major cultural shift concerning punishment meant not only a radical reduction in the use of corporal punishment but executions as well. For example the state of Wisconsin has only executed one person in its history and has not had the death penalty since 1853 (Death Penalty Information Center, 2019). However, states such as Wisconsin were the exception rather than the rule. By the early 1900s only six states did not have the death penalty and within the next 20 years five of those six states reinstated the death penalty (Death Penalty Information Center, 2019).

The historical methods of execution have changed considerably to align with social acceptance of what's permissible and what is considered brutal or cruel and unusual. Hanging has been a common method of execution for hundreds of years but with the advent media depicting brutal imagery combined with changing public sentiment people began to sour on hanging as a method of execution.

Technology also began to play a role in this area of punishment. The use of electricity was fast becoming more and more popular in the U.S. in the late 1800s. In an effort to show the power of this new technology electrical entrepreneur and inventor Thomas Edison developed the electric chair. The electric chair was promoted as a more humane way to execute a prisoner sentenced to death.

## Corrections in Action

At the dawn of the electrical age there were two competing purveyors of electricity on one side Thomas Edison, a widely renowned inventor, developed direct current voltage and on the other side was George Westinghouse who with the help of electrical and mechanical engineer Nikola Tesla developed alternating current. Westinghouse and Edison were bitter rivals competing for supremacy in this business arena.

Edison was contacted by Alfred Southwick, a Buffalo, NY veterinarian and a member of a state of New York Commission studying more humane methods of execution than hanging, in 1887. Southwick told Edison that he had been putting down animals at his veterinarian clinic by electrocuting them. Southwick thought this was a very human way to end an animals life. Southwick thought the same method could be applied to executions. Edison, an ardent opponent of the death penalty, write Southwick back advising him of his abhorrent view of the death penalty. Edison also did not want direct current electricity being associated with something the public may view as dangerous. The initial correspondence did not dissuade Southwick from contacting Edison again about his idea. However this time a business savvy Edison suggested he contact his business rival Westinghouse. Edison's thought was to have the public view Westinghouse's alternating current as dangerous. Southwick contacted Westinghouse and he also turned down Southwick's idea because he too did not want alternating current associated with a "death machine".

Southwick being rebuffed by both Edison and Westinghouse enlisted the help of Harold Brown. Mr. Brown was an electrical engineer who was publically known for his activism against alternating current. Edison seized upon Brown's views and wanting to associate Westinghouse's alternating current with danger secretly funded Browns development of the electric chair.

The first use of the electric chair was in 1890. Convicted killer William Kemmler from New York was the first person to die in the electric chair. On August 6th 1890, Mr. Kemmler was strapped into the electric chair and for 17 seconds 1,000 volts of electricity was passed through his body. Doctors examined his body immediately after the first application of electricity only to find that Mr. Kemmler was still alive. He was jolted with 2,000 volts for 4 minutes (Rosenwald, 2019). This time which caused his veins to rupture. After the 4 minutes had passed he was declared dead.

Southwick thought the execution was successful. He declared, "There is the culmination of ten years work and study! We live in a higher civilization today.

(Holodny, 2019)" Westinghouse on the other hand thought the matter could have been carried out better with an axe.

This method has been modified several times and is used currently used in 9 states usually as a secondary method to lethal injection (Center, 2019). Since the death penalties reinstatement in 1976, 160 people have been put to death via the electric chair. Currently three states, Delaware, Washington, and New Hampshire allow hanging as a secondary method to lethal injection. Three people have been executed via hanging since 1976.

> **Weblink**—Visit the following url to hear execution tapes recorded by state of Georgia correctional personnel during executions via electrocution.
>
> https://storycorps.org/stories/execution-tapes/

From the 1920s until the early 1970s the death penalty was largely socially acceptable (Death Penalty Information Center, 2019). Arguably the only notable development, albeit a very notable development, during this period was eliminating public executions. The last public execution in the U.S. took place in 1936. Owensborough, KY was the sight of the last public execution in the U.S. At the time Kentucky was the only state that still allowed public executions. Over 20,000 people attended the hanging of Rainey Bathea. Bathea, a black man, had been convicted of raping and killed an elderly white woman. 18 months after the execution Kentucky's governor signed a bill that outlawed public executions, thereby ending the practice in the U.S. (New York Times, 2001). Today only Iran, Saudi Arabia, North Korea, and Somalia are the counties that still allow public executions (Worald Atlas, 2019).

> **Class exercise**—Discuss student's thoughts about public executions. What would the purpose of public executions be? If the public witnessed public executions do you think more people would disfavor the practice?

## 1. The Death Penalty Today in the U.S.

Currently, an inmate sentenced to death will spend an average of 16 years on death row before his or her execution is carried out. Of course each jurisdiction is different concerning the amount of time from conviction to execution. For instance, California has the most number of death row inmates in the country, 743 inmates have a death sentence, yet there has not been an execution since 2006. Since the year 2000, there have been 6 executions carried out in California (Death Penalty Information Center, 2019). If we compare California to Texas we can see a stark disparity in the frequency of executions. Currently Texas has only 228 people on death row, 6 of which are women. However, in 2018, they executed 13 people and have averaged executing 10 inmates each year for the last five years. Texas executes more people than any other state in the country. Texas executed more than half of the inmates from all other jurisdictions that allow the death penalty in 2018 (McCullough, 2018). This tally is only about as third as many executions that took place in Texas in the late 1990s and early 2000s. In the year 2000, Texas executed 40 people and averaged almost 28 executions per year from 1997–2007. No other state or the federal jurisdiction came close to executing that number of inmates.

The Death Penalty Information Center identified 10 counties that have prosecuted and account for about 27% of all U.S. death row inmates. These 10 counties represent less than 1% of all the counties in the U.S. and less than 1% of counties that are in states that allow the death penalty.

Figure 11.1

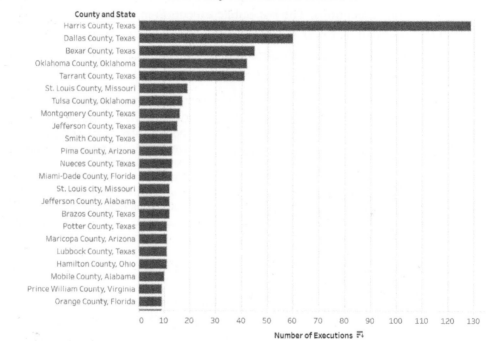

Source: Death Penalty Information Center.

As we can see 4 of the 5 counties most likely to prosecute as case as a death penalty case and then ultimately have that punishment carried out are from Texas. So even within Texas the death penalty as a possible sentence is prosecuted only by a few counties but in a high frequency. Texas as typically led the nation in numbers of executions since the reinstatement of the death penalty in 1976. Figure

11.2 shows that two states in particular, Texas and Oklahoma, have particularly high rates of executions.

Figure 11.2

## Executions by Region

| Region | Total Executions | 2019 | 2018 | 2017 | 2016 | 2015 | 2014 | 2013 | 2012 | 2011 | 2010 | 2009 |
|---|---|---|---|---|---|---|---|---|---|---|---|---|
| South | 1226 | 9 | 22 | 20 | 19 | 22 | 23 | 32 | 31 | 32 | 35 | 45 |
| Midwest | 184 | 0 | 3 | 3 | 1 | 6 | 11 | 5 | 5 | 6 | 8 | 7 |
| West | 85 | 0 | 0 | 0 | 0 | 0 | 1 | 2 | 7 | 5 | 3 | 0 |
| Northeast | 4 | 0 | 0 | 0 | 0 | 0 | 0 | 0 | 0 | 0 | 0 | 0 |
| Texas & Oklahoma Alone | 673 | 3 | 13 | 7 | 7 | 14 | 13 | 22 | 21 | 15 | 20 | 27 |
| United States as a Whole | 1499 | 9 | 25 | 23 | 20 | 28 | 35 | 39 | 43 | 43 | 46 | 52 |

Source: Death Penalty Information Center.

States that have the death penalty do not tend to exercise that option even when someone has been sentenced to death. For instance, there is only a 13% likelihood of carrying out the death penalty. Execution is actually the third most likely outcome for a person sentenced to death. Those on death row are more likely to have their sentenced reversed or lessened or to just remain on death row until they die from other causes (Gramlich, 2019).

There are currently 2,600 people on death row in the U.S. The majority of those people are in states that allow executions but have not executed anyone in decades. North Carolina has had the death penalty as a punishment since 1984. Currently 143 people are on death row there. Yet there has not been a single execution in that state since 2006 (4 people were executed in 2006) (Death Penalty Information Center, 2019).

Many of the 30 states that currently allow the death penalty do not use it. Its use has been frozen either by a governor's **moratorium** or effectively by being blocked by the court system. As an example of its decline in states that allow its use we see that in 1999, there were 98 executions carried out in the U.S. in 20 states. But that in 2018, only 25 executions were carried out in only eight states (Berman, 2019). In other states like Kansas, which allows the death penalty, have not executed anyone since it was reinstated there in 1994. States like Kansas are not unique in fact the vast majority of states that allow executions do not utilize it.

The overall use of executions seems to be largely confined to a few states. Texas of course leads the nation with 13 people executed in 2018. Far behind Texas was Florida with 3 and also Tennessee with 3 people executed in the same year. Florida, Georgia, and Alabama each executed 2 people in 2018 (Death Penalty Information Center, 2019).

# C. OVERVIEW OF THE DEATH PENALTY IN THE U.S. TODAY

In order to provide a clear and focused review of the extent of the use of capital punishment today we will examine the death penalty in the U.S. since it's reinstatement after 1976. Today 25 states, the federal government, and the U.S. military allow for the use of the death penalty. 21 states do not allow its use and 4 states (California, Oregon, Colorado, and Pennsylvania do not allow it per a governor's moratorium). For those states with a governors moratorium capital punishment is allowed by law but will not to use by those governors. A new governor can lift the moratorium if they so choose. As of May 2019, California, Washington, Nebraska, and New Hampshire all had active measures to discontinue the practice. Colorado and Wyoming introduced legislation to discontinue it but those measures failed. Iowa was the only state to consider legislation that would allow the death penalties use where it was not allowed before (Krohn, 2019).

Only people convicted of murder can be put to death. The only exception are for crimes of treason and espionage. The road toward execution begins with the prosecutor. Each jurisdiction is different when it comes to allowing the prosecutor to pursue the death penalty. If the prosecutor does not seek the death penalty then of course that option is not available. This is one of the places where bias can influence who is sentenced to death and who is not. A prosecutor biased for or against a defendant can have a huge impact on seeking the death penalty or not. Even if a prosecutor does seek the death penalty that does not necessarily mean the person will be given a death sentence. In many jurisdictions there must be an **aggravating circumstance** that elevates the crime to a capital offense.

> **Class exercise**—Does your state allow the death penalty? If so under what circumstances can the prosecutor ask for the death penalty? If your state does not allow capital punishment research a state that does allow it and answer the questions above.

> **Weblink**—The following is an interview about a study that looked at the death penalty in Tennessee. Review it and discuss it in class.
>
> https://deathpenaltyinfo.org/resources/podcasts/discussions-with-dpic/discussions-with-dpic-authors-of-death-penalty-study-discuss-tennessees-death-penalty-lottery

In 2018, was a record low for death penalty sentences. 42 people were sentenced to death in 2018. Only 14 states sentenced someone to death and 57% of those sentences came from Texas (7 sentenced to death), Florida (7), California and Ohio each sentenced 4 people to death (Death Penalty

Information Center, 2019). The yearly record low represents a long-term trend in the U.S.

We know that just because someone may be sentenced to death does not mean they will ultimately be executed. There are a number of different reasons a person may find relief from the death penalty. One of course is through court procedures such as appeals. There are any number of appeals that a person can pursue. For instance a person may be retried for a case. They can also receive a lesser sentence such as life without parole. In a few cases they can be **exonerated**. In 2016, 90 people were removed from death row. However 51 of those 90 people were removed from death row due to an appeals court overturning the conviction or a **mitigation** of the sentence being allowed. The other 19 removed died as a result of other means of death not attributed to execution (Davis, 2018).

---

### Corrections in Action

As of the publication of this textbook to 1976, 166 people have been exonerated of their crimes which placed them on death row. Although this this is a very small percentage of the 1,499 people that have been executed during that time period the question of innocent people being put to death is a serious matter concerning the use of the death penalty.

The use of DNA to exonerate death row inmates has gained a lot of publicity. However, exonerations involving DNA are infrequent. Only 20 of the 166 exonerations of death row inmates have involved DNA evidence used to reverse the sentence (Death Penalty Information Center, 2019). Typically exonerations involve false/forced confessions by the defendant, perjury by a witness, inadequate defense, or official misconduct by a prosecutor or law enforcement. Some of those exonerated spent as much as 43 years on death row before being exonerated.

On May 23rd 2019, Charles Finch's 1976 murder conviction was vacated by U.S. District Court Judge Terrence Boyle in Raleigh, NC. Finch now 81 years old was immediately released upon the case being vacated. Prosecutors in North Carolina did not oppose Finch's appeal. Finch's attorney's argued that one of the witnesses was shown an "impermissibly suggestive lineup". The court also found that a sheriff's deputy encouraged other witnesses to give false testimony (Green, 2019).

# D. DEMOGRAPHICS OF DEATH ROW

Figure 11.3 illustrates the drastic rise in executions followed by a steep decline in its use.

Figure 11.3

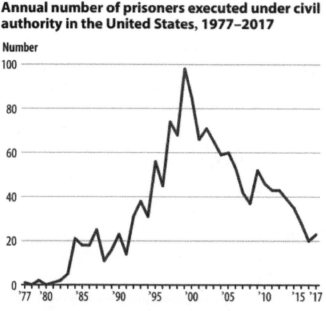

**Annual number of prisoners executed under civil authority in the United States, 1977–2017**

Source: Bureau of Justice Statistics, National Prisoner Statistics – Capital Punishment, 1977–2017. See table 3 for counts of prisoners executed.

As we have discussed in this chapter the number of death sentences and executions carried out has been decreasing. It remains important to examine who is on death row. As corrections professionals understanding the people in custody is a responsibility of the correctional department and subsequently the staff that manage this population.

Eighteen states held fewer people sentenced to death in 2017 than in 2016. Only three states and the Federal Bureau of Prisons saw a net gain in the number of death row inmates. California had the most inmates on death row (742 inmates). Currently there are 2,703 people with a death sentence in the U.S. This number represents both states and federal inmates.

The amount of time a person spends on death row averages 20 years and 3 months. The amount of time from sentencing to execution has increased. Just from 2016 to 2017 the time on death row increased 3 years and 3 months and increased 7 years and 6 months since 2007 (Snell, 2019).

Figure 11.4

Demographics of Those on Death Row

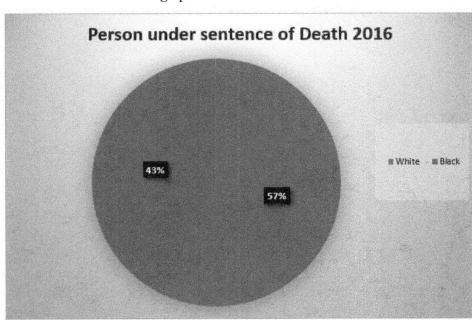

Figure 11.4 represents the racial makeup of the death row population. Even though whites make up a majority of those sentenced to death (1,553) black inmates are over represented on death row. They are over represented because African American males comprise only about 7 percent of the entire U.S. population yet they make up 43% of those on death row. This disparity let alone the racial disparity within corrections as a whole is the subject of much debate and study.

Geography of location is another important focal point for students of the death penalty. Depending upon where a person is can play a major impact in the death penalty being a possible outcome. Of course 21 states do not officially allow the death penalty as a matter of law and 4 states do not currently allow its use per a governor's moratorium. However that states to do allow its use and those that actually use it as a punishment are geographically dependent. Figure 11.5 illustrates this point.

Figure 11.5

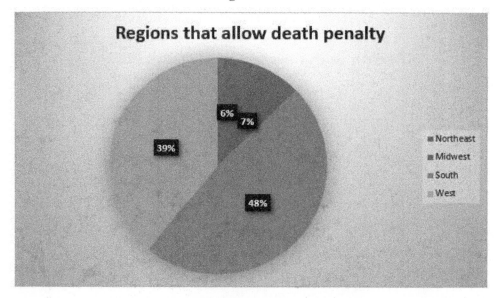

Figure 11.6 shows regionally the actual number of executions by region. This illustrates that while every region of the country (not every state) has the death penalty its use is limited.

Figure 11.6

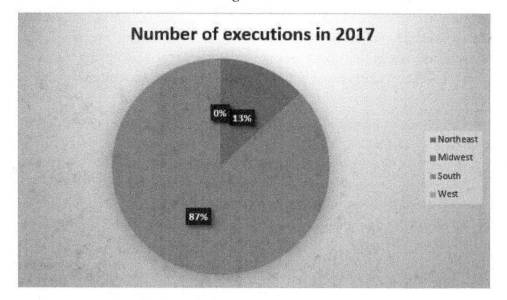

There were no executions in the Northeast or Midwest regions thus they do not register in Figure 11.6. The Southern Region includes: Alabama, Arkansas,

Delaware, Florida, Georgia, Kentucky, Louisiana, Mississippi, N. Carolina, Oklahoma, S. Carolina, Tennessee, Texas, and Virginia.

The average time between sentence and execution has seen a dramatic increase since the death penalty was reinstated in 1976. The average in 1977 was only 3 months between sentence and execution today the average is 243 months. The gap in time between sentence and the carry out of executions is attributed to the appeals process. The time inmates spend on death row is of particular concern to those in corrections. Later in this chapter we will discuss the unique challenges death row presents in corrections as these are typically units of prison.

Just as men far outnumber women in the correctional system so do men far outnumber women when it comes to executions. In 2018, there were 55 women on death row in the U.S. This represents only about 2% of the death row population. Since California has the largest death row population it's no surprise that most of the women sentenced to death in the U.S. are in California (21 women). Only one female is on Federal Death Row. Since the reinstatement of the death penalty 16 women have been executed (CNN Quick Facts, 2019). Texas has executed the most women, but Georgia was the last state to execute a female in 2015.

Figure 11.7 details the age ranges of those on death row. As we know from earlier chapters the age of the inmate can present a host of challenges for correctional staff.

Figure 11.7

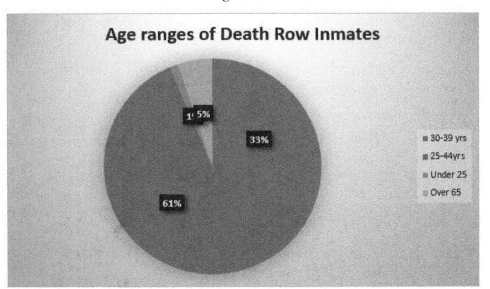

The overwhelming majority of death row inmates are between 30–44 years of age. The average age of arrest for death row inmates was 28 years (Death Penalty Information Center, 2019). Since the number of executions is quickly declining caring for elderly inmates on death row will no doubt be an area of consideration for correctional administrators and line staff.

Understanding the demographic make-up of death row inmates is essential to managing this population. Death row is a unique part of the prison and correctional administrators are tasked with not only carrying out this penalty but of course housing these inmates for extensive periods of time.

## E.  METHODS OF EXECUTION

The methods of execution have varied throughout U.S. history. Though none of those executions intention was to involve pain as part of the punishment. However there are numerous occasions from the past and much more recently where the executions did not go as planned and those condemned to die were arguably in pain. The 8th Amendment of the Constitution prevents "cruel and unusual punishment". It's of course debatable what constitutes both cruel and unusual. However, the following methods of execution have remained despite numerous court challenges:

- Lethal injection—This method is the primary method of execution in all of the states that allow execution as well as for federal executions. In a 2008, challenge to lethal injections constitutionality a three drug combination was approved by the U.S. Supreme Court. In *Baze v. Rees*, 553 U.S. 35 (2008) the court approved the use of the following 3 drug combination:

  1. Sodium thiopental, which is a sedative that induces unconsciousness.

  2. Pancuronium bromide, a muscle relaxer that produces paralysis and stops breathing.

  3. Potassium chloride, this produces cardiac arrest and stops the heart.

  Many pharmaceutical companies have refused to sell these drugs to correctional departments because of its use in executions (NCSL, 2019). 16 states have a secondary method of execution should lethal injection be declared unconstitutional.

- Electrocution—Is allowed as a secondary method in 9 states: Alabama, Arkansas, Florida, Kentucky, Mississippi, Oklahoma, South Carolina, Tennessee, and Virginia. November 1st 2018 was the last time the electric chair was used in the U.S. Edmund Zagorski, 63, was executed in Tennessee. This method was used when lethal injection drugs were not available (Almasy, 2019).

- Lethal gas—Six states use lethal gas, again as a secondary measure to lethal injection. The states of Alabama, Arizona, California, Mississippi, Missouri, Oklahoma, and Wyoming all allow its use. Walter LaGrand was executed in Arizona's gas chamber in 1999.

- Hanging—This practice is allowed as a secondary method in only 3 states: Delaware, New Hampshire, and Washington. The state of Washington disallowed the death penalty in 2018. This is not **retroactive**. Eight people remain on Washington's death row. The state of Delaware does not currently have anyone on death row and the death penalty is very much in question as of the publication of this text. New Hampshire abolished the death penalty on May 30, 2019. Although hanging as a method technically still exists in the U.S. it appears its use will no longer happen.

- Firing squad—This method is allowed in three states: Mississippi, Oklahoma, and Utah. A Utah man was executed in 2010, by firing squad. Although it's a secondary method in Utah inmates sentenced to death prior to May 3, 2004 had the option of lethal injection or firing squad.

The 8th Amendment of our Constitution largely dictates the methods of execution allowable by law. Lethal injection is the preferred method because it seems to represent the most efficient and humane way to end life. However, there have been many recent challenges to this practice as some executions via this method have been botched. Pharmaceutical makers are also not making the drugs necessary for this practice or refuse to sell them for that purpose. The methods of execution evolve just as our opinion of the practice of executing people has evolved. In this next section we will examine the sociology of law as it relates to the death penalty. Executions take place away from the public.

# F. SOCIOLOGY OF LAW AND THE DEATH PENALTY

From the 1920s until the early 1970s the death penalty was largely socially acceptable. Arguably the only notable development during this period was public inaccessibility. As discussed earlier, the last public execution took place in 1936. Thereafter all executions took place behind prison walls where only a limited number of people were allowed to attend. Some members of the press can attend, but no recording equipment is allowed.

The 1960s and 1970s saw much social change. As society changed so did what was allowable concerning the death penalty. Some of the most impactful changes in the history of criminal justice took place during this time period. Some of those changes significantly impacted the death penalty. A series of court cases (see *U.S. v. Jackson*, 390 U.S. 570 (1968), *Witherspoon v. Illinois*, 391 U.S. 510 (1968), and *Crampton v. Ohio*, 402 U.S. 183 (1970) eventually culminated in the suspension of the death penalty in the 1972, case of **Furman v. Georgia**, 408 U.S. 238 (1972). This precedent setting case called for an immediate halt to all executions across the nation. In a 5–4 vote the U.S. Supreme Court held that the way the death penalty was implemented violated cruel and unusual clause of the 8th Amendment of the Constitution. Specifically, the case held that minorities were handed down death sentences at much higher rates than whites, thus sentencing was arbitrary and capricious.

Many states that had the death penalty began immediately to fix the issue. States began to rewrite legislation on how people were sentenced to death as a result guided discretion statutes, which allow for aggravating and mitigating factors to influence jury and judges' decisions were approved. *In* the 1976, the case of **Gregg v. Georgia**, 428 U.S. 153 (1976) permitted the use of the death penalty as a punishment.

Three procedural reforms came out of this decision. The first was to requirement of a bifurcated trial with both an adjudication and a penalty phase. A second result of *Gregg v. Georgia* was appellate review. The third is a proportionality review where the state reviews how the death sentence is applied to and identify any disparities. Not all states chose to reinstate the death penalty immediately after *Gregg v. Georgia*. Still other states that initially allowed the death penalty such as New Mexico eliminated it.

There have been some important changes after the *Gregg* case that limit who can be put to death. A few examples are

- 1977—*Coker v. Georgia*, 433 U.S. 584 (1977): The death penalty for the crime of rape of an adult woman is unconstitutional.[1]

- 2002—*Atkins v. Virginia*, 536 U.S. 304 (2002): A person who is determined to be "mentally retarded" cannot be executed.[2]

- 2005—*Roper v. Simmons*,: 543 U.S. 551 (2005) A person that was under 18 at the time of the crime cannot be executed.[3]

- 2008—*Louisiana v. Kennedy*, 554 U.S. 407 (2008): A person convicted of a sex crime against a child cannot be executed if the victim does not die in the commission of the crime.[4]

The continuation of the death penalty as a punishment looks questionable at this time. The number of executions continues to drop as do the number of people sentenced to death. However, in the near future it appears its use will still be a part of correctional tasks. Currently almost 54% of Americans say they support the death penalty (Oliphant, 2018).

Figure 11.8

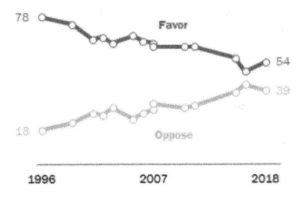

**Death penalty support ticks up after years of decline**

*% who _____ the death penalty for persons convicted of murder*

78 — Favor — 54

18 — Oppose — 39

1996        2007        2018

Note: Don't know responses not shown.
Source: Survey of U.S. adults conducted April 25-May 1, 2018.

**PEW RESEARCH CENTER**

## 1.   Death Row

The term "death row" is actually a slang term. Many know it as the segment of prison that houses those people sentenced to death and are awaiting execution. There were 2,673 sentenced to death in the U.S. as of April, 1st 2019 (Death Penalty Information Center, 2019). States like California (732), Florida (349), and Texas (223) housed the most death row inmates. Many states held between 1 inmate (i.e. Wyoming, New Hampshire) and approximately 50 inmates. Death row is typically part of a larger prison complex. The biggest death row is of course in California. The Condemned Unit, as it's officially referred to, is located in San Quentin Prison near San Francisco. It holds all of the male inmates sentenced to death in California. The prison has multiple custody levels for inmates not on death row. The female inmates sentenced to death in California are housed at Chowchilla Prison located in central California.

Death row is usually managed as a maximum security unit of the prison. However, unlike other maximum units only inmates with a death sentenced are housed there. Death row inmates are typically confined to their cells 23 hours a day. They receive limited time outside of their cells. They are allowed little time outside in the yard. Usually all the time is spent with minimal human contact and inmate to inmate contact outside of their one-person cells is restricted.

Upon sentencing the inmate is not given an execution date. The uncertainty of their final outcome is in question for years, even if they choose not to appeal their case. Capital cases are automatically referred to appeal due to the nature of the potential punishment. As we know a person often spends at least a decade and in many cases much longer awaiting the final disposition of their case. These inmates rarely receive any educational, vocational, or substance abuse treatment. U.S. Supreme Court Justice Stevens was the first court official to broach this topic. In *Lackey v. Texas*, 514 U.S. 1045 (1995). Lackey had spent 17 years on Texas' Death Row. He petitioned the U.S. Supreme court to review his case based on a violation of the 8th Amendment of the Constitution. His attorney's petitioned the court claiming the number of years he had spent on death row amounted to cruel and unusual punishment. Lackey's petition to be heard by the court failed and he was executed in 1997.

The process of actually carrying out an execution is jurisdictionally dependent. It usually involves the governor of the state signing a **death warrant**. This gives the inmate and their attorneys a date of execution. A death warrant does not necessary result in an execution as a **stay of execution** or other court action can delay or remove the person from death row. An inmate may also receive **clemency** by the order of a governor. If no court maneuvers are successful in delaying or eliminating the possibility of the death sentence each jurisdiction has a protocol. Below is a summation of Texas execution procedures:

- Male inmates are transported from the Ellis Unit (i.e. death row) to the Huntsville Unit prior to their scheduled execution.

- Inmates are allowed visits by family, chaplains, and attorneys. Except for chaplains or other religious members all visits end by 12:30 PM the day of the execution.

- The final meal will be served at approximately 3:30 PM or 4 PM.

- Prior to 6:00 PM the inmate may shower and dress in clean clothes.

- All individuals serving as witnesses will assemble at 5:55 PM in the lounge adjacent to the visiting room. Shortly after 6:00 PM the inmate will be moved by their holding cell to the execution chamber and secured to a gurney.

- A medically trained individual (not to be identified) will insert the intravenous catheter into the condemned person's arm. A non-lethal saline solution will flow.

- After this is done witnesses are escorted into the execution chamber. Witnesses for the condemned, the victim(s) family, and some media are allowed as witnesses.

- Once the witnesses are in place the warden allows the condemned person to speak their final words. Once those words are completed, if any, the warden gives the signal to the medical person to begin the injection process. This person is visibly separated from the execution chamber.

- After the inmate is pronounced dead, the body is immediately removed from the execution chamber and taken to a waiting vehicle to a local funeral home for burial.

- The warden shall return the death warrant to the clerk of the county in which the death sentence was given.

Source: Texas Department of Criminal Justice.

This the process for the state of Texas. The process differs from jurisdiction to jurisdiction, but many of these same protocols are followed. The correctional staff that carry out executions are highly trained and vetted. If any mistakes are made there can be serious consequences for them professionally, the prison and prison administration, and the death penalty as a punishment.

In 2014, the Texas prison guard union appealed for better death row conditions because the officers faced danger on such a routine basis that working in such conditions was not tenuous (Long, 2015). Despite the conditions of death row and the dangers it presents to correctional officer's people still form relationships. The nature of the environment can facilitate human connections to form. As a result of such strict housing regulations and small staff to inmate rations officers may spend more time with fewer inmates. Mental health issues can touch these officers at higher rates due to potential inmate on staff violence and as a result of the executions themselves (Long, 2015).

## G. CONCLUSION

Today 23 countries of the 193 recognized nations of the world allow executions. China executes more than 1,000 people each year. Exact numbers of execution in China are difficult to measure as they are very secretive of this activity. Iran, Saudi Arabia, Iraq, Pakistan, Egypt, Somalia, U.S., Jordan, and Singapore executed people in 2017.

Figure 11.9

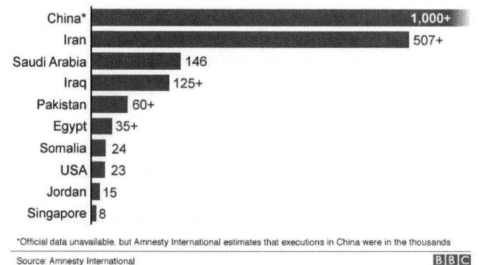

Many question does the death penalty work. In other words is it an effective measure at controlling crime? Specifically murder as that's the only crime a person can receive the death penalty for. If we look at states like Texas, whose use of the death penalty is widely known we see that their murder rate is 5.0 (i.e. 5 persons per 100,000 Texans are murdered each year). If it does deter murder their homicide rate should be amongst the lowest in the country yet when we review the data we see that states like Minnesota, Hawaii, and Iowa have some of the lowest murder rates in the country. In 2012, the National Research Council of the National Academies (Nagin, 2012) release a report based on numerous scientific articles on this topic for more than thirty years. They found the following:

1. Studies claiming a deterrent effect of capital punishment did not factor in the effects of noncapital punishments that may also be imposed.

2. The studies claiming a deterrent effect used incomplete or implausible models of potential murderers perceptions and of response to the use of capital punishment.

3. Estimates of the effect of capital punishment are based on models that make assumptions that are not credible.

The financial cost of death penalty cases far eclipses other cases. For instance Oklahoma spends on average $110,000 more dollar on each death penalty cases than they do on other non-capital murder cases (Oklahoma Death Penalty Review Commission, 2017). The increased costs in Oklahoma are much smaller than the national average with approaches $700,000 more than non-capital cases for each case. The state of Kansas spends an average of $1.26 million dollars on capital cases and they have not executed anyone since the 1950s.

The continued use of the death penalty is debatable. States obviously still use it and the public is still in favor of its use. This even though it's used very rarely. Its deterrent value is questionable at best when we consider general deterrence. Specific deterrence is a certainty. Despite these issues correctional professionals, both line staff and administration, in jurisdictions that allow its use will find ways to carry out this task.

## Discussion Questions

1. Discuss at least two purposes of capital punishment.

2. Explain how public opinion has evolved concerning the use of capital punishment.

3. Detail your thoughts about public executions.

4.  In your opinion does spending a large amount of time on death row amount to cruel and unusual punishment?

5.  Why do you think states that have capital punishment as a sentencing option do not execute people?

6.  What are the financial costs of the death penalty versus murder cases that are not prosecuted as capital cases?

7.  Do you think the number of death row exonerations is a good reason to discontinue capital punishment?

8.  What are the current methods of execution in the U.S.? In your opinion are any of these methods cruel and unusual?

9.  What are some issues death row inmates present correctional administrators?

10. Do you think any psychological harm befalls correctional staff that work on death row? Explain.

## Student Exercises

1.  Research the reasons for and the reasons against the death penalty. Have a class debate based on empirical data concerning capital punishment.

2.  Research contemporary court challenges to the death penalty. Where are the challenges and what are they?

## Key Terms

**Aggravating circumstance**—behaviors that increase the severity or culpability of a criminal act.

**Clemency**—a reprieve of execution typically issued by a governor preventing an execution.

**Death row**—a specific part of a prison where inmates sentenced to death are housed. The unit of the prison is very secure.

**Death warrant**—official court document proffered by a governmental official, usually a governor, establishing a date of execution.

**Exonerated**—the reversal of a conviction for a crime.

**Furman v. Georgia**—precedent setting case which made capital punishment unconstitutional, thereby eliminating its use for a period.

**Gregg v. Georgia**—precedent setting case which reinstated capital punishment in the U.S.

**Mitigation**—lessening of punishment based on circumstances in the case.

**Moratorium**—a temporary stoppage of executions but not sentences of death.

**Retroactive**—making current law apply to cases prior to the enactment of the law.

**Stay of execution**—court pronouncement delaying an execution for some type of cause.

---

1 *Coker v. Georgia*, 433 US 584 (1977).

2 *Atkins v. Virginia*, 536 U.S. 304 (2002).

3 *Roper v. Simmons*, 543 U.S. 551 (2005).

4 *Kennedy v. Louisiana*, 554 U.S. 407 (2008).

## CHAPTER 12

# Future Trends in Corrections

**Chapter Objectives**

- Understand the importance of evidence-based practice in corrections.

- Identify where funding for corrections comes from and the need to use this resource efficiently.

- Understand the importance of recruiting and retaining qualified and effective correctional staff.

- Knowledge of the role technology plays in corrections and the impact it will have in the future.

## A. INTRODUCTION

The trend of using empirical data to support corrections policy and practice is not necessarily new. As we have seen Robert Martinson's research in the early and mid-1970s about correctional rehabilitative programs (i.e. "Nothing Works") was used to usher in a new era of corrections. The transition from the medical model to a just desserts model didn't occur solely due to the work of Martinson but it helped facilitate and legitimize the more punitive model. During the 1970s criminal justice, corrections certainly included entered into the political arena. Today corrections is still part of the political landscape. However, it appears that the days of seeing which politician could be tougher on crime than the next may be coming to a close in many respects. Corrections currently seems to be entering a transitory period where more rehabilitative measures are being employed and fewer harsh punishments are being utilized or conceived through legislation.

In the closing chapter of this text we will examine future trends in corrections. There is serious attention being paid to program evaluation and empirical data concerning correctional policy and practice. Currently, legislators and correctional professionals are listening to and utilizing research and evaluation to inform and direct their policies. Major legislation like the Second Chance Act passed in 2008, and the First Step Act passed in 2019, both emphasized the need for evidence-based practices in corrections. Thereby letting empirical data lead the way to inform decisions about correctional policy and practice instead of political influence. The emphasis on empirical data signals a new era within corrections. The future appears to rely on data to drive decisions. However, large changes within corrections don't depend on research alone.

We will look at social attitudes concerning corrections in our final chapter. Correctional practice often mirrors public sentiment concerning punishment. We have seen in previous chapters how public attitudes toward corporal punishment signaled a shift away from those punishments toward the rise of prisons. The evolving use of the death penalty today is largely a reflection of social attitudes. What shapes social attitudes about an area that relatively few Americans experience? What shaped your views of the prisons? How do you know if they are effective at reducing recidivism? What did you base your opinion of parole on? As a criminal justice student you will no doubt be armed with more education on the topic than most of the general public. Prior to this class where did you obtain your information from about corrections? Where do your parents and those outside of the criminal justice world get their information from? How accurate is that information? These are challenges not only for criminal justice students but also the general public to those that make legislative decisions.

The final aspect we will look at are trends in resources for corrections. Often time's financial resources are primarily considered here. It's true without monies devoted to this area nothing would get done, so that's important and we will examine it here. However, devoting money does not mean much unless there are qualified people to manage correctional populations. The line staff to administration personnel are key to making the system function. The duties demanded within these careers are changing. Line officers are tasked with more than just ensuring discipline of inmates or adherence to conditions of release. They are routinely asked to work with and be cognizant of those with health and mental health issues, be aware of a multitude of different potential resources to utilize, changing laws, substance abuse and use issues, and stressors that impact their personnel lives.

Attracting and retaining people in many different sorts of correctional positions is essential to the effectiveness and efficiency of the system. Agencies are increasingly seeing fewer applicants for positions that were once very competitive. Not only do departments and agencies have to compete with other public sector jobs like policing, but with the rise of the private prison industry and an economy attracts people to other career areas. Working with a correctional population is challenging. Conditions that professionals work in can be dangerous and the working hours can mean working on weekends and holidays. Often the satisfaction of working in the correctional field doesn't come in the form of a substantial paycheck. There are other rewards beyond the monetary.

# B. CORRECTIONS AND EVIDENCE-BASED PRACTICES

For the past several years local, state, and federal governments have aimed to enhance their policies and practices in an effort to provide services more efficiently and effectively. Providing services that are cost effective and that show results attracts more funding and other resources. Research and **program evaluation** is a critical component for making informed decisions. If agencies can show legislators and the general public that their tax dollars are being well spent those agencies and specific programs are likely to continue to be funded. Evaluations provide accountability for agencies. Legislators and the public can see for themselves if programs are efficient and effective. One stark example is the mentality in favor of long prison sentences for any number of crimes. During the "Just Desserts" era to prison population shot up well over 400%. It wasn't just that more people were being imprisoned either but that more people were serving longer sentences. 44 states increased the number of months a person spend in prison since 2000. In some states the average prison sentenced increased 150% over the last 30 years (Courtney, 2019). A vast number of studies focused on prison length and recidivism (Song, 1993) (Roach, 2015). The great majority saw mixed results about harsh punishments and reduced rates of recidivism.

> **Class exercise**—Find out for yourself: Research prison length and recidivism. Report back to the class about your findings.

Evaluative studies reveal critical information about not only complete program effectiveness but where specific parts of programs are effective or not. Just because a program might not be effective overall certain pieces or aspects can prove to be effective. Evaluations can highlight deficiencies and successes. This allows modifications or tweaks that can impact program success.

Today correctional professionals benefit from education and experience in research. Knowing how studies are conducted is very important to understanding evaluations. Many within corrections identify programs and conduct their own evaluations as part of their job duties. Still other agencies and organizations hire people to specifically conduct research and evaluation studies. The goals of the program, the important variables, and the goals of the evaluation must all be easily translatable.

Evaluations can be very complex and detailed. Often times this demands specialized training. Training in research and research methods is taught in all universities and is typically a required component of core curricula for areas of study like Criminal Justice, Criminology, and Corrections specifically. These courses prepare students for exposure to research and empirical data. Often advanced degrees such as a doctorate are required to conduct studies.

## 1. Agency and Program Improvement

The purpose to any evaluation is to improve the agency as a whole or to specifically examine the usefulness of a specific program. There are a number of governmental agencies that assist with program evaluation and research within criminal justice. Here are a few:

- National Institute of Corrections
- Bureau of Justice Assistance for Program Evaluation
- National Institute of Justice
- Office of Justice Program
- National Criminal Justice Reference Service

There are also a number of non-governmental agencies that research correctional policy and practice:

- Pew Charitable Trust
- The Vera Institute
- The Urban Institute
- American Probation and Parole Association
- American Jail Association

There are of course any number of universities that collect and analyze data in this field. You may want to take some time to ask the instructor teaching this class or any of your other instructors to share their research both past and present.

Evaluations must serve a useful purpose. Part of the evaluation process involves making recommendations to **stakeholders.** These studies provide the "evidence" in evidence-based practices. Stakeholders can use this information to make decisions about program implementation, to discontinue a program, or modify a program. A critical aspect of the evaluation is that conclusions and recommendations are based on what was found through the evaluations and not what evaluators or correctional administrators wanted to find. The latter is a potential hazard to evidence-based practices. If the "evidence" is tainted by bias or inaccurate data or measures of the data than a skewed result can occur. Misapplication does great harm to the field and can lead to time, effort, and money being devoted to programs and policies that are not effective at reducing whatever outcome is desired.

Programs and policies based on solid data is a significant trend in American corrections. Correctional professionals from the entry level to administration benefit from understanding what research is. All research is not the same. The value is based on the quality of the study. Corrections professionals need to understand basic elements of study and research. What makes one study more valuable than another? Just as valuable "evidence" can positively impact an agency or a program inaccurate conclusions can damage those with the best intentions.

## 2.   The Public and Corrections

Prior to taking this class many students may have had limited knowledge of corrections. Hopefully at this point your knowledge base has expanded and students have a better understanding about what corrections entails in the U.S. The vast majority of Americans only experience with corrections will be from the news, movies, or from what others say about prisons, probation, or parole. Yet regardless of limited experience or education people will either support or oppose various correctional measures.

A recent poll showed overwhelming support for prison and sentencing reforms. Americans from both major political parties as well as those independently politically affiliated were in favor the First Step Act. In a rare act of political bipartisanship Democrats and Republicans in both houses of Congress passed the act (Committee on the Judiciary, 2019). It passed in the House of Representatives by a large margin (360 to 59) and also by a wide margin in the U.S. Senate 87–12 (Grawert, 2019). Other legislation reforming or mitigating punishment at state and local levels of government have also been implemented.

> **Class exercise**—Research legislative initiatives in your area concerning sentencing or correctional reforms. Report your findings to the class and discuss this trend.

How we punish people is influenced by social attitudes about punishment. The idea of what is "just" punishment evolves as society changes. We can see past movements from rehabilitative models of corrections to retribution. Today is not different. The "Just Desserts" era within American corrections appears to be ending. We are entering a transitory phase as we move away from simple retributive measures and toward rehabilitation and reintegration. This movement is exemplified by certain buzzwords within corrections that seem to be fashionable. Terms such as: reintegration and evidence-based practices have replaced terms like "boot camps", "war on drugs", and "three strikes" (MacKenzie, 2010). Those terms are of course explicitly tied to the "Just Desserts" era. Today those phrases are synonymous of a by-gone era whereby correctional and political figures seem to want to distance themselves from instead of embracing those ideas.

The Pendulum of justice is swinging back toward a more rehabilitative model. The public's perception of justice and fairness has changed just as it changed in the mid 1970s away from rehabilitation and toward retribution. The movement toward rehabilitation and then away from it as our philosophy of what is "just" appears to be our national social rhythm. As surely as we embrace rehabilitation and reintegration it's fairly safe to say that at some point the correctional trend will shift again in favor of retribution or some form of it.

## 3.  Resources

There are a number of different trends we should consider when it comes to resources. As we noted earlier in this chapter corrections is undergoing a transition. Academics, like the professor teaching this class, and others within corrections have been studying punishment. Both societal level responses to punishment as well as individual level responses are really what we've studied since Beccaria wrote *On Crimes and Punishment* in the mid to late 1700s. It's just now there is much more focus on the application of research to corrections. Making policy based on empirical data (i.e. evidence-based practices). So when we discuss resources we must look at areas like **grants** to support research.

There are a number of different governmental and non-governmental entities that provide financial support to aid in research. The National Science Foundation is a large governmental agency responsible for managing, approving projects, and dispersing millions of dollars each year in a variety of areas of which corrections is one. There are of course a large number of governmental agencies that award research grants more specifically within the area of corrections. We mentioned a few of these governmental and non-governmental agencies earlier in this chapter. Without grant funding a very large portion of research could not happen. Researching and establishing a study takes an enormous amount of time and money. Both of these resources can be in short supply. Now that we are utilizing research and evaluation to inform policy it's even more important to expand this resource.

It takes money to operate a prison, manage a probation agency, or operate a treatment program. The average cost to incarcerate one federal prisoner for a single year is about $31,977.65. That's $87.61 a day (Federal Register, 2016). This is no shock as we have covered the costs of incarceration and community corrections in subsequent chapters. However we do not look at trends in funding. In 13 states where the prison population declined since 2010, the total prison cost declined $1.6 billion (Vera Institute of Justice, 2016). For instance in Texas the prison population decreased by 3.3% and as a result their overall spending dropped 7.4% to about $3.2 billion. By contrast 15 states saw their prison populations expand which meant a total increased cost of $508 million. Montana's prison population grew 9.2% between 2010 and 2015. Accordingly prison spending increased by 12.9% in that state during that 5 year period (Vera Institute of Justice, 2016). Just because the population decreased the cost doesn't necessarily decrease. In ten states that saw prison populations decrease spending actually increased $1.1 billion. This seems counter-intuitive: if the population decreased the cost should decrease because there are fewer inmates. That does make sense but if we look at California we see that their prison population decreased dramatically by 20.9% yet they spent 7% more on inmates. It costs $75,560 a year to incarcerate one inmate for one year in California (Associated Press, 2017). The cost per inmate has doubled in California since 2005, even though the prison population has dropped drastically. California will spend $11.4 billion on corrections in 2017. Much of the increase is attributed to the cost of salaries and benefits for correctional professionals.

We discovered earlier in this text that overall the prison population is shrinking in the U.S. Many view this as a positive development. However, just because the inmate population shrinks prison spending might not. The overall trend in correctional spending is a reduction in spending. This has made the use of policy and practices that are effective at reducing the number of people coming back to prison even more important.

> **Class exercise**—How much has your states prison population increased or decreased in the last ten years? Compare the budgets of each of those ten years. Where does your state's correctional department spend most of their money? Compare the percent of money your state spends on corrections to the overall state budget.

The state of Missouri saw a 6.1% increase in their inmate population between 2010 and 2015, yet spending decreased by 1.5%. Doing more with less means state correctional department must look for ways to be more efficient. Missouri's

Department of Correction's have an entire segment of their agency devoted to research, planning, and process improvement.

The devotion of funding or lack thereof is a trend which bears a lot of attention. There is an interconnection of success, if we define success as a lower recidivism rate, to funding. No agencies or program within an agency can be successful if it doesn't have the means to buy proper equipment and employ capable and dedicated people. However, just because a lot of money is spend doesn't mean recidivism rates will be lower. Money can be spend on programs or pursuing policies that have no impact on recidivism and in some cases may actually increase incarceration rates. This is the reason why we conduct research and why evaluations on existing correctional methods are so important. Employing people within corrections that have an appreciation for empirical data but also have knowledge about psychology, sociology, research methods, substance abuse, communication skills just to name a few is extremely important.

Finding quality employees and keeping them are one of the major challenges for corrections managers today. In Chapter 7, we discussed staff subculture. One of the areas we reviewed was employment and retention. The importance of attracting and retaining quality employees bears another look. Looking at trends in correctional employment is not only essential to correctional managers whether for institutional corrections or community corrections but for the budding professional as well. Internships are extremely important not only to the intern but also the agency hosting the intern. Inters of course get a partial taste of what the career entails. This experience can be very beneficial when deciding if the career they are investigating is something to be pursued after graduation. Agencies also get to "test out" a potential employee. Internships rarely receive any compensation so there is limited costs to the **internship placement**. Usually their many be some cost incurred by the agency for limited equipment but the primary cost concerns a **background check**.

Every agency within corrections conducts some type of background investigation on interns and certainly on employment candidates. Each agency has their own protocol concerning these types of investigations. Some simply look for and review any possible criminal history which can take a couple of days. Other background investigations can take months to complete. Whereby investigators not only examine any criminal history, but they may interview spouses, former spouses, neighbors, and university professors. They can review tax records and past places of employment, or residence. Many agencies use a polygraph to determine the truthfulness of a potential employees.

The purpose behind such examinations is due to the nature of the career. Correctional professionals manage a vulnerable population. They are considered vulnerable because the powers a correctional professional has over inmates, probationers, or parolees is extensive. Possible employees with histories or indications of being abusive toward others, have a history of making decisions that would be viewed as unfavorable, and those that might be subject to manipulation by inmates or others could harm the agency.

---

### Corrections in Action

Tiffany Cook is now a former Georgia Department of Corrections officer. She is accused of bringing alcohol, drugs, and cellphones into Hayes State Prison located in Trion Georgia. The prison holds 1,100 male inmates. It's considered a "close" security unit. Ms. Cook was sentenced 7 years and 8 months in prison. U.S. Attorney Byung Pak said, "correctional officers who smuggle contraband into prisons not only betray the institutions they protect, but also jeopardize the safety of fellow correctional officers and inmates." (Department of Justice Northern District of Georgia, 2019).

Cook had been a correctional officer since 2010, within the Georgia department of corrections. In April 2017, she began work at Hays State Prison. In 2018, a prison informant reported to investigators that Cook was smuggling drugs into the prison. When Cook arrived for her shift on July 9th 2018, she was asked by other correctional staff to accompany them to a conference room and upon a search of her person 118 grams of methamphetamine and more than 150 grams of marijuana was seized.

The case was prosecuted in federal court because Ms. Cook was acting as a correctional professional when she committed her crimes. Essentially she was act under "under the color of law" or abusing her role and authority as a correctional officer to further her criminal activity. Often times when law enforcement or correctional professionals commit a crime(s) when they are on duty the crime will be prosecuted in federal court because the punishments are often more harsh in the federal system

---

The responsibilities that correctional professionals have are enormous. Thus the trust employers must have in their employees is very important. Attracting qualified employees to a demanding job is very difficult. Salary is important, but not the only important factor when considering a career. Everybody wants to make a living that can afford them the things they want, but the reality is that corrections professionals won't get wealthy. The drive and satisfaction with careers often goes beyond financial compensation. Correctional professionals work with a variety of people though the course of their career whether inmate or other staff. Some look for and value working with a population (i.e. inmates) that present any number of challenges during a daily shift at work or through the progression of a career. We spoke earlier in the text about staff subculture and there is a value that people find in working with others in a hostile environment, thus development of comraderies. There are any number of different job duties that go far beyond escorting prisoners to chow or observing them in a jail pod.

Recruiting a retaining correctional professionals is can be extremely difficult. We saw earlier in this text that some prisons experience very large turnover rates, some as high as 50%. Prisons are constantly hiring people in all areas, not only correctional officers.

There are consequences to staffing shortages and one trend we see as a result of these shortages is increased prison violence. In May 2016, two Nebraska State prison inmates were killed during a riot. The riot occurred because inmate privileges were curtailed because here were not enough prison staff to monitor inmates outside of their cells and other areas so inmates were spending more and more time in their two person cells (Fiflied, 2016). Another trend to considers the feedback loop created through staff shortages on existing employees. For example due to staff shortages existing officers have to work overtime on many occasions. Sometimes working well over 40 hours per week. The increased pay is beneficial but the latent consequences can be disastrous for families. Also working in stressful occupations for extended periods of time leads to burnout (Fiflied, 2016).

The continued use of technology within corrections has had a dramatic impact on institutional and community corrections. It affects the way we classify and manage inmates. Its use is especially important considering how we supervise parolees and probationer. A common phrase from a by-gone era within community corrections alluded to not being able to" be in someone's back pocket 24/7". Today that's not the case at all. The advent of GPS units affixed to probationers or parolees allows an officer to essentially be in their back pocket and track their every move every minute of the day. That said GPS is a tool for officers and not a "cure all". After all someone can cut a GPS bracelet off or adhere to location restrictions and still commit crimes.

Advanced location monitoring is just one example of technology impacting corrections. We can monitor inmates of those on community corrections for substance use and abuse through a myriad of measures such as skin patches or breath devices attached to cars. These can be important tools that impact behavior, but again are not the solution to preventing recidivism as there remains reasons why people continue to commit crime or why they use and abuse substances. This is why educated correctional professionals are so important to the success of corrections. Now more than ever in the field these professionals require advanced training in a number of different fields.

The last resource we will discuss is the privatization of corrections. The corrections industry has grown by billions of dollars since Corrections Corporation of America (now CoreCivic) was awarded a contract to house inmates in Tennessee in 1984. In 2016, the Obama Administration announced its plan to end the use of private facilities for federal inmates but less than a year later the new Trump Administration reversed those plans (Justice Policy Institute, 2018). Today over 125,000 inmates at the local, state, and federal level are incarcerated in a private facility. Almost 73% (26,249) of people detained via an immigration hold are detained in private facilities. The federal government is not alone when it comes to housing people in private institutions. 27 states also use private facilities to house inmates (Gotsch, 2018).

In many regards corrections has become a business. Companies like CoreCivic, GEO Group, and Management and Training Corporation are for profit companies. In 2015, CoreCivic and Geo Group had a combined annual revenue of $3.5 billion (Gotsch, 2018). These companies are traded on the stock market. They have **shareholders** that are interested in profits and seeing their stock prices rise. Accordingly these companies have lobbyists who try to steer legislation that's beneficial to their companies. This influence may or may

> **Class exercise**—Investigate the price of CoreCivic, GEO Group, and Management and Training Corporation's stock prices. How much money do they make? How many people do they employ?

not be in the best interests of the public. As we begin to close this decade and look into the next the trend towards using private facilities appears to be growing.

## C. CONCLUSION

Corrections is in a transitory period. When we look ahead it appears to more agencies are looking to using programs to are supported by empirical data. The use of evidence-based practices to inform programs and policies will continue to drive those changes. However, it's important to note where and how the data is collected and analyzed. Data driven policy and practice must be based on reliable and accurate data. Just because a study is published doesn't necessarily mean it meets the standards of the scientific method. That's where the consumers of such data come in. They are responsible for sorting through data and studies to determine what's useful and what is not. An educated correctional workforce is necessary for the effectiveness of the field. Without knowledgeable people at all levels the field suffers. If the field suffers the public question the usefulness of corrections. This in turn impacts the amount of resources devoted to the field. It determines not only the amount of resources but the nature of how corrections is administered in the U.S.

## Discussion Questions

1.  Explain what two trends you think in corrections will be the most impactful to the field in the next ten years.

2.  Discuss what concerns you most about the future of corrections in the U.S.?

3.  What do you think corrections is most effective at today?

4.  If you were the Secretary of Corrections in your state what is one change you would make to institutional corrections and one change to community corrections?

5.  What role should evidence-based practices play in policy and programs?

6.  Why do you think it may be difficult for some people to accept changes in corrections that are based on empirical data?

7.  How do you think corrections can do a better job attracting more qualified employees and then retaining them?

8.  How can the field of corrections attract more minorities to the workforce?

9.  Why is program evaluation and why is it important?

10. Explain the importance of the role society plays in shaping corrections.

## Student Exercises

1.  Invite a correctional administrator to class and ask them about the trends and challenges of corrections in your area.

2.  Split the class into groups and debate the "pros" and "cons" of:

    - Privatization of corrections.

    - Technology in corrections.

    - If the general public should determine correctional policy or should it be left solely in the hands of correctional professionals.

## Key Terms

**Background check**—an investigation into a person's past and present behavior in order to determine the suitability for employment or an internship placement.

**Grants**—monies awarded to people conducting research for the purpose of continuing or completing the research.

**Internship placement**—an agency that hosts an intern.

**Program evaluation**—a process by which a correctional program is evaluated through recognized empirical methods in order to determine if or where its effective at producing the intended results.

**Shareholders**—people that own stock in a company. Shareholders receive dividends or payments periodically if the company earns a profit.

**Stakeholders**—people who share an investment or responsibility for the agency or program.

# Index